'This is a book for anyone who loves the ocean – to read and savour, then keep and refer to again and again. It introduces us to the people who use it, protect it and celebrate it. Each page explores our primeval connection with the sea, and the need to save it for future generations.'
– Jo-Anne Richards, swimmer, sea lover and author of *The Innocence of Roast Chicken*

'A swim with the magic of mermaids and myths. This sea-worshipping book calls to the water baby inside us.'
– Sarah Bullen, author of *The Other Side*

deep blue

Why we love the sea

Veruska De Vita

Jonathan Ball Publishers
JOHANNESBURG & CAPE TOWN

All rights reserved.
No part of this publication may be reproduced or transmitted,
in any form or by any means, without prior permission
from the publisher or copyright holder.

© Text Veruska De Vita 2025
© Published edition 2025 Jonathan Ball Publishers

Published in South Africa in 2025 by
JONATHAN BALL PUBLISHERS
A division of Media24 (Pty) Ltd
PO Box 33977
Jeppestown
2043

ISBN 978-1-77619-456-8
ebook ISBN 978-1-77619-457-5

Every effort has been made to trace the copyright holders and to obtain their permission for the use of copyright material. The publishers apologise for any errors or omissions and would be grateful to be notified of any corrections that should be incorporated in future editions of this book.

jonathanball.co.za
X.com/JonathanBallPub
facebook.com/JonathanBallPublishers

Cover by Gretchen van der Byl
Design and typesetting by Melanie Kriel

Set in Baskerville URW

For my parents

contents

xi *Prologue*

in water we begin

- 3 Learning to swim
- 15 Learning to freedive
- 23 The mammalian diving reflex
- 29 A brief history of water

ice

- 41 Breaking records in frozen lakes
- 50 Acclimatising to cold
- 62 Water as healer

freediving

- 73 Greatest depth with a monofin
- 80 Longest underwater kiss
- 90 The black mermaid
- 97 Ambitious human nature
- 104 Shaped by the sea

swimming

- 119 Choppy seas, a mirror for life
- 131 Enjoyment
- 139 Rip currents

147 Cold immersion, chief mermaids and
    pleasure seekers
155 Holiday vibes

protection

163 The changing migratory patterns
    of southern right whales
169 Water, precious water, plastic everywhere
184 Jellyfish and goby fish
188 Agreeing to protect the oceans:
    The High Seas Treaty
195 The human polar bear

connection

201 Our golden kelp forests
206 Around the Buoy
213 Kalk Bay
219 Inheriting the ocean
239 Kosi Bay
242 Swimming with the divas

250 Epilogue
252 Notes and references
258 Acknowledgements
260 About the author

You are not a drop in the ocean. You are the entire ocean in a drop.

– Rumi

prologue

I am three years old. The water goes tap, tap against my thighs. I look at my feet, which seem oddly distant and small, my legs refracted by the water. I run my fingers, wrinkled from being in the pool for so long, along my arms, feeling the peaks on my skin like I've grown scales. On the pool floor, light bounces around, spreads and contracts into shapes – diamonds and squares of aqua and blue and black. Red bikini bottoms pulled up to my belly button. I pull them away from my skin and let them snap back. They balloon from the wetness. I jump and grab on to the side. My feet don't touch the bottom yet, not even in the shallow end, not even if I point my toes. But I let go. Onto my back, water swirls around my head, my face. My eyes are screwed shut and I dare not inhale. And then I am floating.

This is one of my earliest memories of water.

I am 31 years old. It is March and I am newly married, with my husband Franco at Ponta do Ouro on the edge of South Africa, in Mozambique. I've been here before, to swim with bottlenose dolphins that inhabit the area abundantly. The skipper had told us we were lucky; being in the water with dolphins for five consecutive days didn't happen often. Now I swim among silver fish against a backdrop of pale, sandy ocean floor. They are a dazzling mirage. I think there are thousands of them. As they whip past me, I feel ribbons of water brush against my arms and stomach. There is no yesterday or tomorrow. I am here now, today, cradled by crystal blueness everywhere. All around me water bounces like sheets of sunlight.

On the beach I lie on a red towel and I don't care that there is sand on its edges and in its folds. I like the feel of it, the graininess. The sun flits on my skin licking off the water and leaving me brown. It flits on the peaks of waves, rendering the foam white as clouds. Today there are none and the sky is incandescent. It could be on fire, the sapphire centre of a flame.

We are pushing a rubber dinghy into the water; it is big and heavy and the wet sand fights our efforts so that when we are waist deep in the sea we are panting. I climb aboard and sit on the edge next to Franco. It is the first time he is going out in the bay, his first time on a rubber dinghy. As the skipper pushes the throttle, we grab onto the ropes. My husband's hand slips, his wedding band catches on the rope and it slides off his finger. He tries to catch it in the water but it is already out of his grasp and we both watch as it sinks in a straight line downwards. I am superstitious, finding meaning and patterns in almost everything. I wonder if this is a sign. My heart sinks a little bit, his too. But the boat is gaining speed, we are in open water, wet from the rhythmic splashing and we can't help but feel excited.

'I'm going to see a whale shark,' I muse to my husband. I know he doesn't believe me, but it's my birthday weekend and my wishes always come true on my birthday. There is a lull in the chatter and I fix my eyes forward onto the skipper's back where four tattoos rail to be noticed. I decide they are names written in an alphabet I don't know. His head turns left and right scanning near and far for sharks, dolphins, rays. Intently I watch his hand signals as he communicates to other skippers, also with people on board. Fins on, my snorkel and mask in my hand, I am ready to jump in.

He does a wavy motion above his head, the sign for whale shark. I don't even think. Or blink. I fall backwards off the boat and into the water. Fixing mask and snorkel in place I swim towards the enormous fish. I am so close that as it slowly moves its tail I need to get out of its way. He lingers, moving slowly, two prodigal sons following his movements underneath him. He is young, not yet fully grown and yet his

prologue

enormity is mighty. The immensity of this creature is sublime – perfect in its form, perfect in the sea. Just perfect. I have no thought. No fear. My body simply moves where it has to, how it has to.

I am snapped out of my reverie by the splash and pressure of the others jumping in around me. I forgot I wasn't alone. I love that the whale shark is curious and that the fish beneath his belly follow his every move. It is quite gangster. I swim closer to the surface and with my head still underwater look for Franco. I swim to him, we both surface and tread water, giddy with joy. Droplets fly off my face as I slide my mask to the top of my head to kiss him, my lips smacking on his.

At the campsite I shower and then lie on the blow-up mattress in the tent that's been swept clean of sand. Things feel different. I know that I am in a different setting, away from home, but it's as though my perspective has shifted by a fraction of a compass point. A minuscule point, but enough to shift something inside me. It feels good.

It is humid and dark at night. We sit on the beach listening to the waves lapping the sand. Rivulets of luminescence glow green and yellow in the tumbling waves. The white edges of ocean light up at the shoreline. The ocean's rhythm is held in sway by the moon and the spinning of the planet, luring me to sleep. Above, stars prickle.

It is years later and as I sleep fish swim in and out of my mouth. I am submerged, looking up through crystalline water to the surface, which glints in its play with sunlight. I screw my eyes against the light and pierce through the skin between sleep and wakefulness. I've been holding my breath, so I exhale softly and inhale slowly. I turn my head and, on the pillow next to me, is seaweed – my eight-year-old daughter's dark hair.

In the bedroom, the morning sun has made its way down the wall like dry water. I have that familiar yearning to be surrounded by ocean and to feel its pressure on my body.

I have long held a deep love for water, for the sea that carried my father through childhood. For the ocean of my own childhood where I explored rock pools and smoothed my inquisitive hands over shells. The threatening sea of my mother who was born on an island but was never taught to swim. For the future seas of my children as they grow into adulthood on this planet we call home. This book is a love letter to the sea, exposing our intimate relationship with it and the bliss of being in its liquid circumfuse.

Water is deeply primordial. It is a symbol of birth, life and death. We go with the flow of life. We cleanse. We are baptised. In many cultures we go back to water at our death. The crossing of rivers is a rite of passage, a new chapter, a challenge bequeathed upon us. Water gives life, it represents hope, renewal, rebirth. Funeral pyres are lit to then float on the River Ganges. The ancestral chosen ones enter the water and emerge as sangomas.

The equation of life is not static. It renders beauty, death, chaos, and then resurrection. It is its own religion. We return to the earth as bones, as ashes, as air, as memory and as water. A romanticised notion leads me to imagine that our unions with the sea, our cultural associations with the ocean, our relation to aquatic environments as a food source, account for the symbolic importance of water in our daily lives.

My research originated as an inkling, a fascination with freediving. A curiosity for those mystical beings who are able to hold their breath and delve deep into the immensity of blue, and ultimately themselves. What struck me was their facility with depth, the slight motion of their body propelling them downward, the smiles on their faces on their return to surface. They bristled with vitality and an unyielding mental fortitude.

During Covid lockdown, unable to reach the ocean, landlocked and confined to my own house, and barred from doing a freediving course, I began contacting extreme athletes who had reached extreme depths and accomplished seemingly impossible feats. I was humbled by their generosity of time and information, as they shared triumphs, disillusionment, pain, fear, their eating habits and exercise regimes

– the mundanity that makes up a large part of who they are and how they train.

I watched YouTube videos of Alexey Molchanov – the son of the late Natalia Molchanova – preparing for descent: noseclip and goggles in place, gold hood clinging to his scalp, his mouth opening and closing like a fish out of water as he sips every last molecule of air into his throat and mouth.

Like his mother, he is legendary. Scientists who have attached measuring machines to his body say that his facility for diving to depths of a hundred metres and more sets him apart from other human beings. It is so easy for him. His body is built for it. He has a large lung volume and can hold his breath for over 11 minutes if he packs – the motion of sipping more air into the body once the lungs are full; bradycardia – the slowing down of heart rate – occurs quickly for him, and he equalises easily. His metabolic response to apnoea (a temporary cessation of breathing) is akin to that of aquatic mammals.

I connected with him through a fellow journalist, a Russian by the name of Maria Zhelikhovskaya, whom I had met on a press trip to Switzerland years before. Can you help me get an interview with Alexey Molchanov? I asked her. On Facebook she had put out a request for an English-speaking native Puerto Rican she could chat to for a story she was writing. I offered to find her that person in exchange for the interview. She introduced me to Alexey's PR representative who gave me his number and I delivered a Puerto Rican blogger fluent in English.

On Zoom I chatted to Australian Naysan Baghai, a filmmaker whose documentary *Descent* had won at the Sydney Film Festival. A freediver himself, he patiently took me through the process of freediving. He unpacked the bare bones of breath hold, he named the world's best, and shared how he'd had coffee with Alexey when he was in Australia and what a nice guy he was. He also told me about the worst that had happened to freedivers who pushed themselves too far – crushed larynx, coughing blood, shallow-water blackout, death.

I eventually connected with Deborah Andollo, a Cuban freediver who broke numerous world records in the 1980s. Shy of anyone wanting to talk to her about her freediving career, she put me on to an Italian, Nino Piras, who was instrumental in her sponsorship during her heyday. He described her as a butterfly in the water, gliding and in her element. I have not included her chapter in the book as contention about her records is still raw. Nino remembered those days fondly, even shedding tears at the memories, at her determination and unwavering commitment. Because the judging and the timekeeping were questionable, Deborah had to repeat her dive in order to break the world record. She had burst both eardrums, but the following day she did the dive again, setting a new record. It is little wonder that she remains a legend of the sport.

Deborah stopped competitive freediving after her dear friend Audrey Mestre drowned during a dive in the Dominican Republic in 2002. The device that was supposed to carry Audrey to the surface malfunctioned, and there is still speculation about how it happened. Blame is hinted at Audrey's husband and fellow freediver Francisco 'Pipin' Ferreras. Nino suggested that it was also because Deborah was a mother and, realising the extreme risks involved in the sport, decided to retire from it.

I chatted to South African freediver Beth Neale throughout her first pregnancy and then while her daughter was a baby and into the toddler stage. She described to me her own experience of observing her daughter in the swimming pool. By the way she speaks and her anecdotes of being in the water with sea creatures, I am convinced that Beth Neale is a fish whisperer.

As a fan of Hanli Prinsloo for many years, when I found out she was doing freediving courses in Simon's Town, I jumped at the opportunity and flew down. I was nervous and almost cancelled. Yet it was one of the most pivotal encounters of my life.

Through my interviews with Kiki Bosch, the protagonist of *Descent*, I discovered that there are infinite ways of being in the world, of being in the water. In her bare skin and a bikini, Kiki swum next to glaciers, causing a sea captain to weep with emotion as he had never seen a human do such a thing. For her it is so easy.

My youngest daughter led me to Amber Fillary, a South African who holds two world records for swimming under Arctic ice in only a bathing suit. She is in constant competition with Johanna Nordblad of Finland. Cold water is slow, slowing down thoughts and metabolism and movement. It is otherworldly, a Milky Way of liquid flow. For people who plunge into this level of cold, it becomes obsessional.

Geneticist Melissa Ilardo took me on a mind journey to the village of Jaya Bakti and the sea-nomadic Bajau who have been diving for millennia. They walk on the seabed as easily as other people walk on land. Melissa made the groundbreaking discovery that they had evolved differently from other humans through physiological adaptation to freediving.

Zandile Ndhlovu is known as the black mermaid. Beneath the waves she found herself and an alternative habitat where she felt at home. Her journey into freediving has taken her to communities in various African and Caribbean countries where she teaches about the marvels of the sea.

I was fortunate to have interviewed Lewis Pugh in 2009. His remarkable ability to raise his core temperature by close to 2 °C has allowed him to swim the world's oceans, seas and waterways. He continues to bring awareness of the climate crisis to millions of people, and is instrumental in protecting parts of the world's marine environments.

Alessia Zecchini, who holds the women's record for deepest dive with a monofin, is inspiring. Her ambition has made her the best in the world. A star constellation is even named after her.

Taking instruction for breath hold from YouTube videos kept me anchored and helped me improve my apnoea time. I discovered that breath hold opens time. Every millisecond of life is heightened. Between interviews, as I assimilated and ordered information, on evenings when the moon shone bright white amid stars and I was pulled into the infinite breadth and complexities of time and space, losing myself in both the meaning and meaninglessness of it all, I found my way to the couch and to the guided breath hold videos. Seconds turned into a minute, which extended to two and more. I found meaning in stillness.

Diving the depths of our oceans is akin to diving the depths of our own existence. It challenges our abilities and opens our eyes to a different world, teeming with an otherworldly life. Freediver Beth Neale experiences a 'land down' when she hasn't been in the ocean for a few days. Ice swimmer Amber Fillary loves the rush that doing breaststroke under ice gives her. Founder of the International Ice Swimming Association, Ram Barkai, has made swimming in the Antarctic more accessible. They all bring the same things to the surface: their love for the water and an urgent plea for us to keep Earth's water alive.

During these meandering conversations with people who know the sea's depths and shallows intimately, I realised that every competitive freediver, every marathon swimmer, has an obsessive streak, the kind that could become uncontrollable if not channelled into something extreme, where the physical body and the mind enter a state of flow – that state of being that requires a singular focus that is different from the act of thinking.

The conversations would also inevitably arrive at the troubling changes that are occurring in our aquatic environment. While they explored Earth's most inspiring oceanic territories, they noticed that over the span of a few years they saw increasingly fewer fish, and more extreme weather. There was consensus about the rapid, and drastic, changes brought about by the climate crisis. It piqued my interest.

So, I spoke to scientists. They unpacked the perfection of Earth's inherent balancing system. A palaeo-oceanographer shed perspective on our human time frame – we are but a blip on the time scale of the planet. I learnt the extent to which micro- and nanoplastics are causing havoc in aquatic habitats. The migratory pattern of southern right whales has shifted. The jellyfish population has grown enormously.

Kelp forests have more young plants, and this has altered the ecosystem. Our oceans, seas and waterways are in danger.

Interglacial periods, when all the ice on the planet melts, occur every 100 000 years or so. While we are at the beginning of an interglacial period called the Holocene, the problem is that the ice is melting quicker than it should. The rate of global warming – particularly over the last 150 years – is faster than natural climate shifts in previous interglacial cycles.

In our lifetime, we will see climate crisis refugees and the disappearance of many species, and experience extreme weather events more frequently.

The temperature of our seas and oceans is rising. At the time of writing, it was likely that global heating would push temperatures to as much as 1,7 °C above the average experienced before the Industrial Revolution of the late 1800s, a danger that is directly linked to the burning of fossil fuels and intensified by the recurring El Niño climate event. Along with forests, soils, fossil fuels and carbonate rocks – limestone and dolomite – oceans are carbon sinks, absorbing carbon dioxide from the atmosphere, releasing oxygen and keeping the planetary surface cool. Oceans can store large amounts of carbon in their depths for centuries. But the increase in greenhouse gas emissions weakens the ocean's ability to absorb this gas, which in turn raises temperatures.

Our marine systems still support organisms that have been around from nearly the very beginning of Earth's formation. These systems are directly connected to the weather – the oceans and seas are always at play with the atmosphere, that mutable event horizon where air and water meet.

We have come to a point in the Earth's life where we need to make amends. How did we get here? And how do we get back to a system of bountiful equilibrium for all creatures? The first question we know the answer to, the second is open-ended as we can't turn back the clock – we can only change our behaviours and how we consume, to mitigate or at least decelerate the crisis.

There is a global movement to protect 30 per cent of Earth's natural environments by 2030, a complex set of agreements and actions that I am following eagerly. How a vast range of protected areas, including Marine Protected Areas, will be implemented and managed is yet to be seen. My wish is for it to be successful.

In the turmoil of the climate crisis, this is a book about life, hope and love for our oceans.

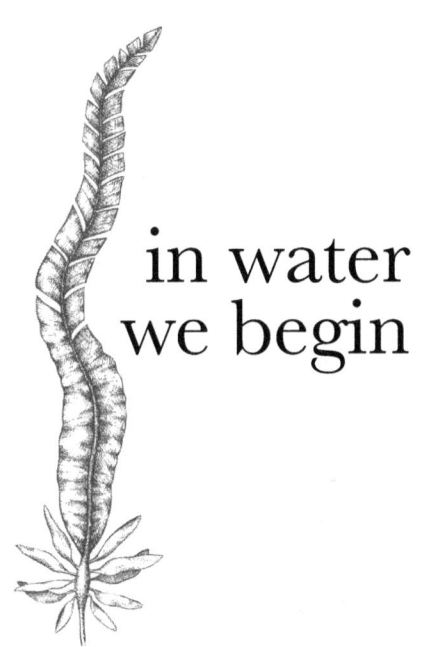 in water
we begin

learning to swim

I was born in Sicily and there man is born an island within an island and remains so until his death, even living far from his harsh native land surrounded by the immense and jealous sea.

– Luigi Pirandello

In the sea, when you swallow water once, twice, you learn quickly how to stay afloat. I was a natural in the water and I learnt to swim that very day.

– Andrea De Vita

The sea is entwined with my family history. My mother and father were born on the island of Sicily, surrounded by the warm Mediterranean. I was nourished on stories, both mythologised and real, told to me by my elders. But it's my father's stories of growing up on its shores that captured my imagination the most, and continue to pull and enchant me.

My dad Andrea has always been a natural in the water and on the first day he entered the sea, he learnt to swim. It is 1948 on the island of Sicily. The air is shrill with the call of cicadas drunk on the August heat. It is three years since the end of World War II and the people of this volcanic Mediterranean island are still picking up the remnants of their lives and sweeping away the dust that had fallen heavily upon them.

On the west side of the island, near Marsala, a school bus rumbles along an asphalt road. Seated towards the middle of the bus, Andrea presses his face against the window. He is three years old and he is on a school trip to the sea. His feet don't reach the floor and he hardly hears the squealing and chatter of the 20 other children on the bus, so mesmerised is he by the hypnotic spinning of the vehicle's wheels and the anticipation of swimming, of touching water, of being fully immersed in it.

The heat presses down thick on the air. He moves slightly to unstick his skinny thigh from the boy next to him. He touches the smooth pigtail of the girl in front of him but doesn't tug because the teacher is watching. The girl has fallen asleep, her head resting on the shoulder of her fellow passenger. Andrea turns back to the view framed by the window. The grey ribbon of road streams past, and beyond that the sea – that ever-present and luminous azure mass that surrounds the island.

The bus slows down and shudders to a stop. Excitement effervesces as the teachers instruct them to gather their things and without pushing make their way off the bus. Andrea fixes his small leather backpack onto his shoulders, aware of the bread and peaches inside it, and shuffles to the front. At the threshold he jumps from the step onto the road, bits of gravel crunching under his shoes, and skips towards the low balustrade separating the beach from the asphalt. The teachers give sharp commands but he does not heed them as he climbs over it.

The beach is a landscape of dunes from which sprout tufts of pale-green grass that flow with the breeze. The wind picks up and blows a reedy whistle through the grass, making it dance. Andrea climbs the dunes, hands and feet sinking into the beige sand. He does so earnestly, excitedly, eagerly, as fast as his young, growing body allows.

Not a single thought of removing his shoes enters his mind, even though shoes are valuable, a sign that you possess more than someone poor. Sand streams into the too-big shoes given to him by his older brother. But he feels important in them and while he is boarding at La Colonia for the summer, the state crèche that teaches and looks after the children of those who live hand to mouth, he need not share his shoes with any of his three siblings.

He feels each grain against his feet but he doesn't care; he is filled with a jubilance that could shake his entire body. The sea is more magnificent than it appeared from the bus window. Running slower now, he fixates upon the wide expanse of blue, the white crests of the waves in perpetual motion, the water's edge lapping with the sound of a thousand tongues.

He drops his school bag, kicks off his shoes and pulls his white uniform shirt up and over his head. He undoes the button of his shorts and wriggles out of them so that he is in only his underpants. The shout of a teacher as he runs into the water and then he feels it – the wetness on his body, the touch of the sea warmed by the fingers of the sun.

His skin prickles and lifts into goosebumps. Wet to the waistband of his underpants, he moves deeper, pushing his toes into the squishy sand beneath him. Suddenly the bottom of the sea disappears and he sinks under the meniscus. Moving his arms and legs, he propels himself upwards to the surface.

He coughs out the little water he inhaled, splutters. He pushes the hair out of his face, but a salty burn behind his eyelids inhibits him from opening his eyes. His body upright, he kicks gently, unhurriedly so that his shoulders are exposed to the slight air moving on the water's surface. As he bobs in the shallow crests, he opens his eyes. Droplets of sea cling to his lashes, distorting the world. He is in a dream. There is a moment, a quietude when the sea is in repose; small waves emanate from the movement of his limbs and with his gaze he follows them to the horizon.

'Viniti, viniti!' Andrea calls to the other children on the beach, beckoning them to join him. They shake their heads and root their feet further into the sand, planting themselves like broken shells left behind at the shoreline.

'Fifoni!' Scaredy-cats, Andrea shouts, licking the saltiness from his lips, relishing it in his mouth.

He looks for the teachers and sees that they are tending to the smaller children, the ones who have barely learnt to walk, so he paddles further out. A swell smacks him in the face and he swallows water again, but he learns quickly to keep his mouth closed. The sea feels natural to him, it is an animal he knows well, one he has known for a long time, long before his experience of it. It is an animal he can play with.

'In Sicily we grew up wild, with nature and the sea.'

Andrea is four years old. The sea is limpid, the sun warm in a sky so deep it is infinite. His mother, father, brothers and sister are a vague memory from days or even weeks ago. It is summer again and he is boarding at La Colonia. Time is merely a set of markers – the rumbling of his stomach before lunch, a teacher calling to him, the lulling rumble of the bus on their way back to the dormitory. Summer is a passing of days that shimmer in a haze of sunlight on air and sunlight on water.

He is in the sea up to his waist, his fingertips touching the water to feel the movement and direction of the tide, like he would lick a finger and lift it to the wind. He cups water to his lips, tasting its bitter saltiness. He swims out until the sea floor is far beyond the reach of his toes. He looks down watching the bounce of light on the sand below and sees a shell. He takes a deep breath, feeling his ribs expand, and then dives, opening his eyes only once he is under. The sea presses against his ears but the shell is close, perfect and whole. He kicks hard, pain pierces his skull, he reaches for the shell and grabs it, the tiny eyes of sand twirling and watching. Swimming back up he bursts to the surface. Andrea is part of two worlds, he knows. The Mediterranean Sea with its beguiling mysteries, and the dry earth with its toil and labour.

'Every animal knows how to swim, especially if it has four legs.'

Andrea is seven years old and his hand is on the flank of a mule, his uncle's beloved mule, guiding her along the road towards the sea. The mule pulls an empty cart, its wheels rattle along the dirt road and bounce over small rocks trapped in the earth. Andrea's older brother Natale is with them. The mule's owner – Zio Nicola – walks in front of them.

It has been a day of grape harvesting, collecting the bunches of ripe fruit in baskets, carrying these on their backs to the cart and then to the enoteca where the dark-red globules will be turned to wine. At nine years old, Natale is strong and carries fifty kilograms of grapes on his shoulders. Andrea prays to be as strong as his brother when he is older.

The day's work has made them tired but the sea will soothe them. They untie the cart from the animal's back and watch her trot onto the beach and then slow down as her hooves sink into sand. Her head pushes forward as she is eager to get to the water. At the shoreline she moves quickly again on the hard sand, tossing the water and then swaying deeper into the sea until she is swimming. Andrea and Natale grab pallets from the cart and run in to join the equine.

They bring the mule to the sea often as a reward for her labour. The pleasure of watching her delight in the waves is reward for them too. The spontaneity of animals is not lost to Andrea's humanness. On their stomachs they lie on the crates and paddle further out, but not too far because Andrea wants to watch the mule as she undulates the water in haloes around her.

Andrea dives down and swims beneath her, observing her kicking legs. He swims up and splashes water over her neck and the top of her head. Her pelt glistens and for a moment she looks like she is coated in fish scales, a mule mermaid. Andrea loves the mule; she is a hard-working animal fit from clip-clopping up steep hills with a heavy cart. In the salty water she is free of bridles and ropes. She cools down. Zio Nicola climbs onto her back and she swims as though delivering him to the sirens of the deep.

'The sea is in her veins,' Zio Nicola cries out as he lifts his arms and plunges head-first into the waves.

Andrea knows that the sea is in his veins too and that the sea is ancient, a gift to land animals, even humans.

'Grapes are picked by hand.'

Andrea is eight years old, his brother Natale is ten. It is October and the season to harvest grapes has again arrived, bringing with it a cool wind blowing away the rapturous heat of the sun's rays. The island settles into a different rhythm of labour and preparation for winter. The harvest is more important than school, and Natale is relieved he doesn't have to sit placidly in the torment of a classroom. The brothers walk to a nearby farm to begin the day's picking. Careful not to squeeze the globes, they pick bunches and fill their baskets, their fingertips staining deep red from grape skin. The baskets filled to the top, the brothers hoist them onto their backs. Andrea is robust against the weight. They trudge uphill between two rows of vines; the soil underfoot crumbles and small clumps of sand tumble downwards like a rockfall in miniature. It is so dry it seems impossible that it could sustain such beautiful fruit.

Their uncle is waiting on the road with the mule and her cart. The boys lift the baskets onto the cart. Andrea pats the mule on her neck and rubs her rump and she responds with a swish of her tail. The morning's labour, a dry mouth, the tang of sweet fruit on his skin opens Andrea's appetite and he plucks a few grapes from their stems and eats them. His eyes closed, he lets the sea smell on the air mix with the juice and flesh and flavours of the grapes on his tongue.

Andrea scrambles back up the slope with an empty basket on his back. At the top of a row of vines he grabs a clod of soil and breaks the large pieces in his hand, some as hard as rocks. He wonders how the plants live in the dryness, when he himself couldn't imagine a summer without swimming in the velvet swathes of the Mediterranean.

Shadows are growing longer; soon it will be the end of day and the end of picking. After all the good bunches have been picked, Andrea and Natale are allowed to go into the fields and take what is left over for themselves. For the last time this day, the brothers carry baskets of ripe grapes down the slope and load them onto the cart, the mule twitching its ears against a fly. The repetitiveness has made her restless.

With their uncle, they walk through the hamlets of Marsala alongside the mule's handsome trot. Doors open, chatter emanates from open windows. One woman, then two, then more, step onto the road to stop them, knowing that they bring fruit that holds sun in its flesh.

A system too rural, too poor, money is never exchanged, unless for a long-held debt, one that goes back a decade or a generation. As Andrea holds bunches of ripe grapes to open hands, they are paid for with a loaf of bread, a bottle of olive oil, a haircut.

He pats the mule with the tenderness of a child, as even a mule lost in the vastness of life and its infinite chores hopes for kindness. It is the winding roads and alleys of this island that will make Andrea and his brother men. At the seashore, water gathers and spills in clipped waves. Andrea reads the breakers as though they are words, each line giving meaning to the story, to his childhood. The hot air ripples across the water's rind and Andrea gives himself to the motion of the sea. It holds him in reverence as he lies on his back floating, letting the water lick his ears and whisper its secrets.

'The sea gives salt to grapes.'

It is after the harvest. Rain falls at night and sporadically during the day, shrinking the sun. Andrea sits alongside Zio Nicola on the passenger cart, eyes fixed on the mule's rump as it swings from side to side in rhythm with head and legs. Her grey coat mimics the greyness of low clouds. Andrea prefers the clip-clopping of her hooves on the dirt roads to the higher-pitched sound on tar – he imagines it's the sound that trees make when they sing.

They stop at one of the farms where they picked hundreds of bunches of grapes. Zio Nicola unhooks the cart and ties the rope from the mule's neck to the gnarled trunk of an olive tree. Its bark, like silvery scales, matches the colour of the air. The silvery bark has seen many days like this, where the air is marbled grey and brown, and the wetness of the world brings the scent of imminent winter.

The farmer takes Zio Nicola's hand and shakes it warmly, he is pleased to see him, Andrea can see how he smiles with all his teeth showing. The farmer looks tired, he hasn't shaved, and the stubble, prickly like a cactus pear, makes him look like he should have grandchildren Andrea's age. The farmer wants Zio Nicola to cut shoots from the new vines and graft them onto the older vines. 'Un ti preoccupare, Vincé, ci pensu io – don't worry, Vincenzo, I know what to do,' Zio Nicola reassures him.

Zio Nicola has his bag of tools on his shoulder and an empty crate that belongs to the farmer, and Andrea follows him into the vineyard. The crate is stamped with the farmer's name and Andrea is glad he can read it: Vincenzo Augustali.

His eyes are on the man's back, lean under his blue shirt, shoulder blades pressing against the fabric. His uncle smells of leather and tobacco and, because it is morning, wine from the evening before. At one of the young vines, Nicola bends down and roots in his bag, pulling out a pair of secateurs. 'Ndria, assapiri d'unni tagghiari – you must know where to cut,' he says to Andrea, who watches his uncle's movements.

Zio Nicola fills the crate with the delicate stems and the two trundle to another, older, part of the vineyard. Nicola takes a single stem and, with a sharp knife, cuts into a gnarled section of vine. He slowly pushes the new vine into the old plant and binds the two with a thin leather cord. He moves along the row doing the same on other plants.

'These ones, their roots are deep and firm within the earth, they know how to fetch water,' Nicola teaches.

It is spring. Andrea is on the cart with Zio Nicola. The mule trots merrily as she pulls them. They arrive at the farm where the previous day they dug a hole, long and wide and deep enough to bury a man in. In a crate, Nicola has bunches of vine stems that have shot roots. For this very purpose, he kept them in water through the winter. Nicola teaches Andrea a new lesson: 'The roots need to be buried deep so that they can drink whenever they are thirsty, no matter what is happening on the surface, no matter if there's been no rain for months.'

It is still too cold for people to start swimming but Andrea doesn't mind the cold – cares for it, even – as long as he can be in the sea. But it is May and he can feel it on his skin; the warmer winds coming from the sea and from the deserts of North Africa. Soon the scirocco will reach the island, signifying summer and with it the blooming of warm currents.

He remembers another lesson from Zio Nicola. 'Vines close to the Mediterranean absorb the salt and give the fruit salinity.'

'In a poor country you grow up quickly; at 15 you are already a man.'

Andrea is 15 years old. On his bicycle he pedals towards the beach, the bar where he has been serving espresso and granita to customers all afternoon recedes behind him. Air whizzes past him yet gives little respite from the August heat. The old town of Marsala with its ancient port and churches hums with people ready for the latter part of the day, the siesta slumber having refreshed them.

A church bell rings marking the hour at 7 p.m. and Andrea knows that he has little time before last light turns the water gold and orange, sunburnt as though it were alive. On the flat road, gaining speed he wheels past the salt mines where pyramids of salt blink like diamonds. Some are covered in terracotta tiles – scales protecting the damp harvest. To one side there are rectangular pools. In some the sea water is navy and in others it is red, having changed over the days to a higher alkalinity.

At a concrete pier he chains his bicycle and then dives into clear aquamarine sea, swimming steadily to the island of Mozia. As he turns his head to inhale, a little salt water gets in his mouth, and then a little more until the soft insides of his cheeks feel ragged. He is used to it and knows that a drink of fresh water will soothe the saltiness.

As he approaches land he breaststrokes, keeping his head out of water to take in the sea pines, still in the still afternoon, and the ruby flowers fully open among fleshy leaves. Alongside the flora, the sandy path he knows well winds along the periphery of the island. The path coruscates with brilliant light in the late-summer afternoon.

When he is able to stand he does so and wades until his feet squelch upon the seaweed-slimy shore. The sun, greedy for salt and moisture, dries his skin quickly. Rubbing his hands on his hair and feeling its dampness, he steps onto the path and sits among the ruins of a Phoenician harbour. He looks out in the direction he came from. His eyes scan the rugged shoreline of Marsala, the pyramids of salt, the buildings in the distance. Here, he is so distant from his daily life. Thousands of years ago there was a Phoenician city on the island. He runs his hands over the hand-carved bricks of the ruins.

My dad's memories and his stories are told to me sporadically but with so much detail that they shine vividly in my mind's eye. My mother grew up inland, in a mountain town called Santa Ninfa, and to this day she has never learnt to swim. Yet both of them have an affinity with the sea; they are bound to it with a shimmering thread that goes back generations.

My earliest memory of Sicily is of water, on a piece of family land. My brother is not yet one and my mother has left him in a nappy as it is too hot for any other clothing. My father's siblings and extended family are scattered and grouped on a concrete slab upon which a house is to be built. My cousins, who are a few years older than me and deeply tanned, run among the tall flowers and the cicadas. On this plot are two perfectly round lakes, water the colour of night sky, with depths that are unfathomable. I am mesmerised by them. I swim in the cool, brackish water of the one closest to the concrete slab so that I have sight of my mother. I kick hard as tingles go up my body at the thought of a sea monster with tentacles like an octopus sleeping in its sunless depths. It is a young child's fantasy so real my toes brush against its slimy skin.

The perfectly round lakes are called the gorghi tondi and somehow they connect to the sea. To me they are mythical, their depths filled with stories and creatures undiscovered. From my watery territory, I watch my cousins run to the most elevated part of the property. I watch them look out, to the blue line of the Mediterranean just below the sky.

As an adult I discover that the gorghi tondi are lakes that formed in volcanic craters. They are such a unique geological phenomenon that the land is now a World Heritage Site.

'Water is life. Water takes life.'

Andrea is 16 years old swimming in Lake Lucerne. He counts four strokes to each inhalation of forest-scented air. It is summer and the inhabitants of the city have dislocated from their daily lives to spend their holiday in the mountains or at sea level where the food fare is more exotic and the days more languid. The city is quiet, imbued with a warm slowness. With his mother, father and siblings, Andrea moved to Switzerland, a country where the ravages of the war barely tore at its edges. He visits the banks of the lake that twines through the city whenever he can.

On a day when the small waves drift dark-blue and clear, so that Andrea can see his feet on the gravelled bottom, in the middle of the lake a man begins to struggle. Andrea swims out, kicking fast. Minutes later he reaches the man who is tired from treading water and is struggling to keep his head above the surface. Andrea puts his arm around his torso and, breathing hard with the extra weight, shouts for help.

'Hilfe! Hilfe!' his voice bounces across the water. With his free arm he waves at a tourist boat that has just left the pier.

The boat reaches them and two stout men pull the drowning man up onto the deck. Water gives life but also takes it. Andrea declines a lift, preferring to glide to the other side of the lake, as he had initially intended to do. A man in another boat witnesses the near drowning and rows out to meet Andrea. The man in the rowboat is a few years older than Andrea, his skin sunburnt red. Noticing Andrea's dark features, the man greets him in Italian and soon Andrea is in the small boat chatting with the stranger. The man was his future brother-in-law.

'Our roots run deep and every vein is filled with water.'

Andrea is in his seventies. Wearing his rubber shoes, he sits on a rock in Umdloti, South Africa. With a knife he picks a mussel and opens it, squeezes lemon juice onto the mollusc and eats it, savouring it. There are far fewer mussels on the rocks than there were a few years ago. The beach that was once pristine has fewer shells and is strewn with bits of plastic. The sea no longer bears enough fruit for the growing human population, microplastics have become a part of the marine ecosystem, the perfect balance of life on Earth is teetering on a precipice. The precious oceans that run in our human veins are being destroyed.

learning to freedive

The free soul is rare, but you know it when you see it – basically because you feel good, very good, when you are near or with them.
— Charles Bukowski

I'm in a beach house on the outskirts of Simon's Town on the Cape Peninsula, so close to the Atlantic Ocean I can hear the seaspray. I am on a freediving and breath hold course led by multiple freediving champion Hanli Prinsloo and her husband Peter Marshall, a muscular six-foot-plus athlete who broke two world records for backstroke at the 2008 Olympic trials, representing the United States. The course started today, a Friday, and Hanli is explaining what happens in the body when you hold your breath. The extra oxygen that is stored in your spleen is released and this allows the body to keep going without fresh oxygen. Carbon dioxide build-up stimulates contractions. Basically, we can hold our breath for longer than we think, and with practice we can extend this.

When Hanli was competing, she would train underwater in a swimming pool and her coach would make her show the scuba diving signal for 'okay'; when Hanli's response was slow, the coach knew she had to surface. During breath hold blood and oxygen rush away from the skin to the organs, but if breath hold goes on for long it starts to affect brain function.

At the end of the day, as we say our goodbyes and step into the velvet night, Hanli tells us, 'If you usually have two cups of coffee in the morning, have one.' Caffeine elevates the heart rate, so less is better. As in many other sports, technique, diet, training, sleep and recovery all affect how well you do. The Marshalls are vegans and Hanli believes that as a freediver it is better to stick to fruits, vegetables and grains. I think they are vegan out of respect for fellow animals, not only for the sake of smoother metabolism. A week before the course Hanli suggested we not eat dairy. I have stuck to this because any practice that reduces oxygen consumption adds precious seconds to breath hold.

On Saturday morning I am lying on a wooden floor on a yoga mat alongside my five fellow participants.

Peter is leading us on a breath hold, and we need to hold for as long as we can. The sliding doors are open, letting fresh air into the room. I've taken a long, deep breath, filling my lungs from the bottom all the way up, and force a few more short breaths into my mouth, filling even this cavity to the brim with life-giving oxygen. It's slightly uncomfortable as my chest and neck feel full, but I relax and listen. My heart rate slows down rapidly and it starts to pump harder. With eyes closed and my sense of smell hindered, my auditory sense heightens and time slows down. Waves crash and ripple, big ones and smaller ones, there is the song of the spray and the wind that works with the water. In my mind's eye I can see the crests, the white foam, the slow continuous motion of the sea, each droplet merged into a mass of pounding blue. I can almost smell its saltiness. Through the open sliding doors, the wind carries the earthy fishiness of kelp and I wonder if I'm imagining it.

I am totally inside my body, the sounds around me keenly sharp. My chest feels expanded but still I let go of the discomfort and bring the sea inside me. Someone near me releases a puff of air, then someone else relents and begins to breathe, in and out. I don't feel the urge to exhale so I continue. I'm in a zone and I could go on forever.

Quite suddenly the top of my abdomen below the ribcage starts to flutter. A rapid rhythmic twitching takes control. Peter explained this to us in his precursory talk and the only way it stops is to start breathing. It is the body's instinctive response to breath hold, a way of forcing breathing, the most natural thing in the world, to start. It's like nothing I've experienced before; the involuntary muscle contraction is almost akin to labour during childbirth but without the pain.

I hold for a while longer, fascinated with what is happening in my body. And then the moment arrives when I can't any more and open my mouth, release the air that has been pent up in my lungs and take a hook breath – a short, shallow, quick breath, the way Hanli taught us.

I sit up and turn around to look at the rest of the group. There is still one person in breath hold – the Polish man. He looks strange not breathing, unnatural, dead but not. The rest of us look sleepy and exhausted like we've been up all night. Not a word is spoken, yet the room feels thick with the thrumming of our thoughts.

The last to let go, the Polish man exhales, and with him so does the room. We are all sitting up, looking at each other knowing that something has changed, something vital and sacred has just happened. There is bliss and curiosity, smiles. What we've just been through is strangely intimate.

The woman behind me, an avid surfer and art gallery owner, catches my gaze and says, 'I came out of breath hold and there you were, still holding. Wow.'

'Three minutes and twenty seconds,' Peter says to me. 'Just before three minutes you were struggling, your face was twitching. I was about to tap your foot in case you blacked out, but Hanli stopped me and let you go on. You got contractions.'

I held my breath the second longest: the Polish man held his for six minutes. For a beginner I did well. Six minutes is the yardstick for freedivers, where you want to get to with practice and conditioning. Contractions are normal and freedivers know how many more minutes they can push themselves from when they begin. Hanli can go for three minutes more.

We stretch, breathe, stretch our necks and roll our shoulders – breath hold is very physical. The Polish man explains that he has done a freediving course in Poland in a swimming pool where the instructor kept their heads underwater and forced them to endure. He said that this time it felt like angels were taking him up to heaven. I nod my head at his description because what I've just felt is euphoria.

We break for lunch, prepared by a cook whom Peter and Hanli bumped into, literally, when they were in Thailand. The food is vegan – carrot sticks, cherry tomatoes, hummus, tabouleh, flatbread – because dairy encourages the build-up of mucus, which is not good for breath hold, and animal product takes long to digest and uses a lot of oxygen. In freediving, every second of breath hold and every atom of oxygen counts.

I root inside my kitbag for my phone and type a fast message to my husband: *I did it! 3 min 20! Second longest in the group.*

Then I take a moment to indulge my pride, to smile secretly to myself, to smell the tang of salt and algae on the breeze. On a wall is a painting by Jake Aikman – a seascape of moody dark blues and tempestuous skies. I want to dive into it. Instead, I stare until I feel I am inside those colours, held by the water, safe in its wise embrace.

It is Saturday afternoon. I am approaching a point where I am about to be unborn, at the edge of everything that I have been waiting for my whole life. Where everything is about to come together. As I pull hard to get the wetsuit up my thighs, over my hips and high enough up my torso to slither my arms into the sleeves, I am squeezing my way back into a birth canal, one that will keep me snug, safe and warm when I enter the water. Physically I feel big and small at the same time, disembodied and detached from my usual world of chores, children, clients and embodied by the anticipation of a dream about to come true. I am so close.

I take a deep breath and duck-dive into the cold waters of the Atlantic Ocean. I am 50 metres from the shore of Windmill Beach upside down, pulling myself down the stem of a kelp plant the colour of olive oil. I remind myself to equalise and ease the pressure from my ears. The water is murky and alive with tiny floating bits. I'm surprised at how loud it is as all around me tiny creatures crackle. The stem of the kelp is not as slippery as it looks, and feels like a firm living rope in my hands, securely anchored to the seabed way below. This is a new experience for me, one I've been wanting to have for ages, one I promise myself I will do again.

Umbrella jellyfish flutter around my head like ballerinas of the deep. The kelp forest is thick, filtering the sunlight and mottling the ocean floor. Parts of the forest have trapped water warmed by the sun and it feels so delicious, so pronounced, against the frigidity of the mean temperature, which has settled at about 18 °C. I'm wearing a too-big 5-mm wetsuit, which I've rolled up at my ankles, and a hood – shivering starts quickly in these waters. The wetsuit hinders my proprioception – my sense of where my body is in the water – and I focus hard on keeping my body straight so it's easier for me to gain depth.

Near the water's surface the kelp blades are bushy but as I go deeper the seascape opens up. Hanli is further below and indicates for me to swim down. She makes eye contact and points – she's found a shark's egg so clear that you can see the embryo inside.

Hanli Prinsloo personifies the ocean. Her hair is dark brown, almost black, and falls in waves around her face. Her eyes are also dark and flicker the way the whites of breakers catch moonlight. Her skin is gently tanned and she has an easiness with water that is beyond human – she glides through it with the grace of a marine mammal.

I kick up to the surface where the waves bob and the wind sings a muffled song in my ears, and take a hook breath. I breaststroke towards my diving partner, a solid-bodied woman who has worked on yachts and has dived in the Maldives. 'You were down there for long. You didn't realise it because you were checking out that mermaid's purse and following that fish,' she says as we bob and dip with the swell.

It's Sunday, the last day of the course. My body feels limber and my breathing is easy; all the exercises yesterday have loosened muscle, mind and spirit. Last night I slept with the lullaby of the ocean still in my limbs. In my dreams I felt whole, held in a thicket of kelp forest, in the crepuscular light of the ocean, both alive and ancient.

The day is overcast and a light wind whips ponytails of cloud across a wide sky. The bedroom window of the Airbnb overlooks the sea and beyond it the rugged silhouette of Cape Point. My diving partner is in the same building and I catch a lift with her to the beach house. She tells me how she has been doing a bootcamp because she works at a blueberry company and has been eating blueberries as though they are peanuts. I listen as the darkening sky spreads a muted grey over the low hills. The flora is so green it looks like it is vibrating. The distant mountains are the colour of blueberries.

In a lull of silence, I do a body check. My ribs and lungs feel good, my arm muscles feel a little tender, on my left foot I have a scrape where the flippers have chafed my skin, but nothing that will prevent me from diving again today.

At the beach house we arrange our yoga mats on the wooden deck outside to stretch, breathe and ready ourselves for the next dive. We lie on our backs in meditation. One of the participants yelps and we all open our eyes and spring to our feet. A baboon has climbed over the railing and is watching us, a large male. 'Hanli, your baby!' I shout and she runs inside. The baboon lopes between us and is inside the house in seconds, exiting from a window with a loaf of garlic bread. He is gone and we are all relieved. It is their territory after all, has been for tens of thousands of years.

My heart is beating fast and I wonder what we'll encounter underwater. Hanli tells us that we probably won't see any large sharks as they prefer open water; the kelp forests are too dense and don't allow them to dash for their prey. If we see a great white shark, Hanli says, 'Look it right in the eye.'

After lunch we pull on wetsuits, grab weights, flippers, goggles and snorkels, and walk along the road to Fisherman's Beach. People on a Sunday drive wave at us. We pass other divers who tell us that visibility is good today.

At the beach Hanli starts to chat with a couple who look to be in their sixties. She's an open-water swimmer. 'Put dishwashing liquid into your wetsuit first, it slides on beautifully,' the swimmer says and Hanli's expression darkens.

'I hope you're not using stuff that will kill the fish,' she answers and I smile, quietly saluting her steely dedication to preserving the big blue.

We enter the water at a large flat granite rock. Peter first pulls on woollen socks, one with a hole at the toe, and then his flippers over them. I'm learning the tricks and this is one that prevents chafing. We wade through the kelp, through the warmth of the forest, until it opens up and there below is a sandy bottom. We swim behind Hanli and Peter towards some smaller rocky outcrops. I dive down, eager to explore the sea life, an exquisite dream of colours. It almost doesn't feel real. The overcast day sheds an even, natural light and I see black urchins, red anemones, blue striped nudibranchs, pink and white sea fans and red roman. Around me plankton snaps and sizzles.

The group convenes at the surface and Peter indicates for us to follow him to a dive site called A-frame. It is part of the Boulders Restricted Zone of the Table Mountain National Park Marine Protected Area, which reaches from the eastern end of Simon's Town Harbour to Oatlands. The site is well known but few know how to find it. Peter tells us to always use the flat granite rock as reference and, from there, to swim out and to the right. Beneath the waves he points to a tent-shaped swim-through – a gap in the rocks – about 8 metres down. Here, marine life is colourful and diverse. I watch the others go, but I decide to explore the area. I follow a fish down to the sandy seabed, watch it slurp something from a rock and then flutter towards another outcrop. I lose track of time. I have become a butterfly in this watery world where the principles of gravity pull me into another essence of time passing. Unlike diving in the kelp forest where kelp blades dapple and darken sunlight, A-frame is luminous and I relish the light.

Now it is later in the day. The clouds are still thick above me and the air cool on my cheeks. We're at another beach, ambling into shallow water where young children splash and play. We swim around rocks to where it's deeper and where a Cape fur seal is twirling and cajoling. It is magnificent, as large as a large man. Far away, a speedboat's motorised sound cuts through the water and it's so ear-splitting it feels like it's slicing through me. If this is how it feels for a small human, it must be utterly bone-rattling for large marine mammals. When the blaring subsides the ocean calms and with it me. I feel free, boundless in this magnificent aquatic world. Soon I will be back in my inland city, locked away from the sea. The thought pulls on my gut as though I'm grieving.

the mammalian diving reflex

Freediving is a sport of self-discipline and self-awareness, where you learn to push your limits and unlock your true potential.

– Herbert Nitsch

Humans have been diving to great depths on a single breath for millennia. Staggering distances have been recorded since the early 1900s, with Giorgos Statti in Greece diving to 70 metres to retrieve a coin, Frenchman Jacques Mayol plunging to 100 metres in 1976 and Austrian Herbert Nitsch reaching 214 metres in 2007 using a weighted sled to descend and a buoyancy device to surface. More recently, William Trubridge dived to 102 metres in 2016, Alessia Zecchini reached 123 metres in 2023 and Alexey Molchanov reached 133 metres in the same year – all using a monofin. A monofin is a fin that both feet fit into, giving the diver a dolphin-like 'tail'.

Professional freedivers continue to extend the limits of their reach, going a few or many metres deeper at each world record attempt. The sport has limitations set by the human body's response to lack of oxygen, increased carbon dioxide and mounting water pressure.

I like to think that the abilities of competitive freedivers point to the fact that humans are semi-aquatic. Our bodies seem built for water immersion, some bodies being more adept than others. Most babies, when put into water, instinctively react by swimming and holding their breath. This reflex has been attributed to the cause of sudden infant death syndrome (SIDS) or cot death, when babies stop breathing.

Beth Neale, a South African competitive freediver you'll read about later, submerged her daughter Neve when she was three months old. Beth tells me that Neve held her breath, exhaled a little, but it was obvious that her mammalian diving reflex had kicked in. 'She is so comfortable in the water that, as a baby, when I went into the ocean, as the water went above my knees and touched her feet, she put her face in the crook of my neck and fell asleep,' says Beth.

From all that Beth has researched about diving reflex in children, what she understood about her own toddler is that the reflex becomes a lesser response beyond the age of six or seven months. Babies experience a laryngospasm, which is when the throat naturally locks, and before six months this happens instinctively. 'With Neve it was still natural until about seven months. At eight months she would come up and cough a little, so I started teaching her,' says Beth. Beth also explains that when the face is immersed in water, chemoreceptors around the eyes push the diving reflex to kick in sooner, which is why during her record attempts she prefers to go without a mask.

Some believe that the diving response stops when a toddler begins to walk, because the need to survive in water diminishes. Yet this reflex is inherent; we can access it and train ourselves to extend our time underwater, to harvest the treasures of the sea and enjoy the feeling of weightlessness. We continue to be seduced by water, whether we're diving, swimming, immersing ourselves in it for our health, simply playing in it as children or exploring its depths and its shallows. We heed its call to explore, find bliss and push our own physical and mental limits.

What happens to the human body during freediving? As the face is immersed in water, the mammalian diving reflex kicks in, slowing down the heart rate and causing blood to move to the thoracic area. This blood shift keeps the vital organs safe and provides protection for the lungs, so that they don't collapse. Unlike other diving mammals, humans have not adapted to managing lung compression – as a freediver swims deeper, the lungs become smaller.

The deeper the freediver descends, the smaller the volume of air in the body. At the water's surface, the atmospheric pressure is 1 bar. At 10 metres, it is 2 bars, halving the volume of air in the body. An interesting thing happens at about 20 metres: neutral buoyancy is reached, which means that one neither sinks nor floats. The freediver is simply suspended. Just beyond this point of equilibrium, hydrostatic pressure takes hold; one becomes negatively buoyant and is pulled downwards, entering a state of continuous freefall. This is what may have happened to freediver Natalia Molchanova – she may have reached this freefall depth and passed out, or she may have become disorientated, not knowing up from down, continuing to soar or drop to the greatest depths of the sea. A poetic ending for someone so in love with the water.

At 50 metres, a freediver continues to freefall and the lungs become more compressed. The lungs are at residual volume – the volume of air that remains in the lungs after maximum exhalation. The lung tissue is under strain and the freediver needs to be careful not to make big movements that could cause injury to any part of the pulmonary system.

At 100 metres, lung volume can decrease to between 9 and 4,5 per cent of surface volume – the lungs become the size of pillboxes. Yet some individuals are extremely tolerant of lung compression at depths beyond this.

Chris McKnight is a research fellow in the School of Biology at the University of St Andrews in Scotland. His primary focus is marine mammals and he spends weeks, sometimes months, tracking and observing seals. This has led him to study some of the world's greatest vertical freedivers. He tells me that the elite freedivers were phenomenal to work with, very keen to have instruments attached to them on their dives. For him, it's fascinating – groundbreaking, even – to learn more about what happens inside the human body when submerged.

Chris and his team develop tools to follow diving mammals, measuring their heart rate and blood oxygenation, and changes in blood volume and brain oxygenation. 'Doing research on humans is a great stepping stone for us because we can ask questions to deeper understand what happens to the body during a dive.' Chris's Irish accent is thick.

He chats to me from his home in Dublin – in the frame of the Zoom call, it looks like a surfer's house: lots of light wood, and everything in it is functional, not just decorative.

He explains that one of the crucial differences between humans and marine mammals is that we have sinuses and they don't. Without air-filled sinuses, marine mammals do not suffer the effects of changing pressure as much as humans do. We need to equalise to match the pressure in the middle ear to that of the depth. Another fundamental difference is that marine mammals don't have involuntary breathing movements, or contractions, and we do. Those who have held their breath to the point of these contractions know that they are uncomfortable and uncontrollable, and only stop once you exhale the carbon dioxide that has built up in the lungs.

'What freedivers who go to depths of sixty, a hundred metres have conditioned themselves to tolerate is phenomenal. They present an incredibly unique model for research,' says Chris. The research hopes to uncover how freedivers condition themselves to endure bouts of exceptionally low oxygen, which could help doctors treating cardiac patients.

'A few of the key things we found was a reduction in heart rate. The freediver's heart rate declined through the descent, just like a dolphin's, until it was 11 beats per minute at the bottom of the dive. In some of the deep dives that went past ninety metres, the heart rate got lower than what we'd expect to see in marine mammals, which was a surprise. Physiologically, deep diving is a stressful situation and I didn't expect heart rate to get as low as that.

'Other interesting changes occurred in oxygen levels. We measured the oxygenation of blood being delivered to vital organs like the brain. At the onset of exercise during descent, these levels, which are normally at 98 per cent, dropped enormously to as low as 25 per cent, which is well below the point at which we expect people to lose consciousness, which is at 50 per cent. One particular diver was tolerating levels in deoxygenation in the brain that far exceed those of marine mammals.

'Brain metabolic rate also drops, so it shuts down. A lot of the body is shut down so that it can better utilise oxygen for the major organs. It goes back to normal in 45 seconds once they surface and concomitant with that is brain oxygenation.

'We also saw a big increase in blood pressure and high intracranial pressure. Deep diving is a complete physiological assault,' says Chris.

What Chris observed, but did not document, while researching elite freedivers was their desire to push the boundary of where their body could go, how much pressure they could withstand and how much further they could fly into the depths, using only the oxygen they took into their lungs at the surface.

While the long-term effects of freediving on the mind and body have not been clearly established, some athletes feel a change in their mood. Chris tells me that after a number of days of doing deep dives, some of the divers had to take a day off because they felt cranky, angry and emotionally vulnerable.

As freedivers immerse themselves deeper into the blue and as research on them continues, it will be interesting to see what is uncovered.

As I move my focus to those who enjoy the sea on the surface, I find a study done by the French Swimming Federation, published in 2024, on the physiological traits of extreme open-water swimmers. It piques my interest as I have wondered how regular and long hours of swimming affect the body. Surfers, and people who swim in cold water, can develop bony growths in the ear canal, or external auditory exostoses, a condition better known as surfer's ear. Swimming influences the lungs by increasing capacity, which is beneficial, but it can also make them swell from a build-up of fluids, which can cause illness. I've heard of long-distance swimmers falling ill with swimming-induced pulmonary oedema (SIPE), which affects those who swim in cold water under high physical exertion.

The French Swimming Federation study showed that the success of open-water swimmers depends on their ability to swim hard and fast for many hours. The researchers found a number of common attributes in 14 elite male open-water swimmers: a highly developed aerobic capacity, which is the body's ability to use oxygen efficiently during prolonged exercise, and elevated lactate thresholds, which allows them to swim longer and faster without muscle fatigue. The conclusion was this: the better a swimmer's body is at using oxygen and managing lactate build-up, the better they can swim.

I think of my freediving and how well the body works with little oxygen, and I go back to practising breath hold.

a brief history of water

While snorkelling in Tanzania I was astounded that so much of the coral reef is bleached. When something starts it's so much harder to stop it than preventing it in the first place.

– Robyn Granger

The sea has tribal memory. Since the beginning, water has been an intimate part of our human story, flowing through the myths and history of many cultures. It is a food source, a life force, an economic resource, a place to play, a mystery to explore, a passage between lands, a pilgrimage, a baptism, a river that carries the dead. It is at once intimately personal and hugely universal. In each ancient droplet there is a tome of memory as old as the Earth.

Arguably, the water on planet Earth has been around since the planet was formed and makes up an enormous water system that is in constant motion. Water is stored in glaciers, in rivers and lakes, in seas and oceans, and in the ground. Water can freeze, be fluid, and rise up to the sky as vapour, to form above the planet as clouds suspended in air. It is a constantly moving system of currents, clouds and precipitation. It flows through everything – animals, plants, soil.

Water is an integral part of life and is present in all creatures on Earth – it makes up about 60 per cent of the bodies of humans, 80 per cent of fish, between 80 and 90 per cent of plants and about 75 per cent of insects. Many chemical reactions that happen in living cells need water, and organisms can't produce food without it.

Our oceans are the planet's biggest ecosystem with an estimated volume of 1 386 million cubic kilometres. One cubic kilometre equals a trillion litres, which is enough water to fill 400 000 Olympic-sized swimming pools. But over the past hundred years or so, industrialisation, the destruction of forests, mining, overfishing, farming, human-made waste, plastic, how and what we eat, and the polyester in the clothes we wear have caused havoc with our marine system. We are killing it with such ferocity and speed it threatens to unbalance life on Earth as we know it.

Everything is connected. We are all made of the same stuff. While there are a million and one factors that contribute to life on Earth, this chapter aims to simplify how oceans and the atmosphere were formed. Billions of years ago, conditions in a primordial sea gave rise to a self-replicating molecule and for the next 1,5 billion years life evolved. There is evidence that photosynthesis began approximately 2,5 billion years ago and over the next hundreds of millions of years, oxygen built up in the ocean and the atmosphere – enough to sustain complex life.

Something occurred that caused a group of microbes known as cyanobacteria to evolve so that they could generate energy from sunlight. The hypothesis is that over a span of 200 to 300 million years, cyanobacteria released oxygen into seawater, which accumulated over the ocean until it escaped into the atmosphere and reacted with methane and compounds that contain nitrogen, Earth's main atmospheric gases in those days. Oxygen concentrations increased and began displacing other gases. This caused a chain of evolutionary changes in organisms, and major changes for the planet. As methane was the main greenhouse gas, trapping heat from sunlight, the more it was displaced by oxygen, the more global temperatures dropped to the point that water turned to ice, creating ice sheets that extended across a large portion of the earth's surface. Scientists call this the 'snowball effect' – more sunlight was reflecting off the Earth's surface causing further cooling.

The presence of so much oxygen in the atmosphere also caused the formation of the ozone layer. The sun's ultraviolet radiation split oxygen molecules into two atoms of oxygen, which then reacted with another oxygen molecule to create ozone – O_3. It was at this time, billions of years ago, that conditions were perfect for an enormous evolutionary step into aerobic metabolism. This is referred to as the Cambrian explosion, which is believed to have been driven by the cooler temperatures and high oxygen concentration.

Some believe that oxygen created a poisonous environment for the species that were adapted to a methane-rich environment. Yet organisms found ways to survive by using the potential of oxygen in respiration. What this caused was the evolution of animal life. Interestingly, when astrophysicists look for life on other planets, they look for the presence of oxygen and water, as they know that these are major factors in sustaining life as we know it.

Cape Town-born Robyn Granger is a palaeo-oceanographer who works for the Royal Netherlands Institute for Sea Research. She studies the ocean to find out what it was like billions of years ago. She focuses on the Benguela Current, a wide, cold ocean current that begins around Cape Agulhas and flows northwards along the west coast of South Africa and the Namibian coast. She unpacks the paradigm that nothing is an enigma, and that by scratching the surface secrets from aeons ago can be revealed. Even if it's a mere idealistic interpretation of the happenings, it gives a sense of what the Earth could have been like millions of years ago, long before humans made an appearance.

She chats to me virtually from Den Helder in the Netherlands. Before presenting her interests, she explains that with academic studies, the more deeply you go into something the more weirdly niche it becomes, honing further into the immense unknown of the world. She gives me a brief history of water, explaining that the water we drink was once part of an ocean. The exact period is indeterminable but as her words build a story, I become enthralled by the romance of it.

All the liquid on this planet was once a river, a sea, a cloud, rain.

Everything has been everything else. It all gets recycled. Materially, all the world's oceans are part of us and we are part of every ocean. The oceans are inside our bodies. Like delicate cirrostratus clouds, the concept hovers around my head, just above my line of sight.

Robyn says that there is general agreement among researchers that the oceans were formed over vast swathes of time. Water was a gas until Earth cooled to below 100 °C, when condensation was able to happen. This was approximately 3,8 billion years ago, about 1,2 billion years after Earth was formed. Once the surface cooled to below the boiling point of water, nimbus clouds gathered and rain began to fall – and continued to fall for centuries. The water flowed into the basins and hollows of the planet, forming oceans and seas. For a sense of scale, early humans seem to have emerged about 2 million years ago.

Robyn unpacks the formation of oceans as simply as she can. She reiterates that it is not an exact science as we cannot definitively answer questions about processes that occurred millions and billions of years ago, but we can put forward useful theories. In this light, it is speculated that the oceans and the atmosphere accumulated over millions of years with the continual degassing of the planet's interior. Basically, water vapour escaped from molten rocks into the atmosphere.

There are many processes involved in how and where the oceans were formed. Where the moon is in relation to Earth and plate tectonics both play a role. When Earth was 2 billion years old, the moon was much closer to it. Earth's rotation was also much faster, so a day was about eighteen hours long. The moon had a stronger gravitational pull on Earth, affecting tides. The gravitational interaction between moon and Earth has always affected the tides and tidal patterns, and with that the movement of water around the planet.

Even today, plate tectonics determines whether an ocean basin is shrinking or growing. The Pacific is an old ocean that is growing smaller, whereas the Atlantic is getting larger. The African Rift Valley is in the process of becoming an ocean again. This is why continents have been in different positions throughout history – the supercontinent Pangaea was surrounded by one enormous ocean, but with geologic movements over time, the continents moved and other oceans were created.

The rotation of Earth affects winds, which influenced ocean currents and the relationship between the surface and the atmosphere. Changes in how much heat from the sun reached the oceans affected their temperature and characteristics, creating conditions that allowed life to begin. The ocean probably needed tens of millions of years, followed by a long period of stability, to create a suitable environment for life. If the oceans were colder, life would not have developed as it did.

How ice sheets form depends on the way Earth moves in relation to the sun in glacial and interglacial cycling, phases that last a hundred thousand years. Triggers cause the shift from one phase to the other. Robyn explains that when Earth is in cold mode, a climate trigger changes it to a warmer system. The Earth changes the cycle as a reaction to where it is in the solar system.

The shift from one phase to another changes how currents flow around the whole oceanic system, slowing or accelerating globally circulating ocean currents. And eventually, at some point, there might be a trigger that causes a water mass to start sinking. There is research that focuses on which triggers were responsible for the glacial to interglacial shifts because they may not all have been the same throughout Earth's recent climate history. This research is extremely specialised, so the conversation shifts back to Robyn's study.

'I like looking at really long records,' Robyn says. 'Atmospheric systems have really long time scale plots. And there is always the question: but how do we really know? Fossils are very beautiful and I like uncovering stuff that is so much older than a human will ever experience. There are these tiny organisms, foraminifera, which are a perfect preservation of an entire ocean and it helps untangle what was going on.

Foraminifera are single-celled organisms, about half a millimetre long, with calcium carbonate shells called tests. They act as the ocean's archives if you know how to interpret them. They are these seemingly insignificant things that are becoming something important, because they can tell us something about the past.'

Some microfossils, like those of foraminifera, tell a story about a large ocean basin, while others reflect the history of a very small system with local climate influences. There are creatures that live in the benthic zone, the deepest section in a body of water, and most of these animals are invertebrates – crabs, anemones, sponges, starfish, urchins, worms and bivalves. For palaeo-oceanographers, these creatures record the goings-on in the sea floor environment. Those that live in the surface levels, at depths of 50 to 100 metres, record the happenings in the atmosphere. The bottom of the atmosphere and the top of the ocean affect each other tremendously because they constantly interact.

Oceans keep the planet cool. They absorb large amounts of heat, and absorb and store carbon dioxide – preventing large amounts of greenhouse gases from accumulating in the atmosphere and raising the temperature. Oceans distribute heat around the globe through currents, with cool waters transported to the equator and warm waters moved towards the poles.

Robyn's focus is on the southeast Atlantic, the west coast of South Africa and further up, where the Benguela Current flows and there is high productivity – the production of large volumes of organic matter by phytoplankton, which supports greater amounts of life in the ocean. Higher productivity affects the chemical composition of the ocean, reducing oxygen levels, which has implications for other systems. The system stays in equilibrium, so if one thing decreases, another increases. It is an equation of addition and subtraction.

'My research is essentially trying to figure out if there were times in the past where there were higher oxygen concentrations in some parts of the Benguela Current and lower at other points, and what this means for carbon dioxide in the atmosphere. Because we know, although science is never certain, that there were times of glacial periods in Earth's history and interglacial, or warmer, periods. The idea is that often other things that are happening in the ocean system link up with that, so you might see that there's more deoxygenation when the Earth was warmer.'

Alongside other scientists, Robyn is trying to put all her bits of research into a wider picture to find the connections. 'I was basically part of a group working towards establishing whether a new proxy method can be used in this region to identify past changes in ocean productivity using foraminifera microfossils.'

Fossil evidence suggests that foraminifera have been around for 540 million years, and there are about 4 000 species still present today in various marine environments. Forty of these species float on the water's surface and the rest live on the ocean floor in mud or sand, or on coral reefs, rocks and plants. They are found in all marine environments, from the icy poles to the balmy tropics, yet each species is very specific about where it lives.

Robyn is looking at shell composition to see whether it records nitrogen changes. 'It's working well. We think that this method of looking at the organic composition of these fossils, which have been preserved for millions and millions of years, will tell us if the oceans were more productive, if there was more nitrogen – and therefore more carbon – coming into the ocean, if we had more carbon sinks or sources. So, it seems like a nice method, and I'm working on developing that.

'Climate and ocean changes are interlinked; they are constantly affecting one another. Using microfossils and using other techniques to look back in time, you can piece the clues together. It's like being a climate detective. It's about uncovering the processes that led to the formation of these foraminifera fossils and the composition of their shells.'

Essentially, Robyn hopes to be able to determine which atmospheric processes were going on, as these affect nitrogen levels. Was more nitrogen and carbon being taken up by our oceans? In a climate that is warming, more carbon and nitrogen tends to be released into the atmosphere, which we're experiencing now. Robyn paints a bigger picture in terms of changes and scale. 'Every little place on the planet is different. Some ocean areas might be taking up more, others may be releasing more. In a warming world, the ocean and climate models predict there will be an increased flux of carbon dioxide released from oceans.'

And, 'Of course climate change is real,' Robyn says. Climate change is ongoing and natural, driven by solar system cycles. Yet human-induced climate change is very recent, having happened in the past one hundred years or so. Robyn explains that these rapid changes will be reflected in records in a hundred to two hundred years from now, and that scientists then will certainly see strong changes in those records. 'We are coming out of a glacial phase but I think we're coming out of it too rapidly; this is what the climate change activists are worried about. We're in a transition. We're not sure if it's going to continue at this speed.'

Robyn is careful when predicting changes and their causes, and says that it's difficult to compare long-term climate records with short-term ones. 'However, all the data that we have from the past one hundred or more years suggests that the changes we are seeing now are directly linked to anthropogenic influence. We know that millions of years ago that was not the case, so in essence we have added an additional forcing – humans – to a system, which now is responding to that forcing.'

As Johannesburg experiences a heat wave like I have never felt in all my life, my anxiety about global warming escalates. I prefer summer to winter, I love the heat, but these high temperatures are worrying. With her wide perspective, Robyn is far more sensible. 'We have a human-focused point of view and a small lifespan. The Earth will still continue if we screw it up. It will still continue and oceans will always be shifting and changing.'

I've heard that scientists can predict the future of our oceans using models that show different scenarios. Robyn explains that no model is perfect, and different models can be used to answer different questions. Some scientists want to focus on a certain period, or a specific region, or are looking to get an accurate range for one or two variables, allowing for larger uncertainty in others. But the more models there are, and the more robust they are, the better the trends that emerge.

In the relatively near future of 100 000 years from now, the ocean basins will have changed very little, as this is such a small time scale. The biology of things, however, will depend on many factors, including whether we're in a glacial or interglacial period; it's difficult to say, but Robyn is sure things will be different. Over larger time scales of millions of years, ocean temperatures will fluctuate. Creatures that prefer warmer conditions will fare better. In twenty or so million years, the Atlantic will persist in its expansion and the Pacific will continue to shrink. A supercontinent will assemble. The oceans will be reshaped, currents rerouted. Ecosystems will rise and fall with the changing chemistry and temperature of the sea. And whichever creatures inhabit those future oceans – whether they resemble anything we know now or not – will carry in their cells the legacy of Earth's long history.

breaking records in frozen lakes

I've had many struggles with mental health and addiction, but freediving has given me a purpose and a way to push my limits.

– Amber Fillary

Amber Fillary puts a finger under the elastic of her bikini bottoms and pulls so that the fabric lies smooth and flat across her bottom. She dips the big toe of her right foot into the water and a zing of cold shoots up her leg. She sits down on the ice, her feet, ankles and shins in the water. The backs of her thighs are cold but she is in her element, in her zone, her happy place. She slides in and feels the softness, the slowness of the water at -4 °C.

It's 29 February 2020 and Amber is about to break the Guinness World Record for the longest horizontal freedive under ice wearing only a swimsuit, a swimming cap and goggles – an accessory she has to wear to protect her eyes from freezing. The 70-metre swim in the dynamic no fins discipline is taking place at Lake Oppsjø in Norway.

She takes a breath and dives in. Slowly she glides under the ice, past the safety holes that have been cut into it every 10 metres, until she reaches the 70-metre mark and calmy floats to the surface. Smiling, she is received with applause and shouts of celebration – she has just broken the record for the longest horizontal freedive under ice without fins, a wet suit or a weight belt. She's beaten Johanna Nordblad of Finland, who accomplished a 50-metre swim in March 2015.

Then, in 2021, while Amber was in the thick of arranging sponsorship for an event to beat the men's record, which stood at 83 metres, she was bested by Johanna. What Amber didn't expect was the outbreak of a pandemic that would thwart her chances to reclaim the record.

I chat to her in February 2021, a year after her 70-metre swim. 'Oh, you're not what I expected,' she says as I appear on video on a WhatsApp call. She looks disappointed. I think she was imagining someone prettier, younger perhaps. Instead, what she sees is someone more or less her age, with dark curly hair tumbling down her shoulders uncontained. What I see is a petite, fit, red-haired woman with a self-deprecating streak. I decide not to ask what she was expecting, and jump right in with the questions.

My first curiosity is to ask her how she feels about her world record. 'I have to wait another year before I can attempt to break the world record, which is currently held by Johanna, who swam further than me in January 2021,' she says, her frustration clear across the WhatsApp line.

'I'm a little bit disappointed. I was in Germany and then I came back to South Africa. Setting up a world-record-breaking attempt is a lot to organise. Also, I don't have snow in my back yard. Johanna lives in Finland; it's what she's used to.'

Amber pauses to drag on her cigarette and then tells me that she has swum under ice four times.

Once she surrenders, diving under the ice is beautiful. The water is slow and the visibility is good because it's fresh water. The light comes in through the ice and she finds it magical. She's part of the element and she yields to it because it's more powerful. 'You can't fight it, or else you're screwed. I do sometimes get scared, but then I switch my brain off and feel that the water is looking after me. It's my space and it's where I get peace.'

Amber doesn't play by the rules. She doesn't do a breathe-up, she doesn't remember ever getting contractions, and when I ask her what she eats after a record-breaking attempt, she answers flatly, 'You're asking someone with an eating disorder what they eat?'

Amber was born in Cape Town and started swimming when she

was very young. In high school she swam seriously for a few years, receiving Western Province colours, but then developed anorexia, which unfortunately affected her performance.

Amber is a recovering alcoholic. She is outspoken about mental health, prone to depression herself. It is the water that releases her mind from its spinning wheel, the cold that calms her. 'It's the best way of getting high without drugs,' she tells me several times, always through a smile, and convinces me to try it.

Her journey of becoming a world record breaker and one of the best athletes swimming under ice has taken her to many parts of the world. She likes to travel and has cultivated a relaxed and loosely tethered bond to places. In her early twenties she moved to England with a pocketful of her father's money, which she quickly drank away. She found a job as a lifeguard at a swimming pool in London. It was massive – double-Olympic-sized – and open year-round. She worked there all through the year, but primarily in winter, and that's when she started cold-water swimming.

'It was kind of mad. There was a swimming club that would swim in winter. The guys would swim naked but would wear a swimming cap, because most of your body heat escapes from your head. The girls swam in swimming costumes. I wanted to do it as well, so I did,' Amber smiles.

A group of people with multiple sclerosis also bathed there. From them she learnt that regular exposure to cold water relieves inflammation and pain. For Amber it relieved much more – cold water became her saviour.

On the screen of the video call I see blue sky and hints of glossy leaves. Glints of sunlight bounce through the camera lens in time with her erratic movements. The cigarette is long extinguished. She flops back on her couch and continues, 'I lived near Hyde Park. In winter, I used to run there in my T-shirt and then go swimming in the lake. I remember running through ice. If it doesn't kill you, it makes you feel the best. Cold-water swimming is addictive because it makes you feel good.'

In her forties she went to Egypt, to the crystalline seas of Sharm El Sheik. She wanted to feel free in the water and was pulled to do a freediving course. She dived to 30 metres but both her eardrums perforated and she had to surface. In the hospital waiting room, as blood trickled from both ears, her instructor suggested she try pool breath hold. A few weeks later, she won a no-fins competition. She returned to South Africa and broke a number of pool freediving records – for static breath hold at 6 minutes as well as horizontal distance breath hold with no fins at 134 metres.

She then entered an international competition, but it was disastrous. 'Mentally I crashed. It was my first big competition. I had worked so hard. I was on my own because South Africa wasn't represented by AIDA. It overwhelmed me,' she says. (AIDA is the Association Internationale pour le Développement de l'Apnée, or International Association for the Development of Apnea. It is the international federation that oversees freediving rules, competitions and records.)

She looked for an opportunity to swim underneath ice and found an event in Finland. When she realised she could do it, she decided to break the world record. There were two problems, though: finding someone who could help set up the record event, and getting sponsorship. Amber got sponsorship from pharmaceutical company Cipla and the same person who organised the attempt for Johanna Nordblad helped her. 'The whole experience was shit,' she says.

After the failed attempt, a freediver friend put her in touch with Arve Gravningen, the headmaster of a school for children with addiction in Norway, and the owner of Fridykker, a company that specialises in services and products for freedivers and underwater rugby enthusiasts. For Amber, finding Arve was a stroke of luck. He understood her mental anguish and her keenness for being marked as one of the world's best freedivers. 'Arve put together an amazing team of safety divers and scuba divers who all volunteered to do it. How cool is that?' she says, her excitement palpable.

I ask her if they helped her because she has a history of addiction and she says yes. I ask her about her training. 'Just in a swimming pool in South Africa.' There's a blasé shrug in her words. 'I focused on breath hold and technique because it's not a weighted dive. So, it's about getting the breath hold right. I went to Berlin to get into ice lakes and to get used to the water. In Norway I had ten days to get the ropes right.' For safety reasons, when swimming underneath ice, the swimmer is attached to a lanyard, which is attached to a rope above them. This rope has to be placed correctly underneath the ice so that the swimmer can progress smoothly. After a pause, she says, 'I just have the ability to get into cold water and just be relaxed.'

'I have goggles on,' Amber continues, 'so my eyes are open – I was told that the water is too cold for the eyes and that they can freeze – and the visibility is okay. The ice thickness was only 25 cm. With global warming it was very difficult to find a lake with 30 cm of ice – a competition requirement.'

For her next event in 2022, Amber trains with coach Allen Stubbs at Jan van Riebeeck High School in Cape Town. By February 2021, she has completed approximately eight weeks of intensive pool training under his guidance. Allen is known for his expertise in training competitive swimmers. When I chat to him on the phone, he tells me that he has known her for a long time but has only coached her for three years. With the calm certainty of someone who has spent years reading bodies in water, Allen fine-tunes her technique. The training is a structured programme to get her physically fit. In the first two weeks they focus on breath hold, swimming 50 metres of freestyle on the surface. In the third week, she swims an underwater stroke, and by the fourth and fifth week she's ready. 'The breath hold is her job, she does that perfectly. She swims 115 metres in one breath in an underwater breaststroke, effortlessly and with no problem. She's ready for it,' says Allen.

Allen changes the programme all the time so that it doesn't get frustrating for Amber. He has also helped her adapt her stroke so that her movement is more efficient and she glides further through the water.

'What I love about Amber is that she's an anomaly. She smokes, drinks coffee, doesn't eat as she 'should', and has a history of alcohol addiction. This is part of what makes her an extraordinary athlete. At South African championship events, you'll find freediving competitors at the side of the pool preparing and stretching. Amber arrives, looks at you and gets into the water. She's in the water for 15 seconds, takes three or four little breaths, then one big breath, and off she goes. A lot of the coaches are scared of coaching Amber because she's gung-ho,' says Allen.

During training, buoyancy is also a factor because she doesn't use weights. Swimming under ice with weight is easy, whereas having no weight fastened around her waist means she has to blow out a lot of air when she's submerging, leaving her with half a lungful. Allen trains her to count her strokes and stay in rhythm until her timing is perfect. There's more control in her swimming compared to when she started, a practised quiet that wasn't there in the beginning. With Allen's guidance, Amber has learnt to slow everything down – her heart rate, her breath, her thoughts, her stroke.

The next part of Amber's training is in Dahab with breath hold coach Brian Crossland. Her five-days-a-week regime consists of gym and weight training, an hour of pool training, and visualisation exercises to hone her mental focus. For the ice dive, Brian flips the usual breath hold training because in very cold water a long preparation isn't possible. The mammalian diving reflex needs to kick in without a warm-up.

Brian tells me that Amber's body relaxes the moment she touches water. She doesn't react to high levels of carbon dioxide like other freedivers do and her recovery is immense; she starts talking the moment she pops her head up at the end of the ice swim.

Like her other coaches, Brian describes Amber as an anomaly. 'She is very determined and, as a coach, if you understand her you get amazing results,' he adds.

Her training then takes her from Dahab to Berlin, where she spends a few weeks acclimatising to cold water.

breaking records in frozen lakes

Fast forward to 26 February 2022, and I'm chatting to Amber over a WhatsApp call when she's in Norway for her record-breaking event. 'I don't want to get too cocky or too confident until it's over. I've been having bad dreams. I hope I don't lose focus,' she says. She's been there for a week and I can hear she's uneasy, the familiar self-doubt back in her voice.

'The first day I got here I was nervous about the cold so I just got into the water. I'm hoping I can do the hundred-metre dive tomorrow or a hundred and five. I think for the record I'll do the hundred metres really good,' she says. I imagine her pacing in her small rented flat.

She's an hour and twenty minutes' drive outside Oslo, and a thirty-minute drive to lake Mysutjernet, so it's simple for her to train daily. Arve, the headmaster and freediver who helped Amber with her first world record, and his dad have been helping her. 'I am so blessed, so blessed. Arve's dad picks me up and drives me to the lake. Then it's a five-minute walk to the starting hole. There's even a sauna.'

What's different from her first world record attempt is that this time she doesn't have a lanyard attached to a rope that guides her along in a straight line. 'It's one less thing to worry about. I follow the line on the bottom of the lake, it's shallow so it's easy to see. Everything else is the same – even the nerves,' she explains.

'I do wonder why the hell I'm doing this again. In Egypt I thought, what the eff am I doing, spending all this money, holding my breath underwater?' Her apprehension crackles down the WhatsApp line.

'Hopefully it goes okay. I'll be relaxed afterwards. I've got another week of nerves. I want to have done the distance before I do the record. I'll just see what I do tomorrow or the next day and I'll stick to it. Even if I do ninety, it's still a good dive and that will be my distance.'

I ask her to take me through her process step by step. 'At the lake, I get into my costume and then get my head into what I'm doing. Then I get into the water. I swim and then I get out. I'd like to do more but it's just too cold. That's why I get so nervous – there's no warming up,

I just have to get in and do the distance. There's no playing in the water, because it's hovering at zero degrees and it takes too much energy. Yesterday I didn't feel so cold so maybe I'm getting acclimatised.'

The sauna is at the starting point of her dive, so afterwards she puts on her neoprene shoes, walks back to it and steps inside. It takes her two and a half minutes to stop shivering and get back to normal body temperature. 'It's my hands and feet that get cold. Sometimes my hands can hurt a little bit as they defrost. It's not that bad because I don't spend much time in the water.'

I ask her what she does with the rest of her day. 'I have a really nice apartment. I do YouTube work-outs in the morning with weights I've borrowed from Arve. I read and I watch TV. I go to the toilet a lot because my stomach is working overtime. I visualise my arm strokes for the distance, just over forty.'

How is the preparation for this record different from the last time? 'I've got a little bit too much time to prepare; the last time I didn't.'

I chat to her again on 5 March 2022 and her nerves have been replaced with pure exhilaration. She has just broken the men's world record for the longest under-ice swim with breath held and without fins or a wetsuit. 'I did it! I could've gone to a hundred metres but I stuck with ninety because that's what was prearranged with Guinness. But I could've gone further.'

The achievement is an early birthday present for Amber, who turns 50 in April. It makes her a multi-world record holder. She also carries the torch for the longest under-ice swim with breath held (no fins and no suit) in the female category, as well as a record for the longest underwater walk with breath held.

I'm not surprised that cold water holds something like solace for her. It does the same for many people. The moment your face meets its surface, the mammalian diving response awakens. Blood draws inward, away from the fingers and toes, towards the heart, the lungs, the brain. You'd think it would feel like retreat, but instead it brings a strange interior warmth, a kind of surrender. I know because after my many chats with Amber I start cold-water dipping. Thought slows. The noise dims. What's left is the pulse of the present. In that suspended moment, we are stripped back to our most essential self – not athlete, not survivor, not seeker, just a body meeting the cold with focus and resolve. There's something liberating in that simplicity. Something that feels like truth.

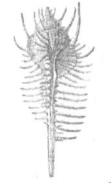

acclimatising to cold

THIS IS ANTARCTICA, unpredictable, harsh and hostile. Yet out of this world beautiful. We will continue the swim tomorrow afternoon. We hope for warmer water. 0C would be great!
— Ram Barkai's Facebook page, 12 November 2024

Ram Barkai is close to seventy, yet he exudes the fitness and vitality of a man twenty years younger. He is tanned and has a full head of salt-and-pepper hair. His enthusiasm shines in his eyes. Ram has had a number of life transformations. His appetite for risk is huge. He's been married and divorced twice, has four children and was the CEO of South African financial services company Cadiz Holdings. He holds a Guinness World Record for the southernmost swim of 1 km in Antarctica. In 2009, following his passion for endurance swimming – cold-water swimming, particularly – he founded the International Ice Swimming Association (IISA).

His vision was ambitious and multifarious, defining, formalising and regulating various aspects of the sport. One of the biggest things he's done for ice swimming is to define it: swimming unassisted in water that is 5 °C or colder, wearing a standard swimsuit, silicone cap and goggles. The development of safety and swimming rules and maintaining records of ice swims worldwide are other contributions the association has made to the sport. It is also campaigning for ice swimming to be included in the Winter Olympics.

Ram regularly takes swimmers to the Antarctic to swim ice miles, and organises a number of other races in the extremely cold winters of Russia and Switzerland.

Born in Israel near the Sea of Galilee, Ram spent his childhood fishing, swimming, sailing and windsurfing. He spent more hours there than he did in the classroom. He felt at home in the Sea of Galilee and while he never really learnt properly to swim, he had no problem spending most of the time in deep water.

As an adult, his life became more adventurous. In the Israeli army he was a senior commanding officer in a tank regiment. He went back to civilian life as a tractor driver on a kibbutz. One day he found himself caught in a field of flames and, while he survived, 20 per cent of his body was burned. He needed many months of hospital treatment, but the experience may have triggered his later fascination with cold water.

He left Israel to follow a woman to South Africa. At 30 he went to work in Japan. It was during this time that he injured his knee doing aikido and sought a low-impact activity for rehabilitation: swimming was the obvious answer. It was the first time he'd swum in a pool; he was 38 years old. 'I realised that's really what I wanted to do, and when I came back to South Africa in '96, I started swimming in the ocean.'

There are some people who just manage the cold. Ram Barkai is one of them. He likes it, welcomes it, plays with it. Ram and the cold have an affinity. He found the cold when he moved back to Cape Town and began swimming at Clifton and Camps Bay. In turn the cold found him, offering him the type of mental challenge he craved. As a teenager he discovered the speed of windsurfing, the elements of wind and sea. This is what aliveness felt like for him. The cold – the places it takes him, both mentally and physically – has become his ally.

When I ask him why he started and why he still does it, he answers: 'I think I am attracted to challenges. I don't like to be told that I can't do things. And also, I think I actually like the cold in some masochistic way because it's never easy. But I find that I actually enjoy it and I can handle it, and it's very mental as well, which I like.'

Ram likes the combination of mental and physical toughness. Yet, he doesn't think he's suitably built for the cold. 'I'm quite skinny, I can't really put on a lot of body fat, even if I try. But I do have a fast metabolism and I'm an active, restless person.'

He believes it's his mental stamina that pulls him through when he swims in the icy waters of Antarctica. When he started ice swimming, for four years he was called the maestro, the guru of the sport. Now, there are many people doing it all over the world and there are many experts, each with their own opinions, advice and techniques for ice swimming. Ram too has his own.

He's been on a healthy diet for 25 years, ever since he found out he had coeliac disease, an autoimmune disorder in which the ingestion of gluten – a protein found in wheat, barley and rye – triggers an immune response that damages the small intestine. In some way, it was a blessing in disguise because his eating changed dramatically: healthy food and very little alcohol.

But he tells me that according to Professor Tipton, who's considered to be one of the gods of hypothermia, you have to have the optimal ratio between being fit and fat. There is no way of being polite about it because there is little doubt that natural fat provides insulation – especially brown adipose tissue, which is also known as 'brown fat'. Ram clarifies: 'It doesn't mean that if someone is on the fatter side that it's easier for them, because then there's the mental stuff, the pain and the discomfort. But I can definitely feel when I lose weight that my ability to withstand the cold for a longer period drops.'

As a rule of thumb, 20 per cent body fat is ideal, but it's distributed very differently on different people. It's distributed more evenly on women; on men, it sits around the belly. But the more body fat, the heavier the person and the slower they are in the water. This is why the relationship between being fit and having some insulation is very important.

Then there are the skinnier, athletic, professional swimmers who cover the same distance much faster, even in very cold temperatures.

They can do a kilometre in approximately 13 minutes, while others, on average, will cover the distance in 18 to 20 minutes. The skinny professional swimmers stay warmer because they spend fewer minutes in the water. In temperatures that hover around 0 or 1 °C, every minute in the water is critical, and every extra minute in the water even more so. Ram has seen thousands of people swimming and he has observed that the skinnier they are, the colder they get.

Then there are people like Ram who just manage the cold. It doesn't scare him. He understands it. He's learnt how to deal with it. He knows how to acclimatise. 'I always say that if you're a good swimmer, which means that you can swim a few kilometres no problem, then the cold is primarily mental.'

I tell him that I've been chatting with Amber Fillary, another superhuman who embraces the cold. His eyes light up because he knows Amber, respects her abilities and confides that she wants to do the ice swim but that he's worried she's too skinny. 'But her mind is strong,' he says as he taps a forefinger to his temple. I agree with him; her state of mind is perfect for this kind of ambitious, high-risk endeavour and she's had numerous encounters with extremely cold water.

I ask him how long it takes to acclimatise. 'Generally, we swim at least once a week in the Atlantic Ocean in the summer or sometimes when there are nice days we swim in the ocean every day. I can, because I'm going to Antarctica in six weeks' time and I need to get my body back into zero minus one degree temperature, which is quite brutal. If you're experienced and you're fit, a few weeks to a month is good enough to smack you back into a reasonable condition. Acclimatisation, again, depends on what you're trying to do. If you're trying to do a short swim, it's not a problem. If you're looking to do a half an hour or more swim, then it's different, then it's harder. Then you have to acclimatise more. If you have never been in the cold and you are a warm-blooded person from Durban, it takes longer. You need to gradually get into colder water and increase the distance.'

Ram finds acclimatisation interesting as it's a vital part of conditioning the body for an ice mile. 'I spoke to an Israeli woman who recently did an ice mile. She swam the English Channel, the North Channel – big distances in cold water. She's a tough swimmer and she's not skinny. She said the ice mile was very hard, a very different type of hard – a lot of mental pain management, very intense.'

Ram knows that the experience is intense, and he's always interested to hear it from other people too, to enrich his own experience. He says, 'Never fight the cold because the cold always wins. Never show your fear.'

Sometimes when he swims with people, he can see that they're scared of the cold. He can smell it, it's the way they behave, their movements, the look in their eyes, they are petrified and they panic.

He explains to me that being scared of the cold is like being scared of the dark – you will see monsters, hear voices, footsteps, you will think that someone is following you, chasing you. If you're not scared of the dark, you stop seeing shadows and hearing voices. It's the same when swimming in ice-cold water. 'The minute you start getting scared, chemicals are released in your body that prohibit you from doing things.' Ram provides another analogy: 'It's like riding a horse. The minute it senses you are scared it will kick you off. It's the same with the ice.'

But the pain of cold is real. It seems that Ram has a large capacity for pain and this is when his mental stamina kicks in. Ram says that he follows the adage of when you panic, don't panic. He deals with the cold by dissociating himself from it. It's as if he has a switch. 'It doesn't mean that sometimes I don't panic. But when it starts to overwhelm me, I just bring it down and relax. I say to myself: how far are you from shore? Can you swim? Can you breathe? Can you see? Yes, you can. If it's simply an overwhelming feeling, great. If it's bigger, then get out.'

Swimming with fear and panic is part of the acclimatisation. 'I always say that part of my mental training is to go and swim in the sea, regardless of the conditions. And I've done it for many years.'

'Obviously, sometimes the sea can get very dangerous, especially here on the Atlantic seaboard. It's very uninviting, there's wind, sometimes it's much colder outside than in the water. Many times, I've swum in waves or in a howling southeaster. It's almost to say to myself: I'm not scared of this horse.'

He tells me that often he sees shadows and waves that look like dark fins – shark waves. There is a lot of kelp too and he touches jellyfish. Many times, Ram takes newcomers to the kelp and to the seals. He teaches them to not be afraid because the moment a mammal senses that you are nervous, they may see it as aggression, and attack. 'I've swum in the sea with seals a few times, and with dolphins. It's quite scary because they're so quick. Seals have big teeth and they come very close.' In these situations, Ram tells the newcomers: 'Put your head down and swim.'

He is regularly asked about sharks, especially around False Bay, Robben Island and in the Atlantic Ocean. He thinks that 90 per cent of the time great white sharks aren't interested in swimming humans. Also, you can't swim being worried about sharks. 'You can't be worried about what's going to happen because your muscles will get stiff, your mind will get stiff and so will your confidence.'

Ram has seen bad things happen in the water and he's learnt from them. Like any extreme sport, there is a lot of pioneering. Many mistakes are made and things are learnt through experience, as one goes along. He tells me the difference between stupidity and bravery is in the outcome. 'So, I'm alive, so I'm still brave. But as you gain more experience you realise that you don't want bravery, you want safety.

'It's part of the parameters. Going around the world doing extreme stuff, you meet a lot of other people who do extreme stuff and you have to be very analytical. You have to calculate everything. You have to be very professional, otherwise you're going to die very soon.'

Like others who regularly swim in icy water, Ram's body reacts with anticipatory thermogenesis – his body temperature rises in anticipation of extreme cold. It is a reflex to cold and some bodies do it quicker and better than others. But not everyone experiences anticipatory thermogenesis, some people start to shiver and their core temperature actually drops.

Ram has done a few swims for Discovery Channel and on one of them he swallowed a small capsule, a measuring device, that transmits core body temperature. He had to take it two hours before the swim for it to make its way through the intestine to get to his core area. The capsule is disposable and passes through after eight hours. Ram's normal core body temperature is 36,5 °C. Just before he entered the water, his core body temperature rose to 38 °C. The extra warmth around his internal organs allowed him to immerse himself in zero-degree water, in a lake in Norway covered with floating ice, for about half an hour.

He compares this anticipatory reaction to when he was in hospital with his burns. 'When the doctor started removing the bandages twice a day, it was extremely painful. I remember saying: it's sore. And the doctor saying, I haven't even touched you. But I felt the pain because they did it to me every day, twice a day. A very similar thing happens when you swim in cold water regularly. You anticipate it and your body reacts.'

The lake swim was a challenge because there were many large sheets of floating ice that he had to push away while he swam. He swam for just over a kilometre and when he finished he could feel he was close to the edge of hypothermia. When he got out of the water, his core body temperature was at 35,5 °C. They put him in a car and drove him to a cabin where he had a hot shower. In the shower, his body temperature continued to drop, a phenomenon that is quite normal after a period of cold exposure.

His core temperature got to 30 °C, at which point they stopped reading his temperature to him, perhaps not to alarm him. 'I was standing there in the hot shower and at some point, I could feel that I was starting to turn the corner – my mind started to focus, because when your core temperature drops you start to have an out-of-body experience. I started to warm up and I felt euphoric.

'I said, guys, I'm great. Where's my whisky? I usually have a whisky after recovery, and the doctor said, not yet. Your core body temperature is 33. Okay, so my core body temperature was two and a half degrees lower than when I finished the swim, and I felt fine. The fact that the core body temperature drops mostly after the swim is normal, and this is why recovery is very tough. Sometimes the recovery is the scariest part. You have to wait. You can't accelerate it. It can kill you.'

Ram recuperates relatively quickly, within half an hour. Other people take about an hour, and some people can take two hours to come out of a very tough swim. This is why when he is leading an ice mile swim he watches the participants closely to make sure they're okay. 'When they come out of the water, I look at their eyes, they are vacant, they're in a zone. I talk to them, they can hear me, but they can't talk back. When they're out of that zone, they're still very cold. They're still in danger in terms of core body temperature but their sense of humour is back. I wait for that and the eyes, that vacant look to suddenly focus. Then I know they're okay.'

Ram doesn't know why his recovery is quicker. The moment he knows his brain and his body are fine and he's out of the dangerous part, he intellectualises the rest. He doesn't fear being cold as long as he's in control.

It's November 2024, and from his Facebook posts I see that Ram Barkai is in Port Lockroy, in the Antarctic Peninsula, with a group of daring swimmers. They're waiting and hoping for the water temperature to rise as it's hovering obstinately between -1,4 and -1,8 °C. It needs to be a little warmer for an ice mile.

There's a photograph of Ram in a red jacket, its hood thickly fur-lined. In the background are mountains of white and blue ice, the sky is equally white and the sea is the colour of lead. It is impossibly beautiful; it almost doesn't seem real. In the background is a rubber dinghy with seven people on it. Three of them are in regular swimming costumes, two of them dangle their legs over the side, ready to jump into the sea.

A few days later, in another post, Ram writes that all the participants successfully completed an ice mile. The trip marks another personal first for Ram – it's the first time he has swum 1 km in -1 °C water with a pacemaker.

I'm curious to know what it must be like to live with Ram, so I reach out to Samantha Whelpton – Sam, his significant other. She's almost thirty years younger than him and just as warm and congenial. She considers the question and then says, 'That's a very big question!'

She tells me that the mornings are important to them when they start their day with coffee in bed and a rusk, hers normal and his gluten-free. They both work from home so sometimes there is overlap with work and play, especially as Ram has regulated ice swimming, what Sam refers to affectionately as 'this crazy sport'. She describes Ram as a family man who is very close to each of his four children, always making time to see them wherever they are in the world. As part of their trip to Molveno, Italy, in January 2025, they spent time with one of Ram's children who lives in Munich, Germany, and went to Newcastle, England, to meet up with Ram's youngest daughter and her friends. Molveno is where the sixth Ice Swimming World Championship, organised by the International Ice Swimming Association, took place. Over five hundred athletes from all over the world competed in various distances for different disciplines, including freestyle and butterfly, in water temperatures below 5 °C, wearing standard swimwear, cap and goggles – in other words, very little. Both Ram and Sam competed.

I ask her what he's like on expeditions and she tells me that there is a decisive shift in his demeanour. 'His military background comes out. He's shouting instructions, giving orders that are clear, precise and to the point. Safety is very important to him.'

He will pull people out of the water if he sees that they're in danger or won't cope with the Antarctic cold. 'When shit hits the fan, you want someone like Ram by your side,' she says.

On their expedition to Antarctica in November 2024, a group of swimmers were in the water when the weather turned. Ram had to make a difficult decision: to pull them out before they had completed their mile. They were disappointed that they hadn't finished because it was a big goal. He reminded them that they were in a hostile environment, where not many people have been, and that they had to accept the conditions they were dealt with on the day. They tried the swim on five different days. 'It was so stressful because you don't know when you're going to swim,' says Sam.

Ram has pioneered swimming expeditions to Antarctica and what Sam has observed is that their team and the ship's crew have learnt from Ram, especially how to keep people safe. Having a clear, marked-out point is one of the big safety measures. 'In the Antarctic, you lift your head out of the water and all you see is white, if someone says *go there* and points you can't see it. With a clearly marked point you can swim in that direction, you have a point to swim to,' says Sam.

'Ram always reminds me that the swim is not over until you've recovered and that is the most valuable lesson I can pass onto swimmers. It's so mental and I always think of what Ram says: When you panic, don't panic.' Sam is also a marathon runner and she believes that when runners cross the finish line in an ultramarathon like the Comrades and then collapse, it's all in the mind. 'There's no reason to fall when your body has just managed to run 88 kilometres,' she surmises.

Her mindset about recovery after swimming in very cold water is the same. 'You're in control of it and it doesn't have to be terrible.' On one of the days on the November 2024 expedition, when it was almost Sam's time to swim, one of the other participants, a woman, had a hard recovery. Sam turned to her swim buddy and told her not to look – seeing someone in distress because of what you're about to do messes with the mind, it shoots your confidence and will probably affect your performance. Ram went to Sam and told her that she still had lots of time. So Sam went to help the struggling woman, and held her hair while she vomited.

59

Sam always aspires to have a recovery that is okay. 'There is a dark patch afterwards where you ride the pain train. For me it lasts about twenty minutes, but lukewarm water on my hands does help to soothe me.' After an ice mile – and she's successfully done three, earning her a Guinness World Record – she's numb from her shoulders down to her fingers and her hands feel like spades. She experiences pins and needles in her stomach area and chest, even in her breasts, for a while. She shivers a lot, but she actually enjoys it; her body even starts to shiver in anticipation of the cold. 'I have intense shivering and muscle tension, and then it subsides. I still don't have sensation in my middle fingers, but I know it'll come back. It comes back from the outside in, my thumbs and pinkie fingers first.'

When Sam swam the English Channel, which she measures as a double Robben Island swim, at the end she took off her goggles and sank underwater. She doesn't remember doing this and she doesn't remember the recovery. 'I don't want to be in that position again,' she says.

Sam and Ram met while swimming. They were both part of the Sunday hot chocolate swimming group in Hout Bay. It was 2015 and they were doing a 10,5 km swim from Lighthouse to Big Bay. It was cold and Sam was one of only five people who finished the swim that day. Ram was already a swimming legend but Sam saw him get onto the boat mid-swim; he didn't finish the race. She asked him afterwards why he stopped and he said, 'I just got bored.'

'That is a standard Ram answer,' she says. 'But his attitude that day was right; if you're hating it, it's not your day.'

That swim was Sam's second long-distance swim and she says that when you're young, ignorance is bliss. 'I wonder if I would do that swim now. I've become respectful of the cold, I'm humbled by it, and scared of it,' she says. 'The cold will always win.'

On the same November 2024 Antarctica trip, Sam swam next to an iceberg during her 250-metre test swim at Portal Point. 'I was so lucky. As I swam alongside the iceberg I tried to get as close as I could.

It was exceptionally cold. It was flat on top and then went down very deep. I tried to look down as far as I could. I remember feeling incredibly happy,' she describes. 'The water looks black but it's so clear. It's three hundred metres deep and you just know that there's stuff swimming underneath you. We spotted orcas on that trip.'

When Sam's mother was eight and a half months pregnant with her, she was still dipping and swimming in the sea. Sam reckons this is part of why she loves the sea so much. 'The sea makes you feel small, it puts a perspective on things. After the day-to-day stresses of life, the sea brings you back to what's important.'

water as healer

The moment you stop fighting it, it becomes quiet. And of course, this is a more meditative thing, but it's a moment to really go back to yourself and centre yourself. It creates a moment where in you, you can just be.

– Kiki Bosch

It is March 2021 and Kiki Bosch is in Mexico. More specifically, she is driving back from Valle de Bravo, two hours away from Mexico City, to her lodging. The streets are bustling, noisy with people shouting and vehicles hooting. It is festive and colourful, and she feels good, having just had breakfast. She is here to work with people with addiction, and they come from all over the world to be guided by her. A video of her swimming between the icy plates of Silfra in a G-string bikini got millions of views on YouTube and within a week launched her into fame. Silfra is a fissure in Iceland located in Þingvellir National Park, about 50 km northeast of Reykjavík. It is famous for being one of the world's clearest diving and snorkelling sites, with visibility exceeding 100 metres. Silfra is a rift between the North American and Eurasian tectonic plates, meaning divers literally swim between two continents.

Numerous documentaries have since been made about Kiki and she has appeared in magazine and newspaper articles in many countries. She has done, and survived, what most people could never do – swim in waters so cold it would give anyone immediate, irreversible and probably fatal frostbite and hypothermia. As far as humans go, she is divergent.

In Mexico she boards in a house owned by South Africans. Her room is so simple, so minimalist, that to call it spartan would be generous. There is no bed and a hammock hangs from the ceiling – her choice, because this is how she likes to sleep. There are three cushions on the floor that she uses for seating. A small shelf for storing her things. There is an adjacent room that she uses as her office. Outside the bedroom, through a sliding door, is a small patio where she keeps her ice tub.

Beyond that is a verdant backdrop of lush, tropical trees, a rosy sky poking through the foliage, and beyond that tower dark-grey mountains, like giants protecting the valley. 'You sound like the house owner,' she says, 'she's also from South Africa.' Other voices make their way to my ear; the house sounds busy and youthful. I picture bare feet and shaggy hairstyles – that carefree laissez-faire attitude of young travellers not yet rooted by careers and children.

'I haven't done much freediving in Mexico. I'm focusing on the vagus nerve and helping people with addiction and mental illness.' Her sing-song Dutch accent slides off her vowels.

The moment you plunge into cold water, a cascade of physiological responses ignites, and at the centre of it all is the vagus nerve, the body's great regulator. It stretches from the brainstem, weaving through the heart, lungs and gut, acting like an internal conductor of balance. In cold water, it sends out a call for adaptation – slowing the heart rate, redirecting blood flow to vital organs and triggering a deep, involuntary breath that feels like both a shock and a release. This is part of the diving reflex, a primal survival mechanism shared with marine mammals. The vagus nerve links to the parasympathetic system, the rest-and-digest mode, creating a paradox: the cold may jolt you awake, but it also soothes, grounding you in the present, making the body feel simultaneously alive and deeply calm.

Kiki tells me that she spends two or three days in Valle and then teaches in another spot. On the course, which uses cold-water and ice-bath immersion, are mostly people from the US and Europe, with some locals, but they're not fully in the programme. I ask her if she's doing the Wim Hof method and she says that what she's doing now is a deeper experience.

'Those on the programme are on a quest for liberation out of their circumstances, they want to be free. I never put any attention on any person who uses. My responsibility is to make them feel safe in my environment and in the dialogue. If I tell you, you are this or you are that I am automatically oppressing a part of you that doesn't even have a voice. For the participants it's for them to find that voice.

'Part of the programme is to help individuals find or re-find their place in the world, and this determines how they navigate their circumstances, how they recreate their reality. We need to know how to express ourselves in our environment. This inexperience of emotional expression is part of our generation. It has never really gotten priority. It is human to not see a way out, so dialogue is very beneficial because people open up more. At the moment, we're just really planning the way in which to integrate all of it. We only take seven people at a time.'

For the participants, enduring ice baths is empowering and an opportunity to observe their pain from a different point of view. 'It's important to override your receptors of how you feel the cold. That in itself is a massive success. One participant went from 30 seconds the first time he went into an ice bath to 30 minutes in the second week. He understood that the bath was a physical space and so was the pain in his life. He had a steady heartbeat and a steady breath. When people are resilient, they can learn how to meditate very quickly. They just need the right guidance. An ice bath doesn't give you space to think, you're in survival mode. They have to find the breath. And that is the life experience.

'I am really happy when a participant tells me it has saved my life. It opens so many windows and doors. There is so much trust in me that I'll take it to the right places, and I want to do this. Working on this programme has brought me a lot of fear. It kind of happened and I rolled with it and then I was afraid of it. I really want to vanish into the background,' she sighs, overwhelmed.

She has put her freediving on ice for a while but hopes to make a few diving trips while in Mexico. I think this is partly because breath hold was causing her to lose peripheral vision. She caught a herpes virus when she was a child, and long periods and frequency of breath hold have reactivated the virus.

'At the moment, I'm focusing on this part. I love what I want to explore. I am all I think I am but I'm also all you think I am,' she says, aware that the world sees her as the girl in the G-string swimming gracefully in one of the most dangerous and exciting dive sites in the world.

I am curious, so I ask her about freediving and how it affects her experience of time. 'Breath hold and freediving are beautiful ways to connect to nature and human nature. Time doesn't exist. Time is literally your breath. Once you're down there you're part of nature. Freediving is such a short space of time but I have some of my best memories, I have no clue how long I was down there but the feelings and connections were so much more.'

While she has been a swimmer her whole life, Kiki's journey into extreme cold-water swimming sprouted from one seminal, traumatic event. She was working at a dive school in Thailand. One night she'd been out with a group of friends and co-workers. A male co-worker told her he'd walk her home. Little did she know that he'd spiked her drink. As she lay unconscious, he raped her.

She was confused, ashamed and horrified. She didn't let the authorities know. What made the experience more horrific is that her perpetrator did the same thing to another woman. That sent Kiki over the edge. She was flipping between being okay and devastated, barely functioning.

She moved to Australia and it was there, in winter, when the Pacific Ocean swirls at 16 °C, that she discovered cold-water swimming. It stilled her mind. The thoughts stopped. She found peace. 'After the rape, the ocean didn't feel the same any more. It was an enjoyment that I couldn't give myself any more. When I swam in the Pacific Ocean it created a space in my mind, quiet moments of pure being. There were different emotions and different ways of being that became more clear. Like, hey, I am here in the water and just for a blissful moment calming myself down. I just had to breathe. There is always a way of breathing through it. No matter how cold life might be at certain moments, there is always a way to breathe through it,' Kiki explains.

She enrolled for a course with Wim Hof, an extreme cold exposure athlete from her native Netherlands, training her body to withstand cold by hiking in snow wearing next to nothing, and practising breathing techniques. There is a video clip of her in hiking boots, shorts and sports bra carrying a backpack as she hikes on a snowy mountain. She passes hikers wrapped to the gills, who stop and stare at her. Kiki isn't shivering; she is relaxed and focused. The Wim Hof technique taught her how to become resilient to cold by mastering her nervous, cardiovascular and immune systems.

With the desire to go to Iceland and experience deep cold, she committed to acclimatising her body. She and her boyfriend were living in London at the time and she did this by jumping into an ice tub, which she kept outdoors, exposed to the English winter, every morning soon after waking. Her daily morning routine was wake up, meditate and then sit in her outdoor tub for a few minutes. She explains that the environmental temperature was between 2 and 8 °C and the water in the tub probably the same. I imagine the contrast between feeling perfectly warm under a duvet and entering icy water, the shock to the body. I admire Kiki's mental focus; it must be both subtle and immense.

'The body can condition quite quickly; it takes about three to four weeks. You start gradually and build up. So, 30 seconds to a minute, then to two and so on. Your mind is the most important part of cold-water swimming. You trust your body with your conscious mind. You sense the cold instead of feeling it. Within myself I have a place where I can go with my breath. Sitting in an ice bath is the pinnacle of mindfulness. It's finding these places in your body where you can breathe, where you can feel warm. Seeing the body with your eyes closed,' she says.

It was at this time that Kiki signed up to do a Wim Hof method instructor course. 'I intently started to visualise. I had the motto, train at your worst, in sub-optimal conditions. No matter what happens you can trust that.'

Finally, in April 2017, Kiki swam, unassisted by a wetsuit, in the Silfra fissure in Þingvellir National Park. Her boyfriend shot the footage. It shows a sylph-like Kiki wearing only a bikini, a mask and fins, gracefully swimming between the tectonic plates. What makes the video so alluring is the cinematography and the fact that the water temperature is a glacial 2 to 4 °C, yet Kiki looks calm and in control. 'We were just enjoying ourselves. My boyfriend was filming and I was diving. Within a week the video went viral with 30 million views and I became this person who just does it.'

Just like that Kiki entered the public eye and became a phenomenon in extreme human ability. Kiki achieved what for many humans has been insurmountable; a handful of people have died in the fissure while diving and snorkelling, their bodies unprepared for the extreme cold and the perilous environment. 'The video was an explosion. The interest in what I had achieved took me by surprise.' Even now, as Kiki speaks about the video, her voice is frosted in astonishment.

The Silfra fissure is not the coldest place she's swum. Kiki has taken it further, maintaining inner calm and manipulating her outer perceptiveness to swim in even colder waters. She has swum in a glacial lake in Greenland, where the water is near freezing, close to an iceberg. Again, she was wearing only a bikini, mask and fins. The glacier radiated waves of cold as water moved past it. As she describes this, the calmness it brings to her, even through memory, is remarkable.

In Sydney, Australia, 23-year-old film student Naysan Baghai was searching for a topic for a documentary. He came across Kiki Bosch on a #MeToo social media thread and the pieces of the puzzle started to slot together. Her story had layers as it blended freediving with a greater universal theme.

Their first meeting was at an airport in London while Kiki was in transit, and what followed was a month in which the crew shared a cottage in the English countryside to get to know each other, building the energy and the chemistry that would make filming more effective. After a month, they all understood each other and knew how to play to each other's strengths.

Naysan talks to me via a virtual call. His features are Persian. He tells me he was born in Canada and then he and his parents moved to Australia. His accent has North American undertones. 'It was two years between when I met Kiki and I rolled the cameras. When it was time to film Kiki describing the rape and what ensued, she was wary of the fact that I'd bring it up. There was an electrifying moment in the filming where we could all feel Kiki purging emotions. There was a standing ovation afterwards and we all decompressed.' In his voice, Naysan conveys the emotions that pricked those minutes.

Another pertinent moment during filming was when Kiki entered the waters near a glacier. 'The captain of the ship didn't believe that she could do it. He said that a person would die if they swam in such cold waters. When he saw Kiki swimming so close to the glacier he started crying.'

Naysan's documentary *Descent* won first place in the novice category for Best Australian Documentary at the 2020 Sydney Film Festival. *Descent* tells the story of Kiki's journey from the night she was raped in Thailand to her discovery of the beneficial effects of cold-water swimming to her working with Wim Hof to the international buzz created by her YouTube video.

In the documentary is a scene from the filming of a commercial – it shows Kiki walking on the sea floor. The production crew did numerous takes, causing her to become dangerously cold. The crew, not knowing what to do, put her in a hot shower. This is something Kiki never does, preferring to warm up naturally by wrapping herself in a thermal blanket or poncho. Many of those who plunge into cold water choose to raise their core body temperature slowly, in warm clothing, with a warm, but not hot, drink, so that the body doesn't go into rewarming shock, which can lead to low blood pressure and fainting. Throughout the documentary it is clear that Kiki understands her body, making this part particularly difficult to watch.

When Naysan decided to become a professional underwater cinematographer while at film school, he complemented his education with freediving and scuba diving courses. 'A lot of the dives that were part of my self-prescribed training programme were in deeper, colder and murkier waters, and my non-diver friends began to question my sanity, asking me, "Why do you do it?" That question made an enormous impression on me. When I met Kiki and learnt about her story, I finally crystallised the concept and theme for *Descent* – the psychology of people who specialise in challenging underwater environments.

'Most of my dives are mental health dives. A lot of my best freediving friends have high-pressure jobs so we tend to burn out very quickly. Diving means no cameras, no goals, just pure relaxation. I will do the same dive again and again and stay at the bottom for as long as possible. You are receptive to how your body is feeling and what you want to do in the moment. It's addictive and this is both good and bad. I brave the water without a wetsuit and it's a lot more pure. It's a liberating feeling at times. Part of that was inspired by Kiki.'

When Naysan did his first freediving course, it was miserable. 'At 14 metres I perforated an eardrum, the estuary was murky and it was a bull shark habitat.'

Naysan did another course and it went well. His breath hold reached the five-minute mark. But as he continued to practise he noticed a decline in his short- and long-term memory. Naysan has a photographic memory and perfect pitch, so the effects of breath hold began to worry him. 'My sense of pitch was completely disturbed. Memory is not impervious to holding one's breath for extended periods and often. Nor is it impervious to the impact that depth pressure has on the body.'

Naysan has been shooting with a camera while breath holding since 2017, but he made the decision to not push himself to go deeper. 'Freediving and filmmaking have a yin-yang thing in my life. You have to have balls to break the rules and do something more expressive that has meaning. To achieve a level of Zen-ness where I'm not mentally frantic, that would be my Mount Everest.'

After the filming of *Descent*, Kiki lived in a cave for some time. She lived there to be in nature, close to the sea, touching the earth, hearing the murmurs of insects and animals. Not one to be a recluse, she would go out with her friends and then go back to her cave. The cave dwelling was not about isolation or exclusion of the world, but rather about experiencing the temperament of the landscape.

Kiki describes it for me. 'I was finding ways to reflect the way I felt. I would sleep in the cave and then go out. I would be home before sunset and up at sunrise. It was the real rhythm of nature and it was so profound for me. I would take time in the morning to watch the ocean or meditate. My most profound realisations were during that time. I would meditate for one or two hours before going on with my day. You feel into a new way of being by constantly challenging it in micro-moments doing little things every day that teach us more about being human. There is freedom in that. I fall back on my connection to nature in order to shift and change with the tides.'

In Mexico, Kiki invites people into the intensity of ice baths, letting them experience how the vagus nerve acts as a built-in tuning fork for calm. The shock of cold water gives way to steadiness. In her own way, she offers the participants a way back to the body's own wisdom.

freediving

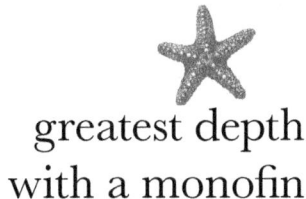

greatest depth with a monofin

The sea is the essence of life, and every dive is a chance to experience its power and beauty.

– Alexey Molchanov

Alexey Molchanov is the man who has been deepest with a monofin. A monofin is standard equipment for elite freedivers who aim for depth or distance. Compared to bifins, where a diver wears a fin on each foot, a monofin is worn over both feet. The result is a sleeker silhouette, like that of a mermaid or a dolphin, that propels the diver further with a lot less effort. A monofin mimics the dolphin kick, engaging the whole body – from chest to toes – in a fluid wave motion. With each undulating movement of the body, there is less kicking and more slipping through the water, allowing divers to conserve more oxygen.

On 30 June 2023, at a competition in Villefranche-sur-Mer, France, in the constant weight with monofin (CWT) discipline, Alexey descended to 133 metres, setting a new world record.

I chat to Alexey two years prior to this, on a day in 2021 as he's walking his dog in Moscow. In the first few seconds that he puts me on FaceTime I see it's a glorious, bright day and he's in a park of concrete pathways, wooden benches and leafy trees. 'I don't like to keep still,' he explains, and I understand that for this interview he is giving me some of his very precious time. He talks about his childhood and his mother, but we don't talk about how she went missing a few years ago; it is an unspoken agreement. I decided before the interview that

I wouldn't ask about it, wanting the conversation to be about him and not the famous Natalia Molchanova.

Natalia Molchanova is an icon of the deep and her disappearance made world news. In 2015 she was teaching two inexperienced divers in the open waters of the Balearic Sea, off the island of Formentera on the east coast of Spain. Between their dives, she would do a few of her own training dives, and after one of them she didn't surface after a few minutes. (The year before, she'd dived to 91,44 metres – that's like looking down a 30-storey building – and emerged after 3 minutes and 29 seconds, so she was fast.) The others waited a few minutes more, knowing that Natalia could hold her breath for long, but after ten or so minutes had passed, they knew something was wrong. They radioed for help.

An underwater search ensued but was halted four days later when there was no sign of her body. She never surfaced, never returned to her husband and son. No one will ever know if she blacked out, was injured, or got caught in a current or tangled in a stray fishing net. Her famous saying – 'freediving is not only a sport, it's a way to understand who we are' – reveals much about the way she challenged herself. She was training for an upcoming AIDA Individual Depth World Championship event happening the following month in Cyprus. She was 53 years old, with a long string of records. She died where she was happiest.

Alexey Molchanov has followed in his mother's freediving footsteps. Stocky, muscular, in his thirties, Alexey is well-respected and well-liked in the diving community. In his native Russia, he's a celebrity.

'I've been in the water all my life; my mom taught me how to swim properly and at a young age I was competing regularly. I started freediving in open water when I was five, in the Black Sea. There was some archaeological research and we joined the team but I was, of course, just playing around and helping a little bit. Every year we went to the sea and I think this determined my path to becoming a freediver,' he says, his rhythm in time with his walking, his English accented with Russian icing. 'At one point in my life I chose violin and studied at a music school for several years. Then my mum asked me: swimming or violin? And I chose swimming. I'd like to pick up the violin again someday. I'm actually deciding whether I should get a classical one or an electronic one. Something light that I could travel with, take with me while I'm competing. I want to have a little bit of a rest from my busy work and have something outside of freediving again.'

The conversation travels back to the water and Alexey tells me that he became a freediving student at 17, after he finished school and went to university. His mother joined him, both of them falling for the joys of freediving long before it became a sport in Russia.

'Now, I'm involved in competitive freediving and teaching other people. The fun side of freediving for me is playing with the camera. I've taught the most in Dahab of course, it's like a cradle for Russian freedivers. It's close to Moscow, like a five-hour flight. You have unlimited depth, so for me Dahab is the place where I've been teaching the most and have participated in freediving festivals with my mother – these are some of my fondest memories,' he says.

He has taught in many beautiful places. 'Teaching during adventurous trips, like when we went to Tonga to dive with humpback whales, you are doing this adventure and sharing the experience, this is the best combination. The most incredible experiences would be for me the most exotic – I've had a lot of experience in warm waters with bull sharks, with humpback whales and sea lions. I would repeat them any time,' he shares.

The most exotic experience was the one he had in the cold waters of the Arctic Ocean. 'It was -2 °C on this island in the Russian Arctic during an expedition with Luke Hardy. It was a Russian-French-American scientific documentary expedition to highlight ecology problems and to see if there were any changes to the Arctic in terms of ice. I was lucky to be there. We had a chance to dive near an island where there was a colony of walruses. What we learnt is that no one had ever been to that island so the walruses had never seen humans in the water with them – we were diving in a place where no one had gone diving before.

'And there was really almost no visibility so we were very close to shore and at some point, the walruses came really close to us even though we were keeping our distance because we didn't know how they would behave. But there were some young ones that came close, they didn't seem aggressive, one of them bumped into my camera underwater. He was next to me, about one metre away, and we stared at each other for about five seconds. I was nervous a bit, but I could see that he was as well. He then got onto a rock about five metres away and he started to pose for me to take pictures of him. It was a short moment but a really amazing experience. They were so curious,' Alexey recounts.

Alexey dives in warm and cold water, perfecting the preparations required for both environments. He explains that in cold water he is thinking about time limitations and preserving heat. On 16 March 2021, Alexey descended 80 metres in the waters of Lake Baikal in Siberia, setting another world record. He wore a 7 mm wetsuit and yet, when he entered the water to prepare, he was already starting to cool down. He knew that if he wanted to perform well and have good hypoxia resistance, he would need to start the dive within a specific time frame. Every second counts: 'If you get cold and it's about records it's a problem. You need to plan through all the details – how you prepare, how you put your socks on, your gloves, how you take your suit off afterwards, do you have a tent. Those are important,' he says.

In terms of relaxation in the water, the warm and cold environments are similar in some ways and very different in others. 'Technique-wise it's the same – you breathe the same way, relax the same way, swim the same way. In cold water there is a wetsuit and this adds more effort. When I was diving in the lake, I calmed down my breathing and took a deep inhale before the dive. Everything is the same but it's harder to execute because you could be more tense, because of the cold on your face. But if you can relax with those sensations, you can actually feel your bradycardia [the slowing of your heart rate], and the sensation can be warmer than in warm water. So, if you plan everything and you are warm, you can have a faster blood shift and bradycardia than in warm water,' Alexey explains.

How freedivers train for world records depends on the dive. Alexey has accumulated thousands of hours of pool training in his life, so he has refined his breath hold technique. He maintains his lung capacity and flexibility with pool training and with dry exercises – out of the pool. Pool training is mandatory but mostly for freedivers who are starting out. 'For me, I train in the actual conditions or someplace similar, it's about fine-tuning. The main part of my operation was going to lakes in December and January and diving there even before they iced over. So, it's adaptation. I was used to the water, I was used to the temperature, that's why it was relatively easy,' he says of his training in the run-up to the Lake Baikal record.

Lake Baikal is the deepest and oldest freshwater lake on Earth, holding over a fifth of the planet's unfrozen freshwater. It is cradled in the mountains of southern Siberia, a place of immense beauty – a contrast of stark white and dark grey and deep blue, with areas covered in spruce, pine and larch, coniferous trees that thrive in harsh winters. Because it is isolated and over 25 million years old, there are species in the lake that are found nowhere else. Alexey's freediving takes him to magnificent places.

Our conversation is interrupted by a muffled barking. 'Oh, my dog is aggressive. She is such a sweet puppy and then for some reason she barks, I don't know. I can take her for an hour's walk and I am exercising, so it works really well for me.

'So, adapting to a cold lake was the most important for me in this particular dive. I was adapting several months before so on the day of the record I was relaxed, which is the most important part for me.'

I want to see this for myself, so I watch a YouTube video of his dive. He enters Lake Baikal from a perfectly square opening that has been cut in the ice. He sips air, packing as much oxygen as possible into his lungs. The lake's frigid waters rest at a mere 3 °C. Nearby, on the ice, are spectators and camera crews – all of them wrapped in thick puffer jackets, scarves, beanies and gloves to keep out the Siberian air that is -6,5 °C. Everyone's excitement is so evident.

After the countdown, Alexey puts his face in the water and then slowly duck-dives down. The underwater cameras show water that is a glacial green and Alexey glides through it effortlessly, his monofin giving him the hydrodynamics of a sea mammal. In 2 minutes and 54 seconds, he descends 80 metres, flips around and returns, setting a new world record for the deepest under-ice freedive.

He dedicated this record to Lake Baikal, calling it 'an amazing place of ecological significance, a living organism to be looked after'.

I've heard from others in the community that Alexey's body is perfectly adapted to water and long periods of apnoea. If he 'packs' by sipping more air into his already fully inflated lungs, he can hold his breath for 11 minutes, which is extremely long. There are those who have held their breath for longer. In 2008, magician David Blane held his for 17 minutes, in a tank of water, in front of an audience. He noted that during the months that followed he experienced gaps in memory and hallucinations at random moments, as he was getting on with his day. David pushed himself to the brink, almost. Depriving his brain of oxygen for that long has left scars. Budimir Šobat broke this record in 2021 by holding breath for a staggering 24 minutes 36 seconds.

Despite being born with a talent for depth and apnoea, Alexey still conditions his body to tolerate high carbon dioxide levels. He does this by holding his breath while walking. He practises attention-control techniques. 'As you progress as a freediver, you learn to move your attention around your visual field, around your body. I work with this meditative state of mind.'

He doesn't follow a special diet. Outside of competition periods he focuses on healthy eating, taking in a variety of foods, as that is what his mother taught him. 'In general, I avoid unhealthy products like sugar and bread, but I'm not strict about it. When I'm training a lot, I have a high metabolism and I need to recover fast, so I'm not too fanatical about diet,' he says. 'For depth I need strong muscles and more power. I'm not reducing calories intake because for deep diving you've got to have enough power and speed of recovery – it's different to static breath hold.'

His diet does change before a competition, though. The evening before diving he avoids food high in fat and protein, as these are hard to digest. On the morning of the dive, he shifts to carbohydrate-heavy porridge or oats. 'The idea is to get to the dive without feeling hungry, but not feeling heavy. For me this works, but it's not one rule for everyone.'

It is clear that for Alexey, water pulls at his core. He's built a career and a business around freediving, which for him is a way of life. Like his mother, he is of the water, his body perfectly adapted to the pressures of the deep. He has his mother's genes as well as the insights she shared with him. Over the years he has become immersed in the intense practice of freediving to the point that he has reached the furthest depths in history in lakes and seas, wearing a monofin that makes him part-dolphin. I have little doubt that in his practice there is intuition and also constant calibration. He strikes me as being a perfectionist.

longest underwater kiss

Like water, we learn to flow, adapt, and embrace the currents of life.
— Alexey Molchanov

You've already met Beth Neale in 'The mammalian diving reflex', where she describes how her daughter Neve responds to being in water. I've watched my own girls learn to swim, from a young age feeling their way in a fluid world, the ease with which they adapt. I've held their hands as we've played in the tumbling waves.

In this chapter I'll take you to my very first encounter with Beth, our subsequent conversations and that longest underwater kiss.

I'm sitting in my car outside a gymnasium; my daughters are inside practising vault and bar and strengthening their core muscles in time for competitions which, if all goes well, they'll compete in during August. The dust and dry air make me sneeze. I've never enjoyed winter in Joburg.

I watch the dust particles float until they settle on the dashboard. I have a chunk of undisturbed time ahead of me so I dial Beth Neal. As I wait for her to pick up, my attention moves beyond the windscreen, past the peeling bark of the eucalyptus trees to a sky marbled with dusty yellow, and then to a pale three-quarter moon. I get the strange feeling that I sometimes get when I feel the immensity of it all. I am a spectator marvelling at the perfect tension that holds the moon to its tango with Earth. I marvel at how it hangs there, in perpetual orbit, like it has done this forever and will continue to do so, perpetuating the tides, perpetuating so much more. That is its purpose. In my hand, the ringtone continues and, with bated breath, I hope that she picks up.

'Hello.' The voice is slow, fluid, like the person it belongs to has just done a relaxing yoga class. I introduce myself, tell her that I'm writing a book about freediving and ask if I could interview her.

As the conversation flows, I can feel us becoming friends; there is an immediate connection. She is warm and so at peace with the world, so in her element.

'Every time, after I'm in the water, I get a land down. I imagine it's like coming down to earth after skydiving or a performance.' I can hear her smiling. In my file on the passenger seat I have a photo of her – long blonde hair dancing in the water, pink wetsuit zipped down to reveal the slight curve of cleavage, blue eyes open to the camera – a portrait of a laid-back mermaid.

In my mind's eye I see her in the ocean. Luminous sunlight streaks down to surround her like a protective chamber. Followed by the image of one bare, wet foot then another smacking down on concrete as she is pulled to land. A 'land down'. A brutal, unwanted, but necessary union with bricks, institutions and all other things that are human-made. 'I can't wait to get back into the water. It's my happy place.' Her manner and her speech are unharried, she metabolises thoughts to the slow flow of water.

One of her earliest memories is standing on the rocks in Leisure Bay and watching the waves crash, wanting to be a part of them. The ocean on the KwaZulu-Natal South Coast is wild with big breakers, and that's what she grew up with.

At the age of 11, Beth told her parents that she wanted to be a dolphin trainer, so they took her to Sea World in the United States. Instead of loving it, as her parents had presumed she would, she was devastated. 'I saw the cruelty of dolphins in captivity. I saw a beluga whale, this sentient being in a tank. It was from that experience that I wanted to tell the story of what's happening to wildlife and our impact on wildlife.'

The first time she experienced flat, calm, tropical ocean was in Ponta do Ouro in the south of Mozambique, a small town close to the South African border. A town that dwells in my heart too – the place where I swam with a whale shark.

'In Ponta do Ouro, when I was 18, I learnt to scuba dive. When I got to see a coral reef for the first time and the animals in the water, it changed my life. It was a world that I wanted to be a part of. It was also where I swam with wild dolphins for the first time, which was hugely emotional and spiritual for me. That set me off on my trajectory although I didn't know clearly how I was going to use my passion for the sea.'

She scuba dived a few more times after that but didn't feel a connection to the water. The passion was being underwater with sea life and she became a filmmaker so that she could record these stories. At university, her honours project was with the Two Oceans Aquarium in Cape Town and the outreach programme it runs for children. She took a camera underwater for the first time and that led to her enrolling at the Wildlife Film Academy, where she learnt the skills to film wildlife.

A relationship took her to London. It was in the middle of the recession – 2008 – and while she had built herself up as a filmmaker in South Africa, in England she had to start from scratch. One gloomy day as she lay on the couch watching *The Big Blue* – a movie about freedivers Jacques Mayol and Enzo Maiorca – she googled 'freediving London' and found a course.

Beth's first formal freediving experience was at a gym in London, in the middle of the city. 'We got in the pool and it was my first time wearing a monofin. I remember it was a group of elite triathletes, they were fit and strong while I was probably the unhealthiest I'd ever been and they could not understand how I could hold my breath for longer and do more lengths underwater. I was naturally good at it.'

It's getting stuffy in the car. I turn on the ignition and roll into the shade of a Tipuana tree.

Beth is impressed that I interviewed Alexey Molchanov, the men's world record holder for deepest dive with a monofin, and tells me that there is a movie out about his mother Natalia Molchanova but that it's in Russian. I spot my children emerging from the gymnasium and I tell Beth I'll call her tomorrow.

As I lie awake in the dark, in my quiet time just before I give in to the warm trammels of sleep, I wonder about Beth, what her days are like, the privilege she holds of being able to tell the stories of marine animals.

I call Beth the next day and her voice is animated. 'We were filming a whale mom with her baby, with the drone. I'm standing on the beach now and you can see the humpback whales from here. The baby is so newborn that the mom has it on her back. The baby swims away for a bit and then goes back onto her back so that she can push it up to get a breath. I'd much rather be in the water with them but this is good enough. I can see another whale on the horizon.'

The wind whips at the microphone and I feel a pinch of envy as the ocean sounds travel down the airwaves to the shell of my ear. Beth is at Aliwal Shoal, a Marine Protected Area (MPA) near Umkomaas. The MPA extends for 18,3 km between the Mzimayi and Umkomaas river mouths, and 7 km offshore to include a number of shipwrecks. No fishing is allowed, which keeps the ecosystem pristine.

'I stopped eating fish when I was 15. I watched a documentary called *The End of the Line* about the reality of overfishing. Now I teach children about overfishing, most of them have no idea what effect this has. For me every fish counts. There's a whale having a big fat jol over there!' Her excitement is tangible as I picture her, eyes fixed on the creature as her partner Miles Cloutier pilots the drone.

'A lot of people think that fish don't feel pain and that they're stupid. Even how we talk about fish is strange, we group them with agriculture and plants. In South Africa there's the department of fishing and agriculture. People grow fish in fish farms, which takes away from the beautiful creatures that they are, making it easier for people to catch them. There are pictures of fishermen holding a big fish they've caught, and smiling, posted all over social media. You wouldn't get away with that if it was a giraffe or a zebra. It's completely acceptable with fish,' says Beth, unpacking her argument, one that she has refined and recounted many times.

'Fish are intelligent. There's BBC footage of a Japanese puffer fish that builds this intricate nest design to attract a mate. People need to change the way they see fish, sharks especially.'

Beth is a big fish activist, channelling her love for marine life into ocean conservation and outreach work and telling inspiring stories. She is a witness to the depletion of our oceans and is committed to educating the new generation about sustainability. She explains that South Africa has the Southern African Sustainable Seafood Initiative (SASSI), which places fish on a green, orange or red list depending on how endangered they are. There are fishing practices that can collapse the entire fish stock.

'Another big thing is bycatch. For every kilogram you catch, ten kilograms of bycatch is caught and that's what gets thrown away. There are so many detrimental fishing practices. There's even dynamite fishing. I've been thinking a lot about it and also seeing on Facebook about the Chinese trawlers in the Galapagos. I've been putting it into perspective for kids – one trawling net is the size of 12 football fields – putting it into terms that they understand. When they have a piece of fish on their plate, they need to find out what type of fish it is, how its family is doing and how it was caught. You have to know answers to these questions first. And you hope that even one in the group will get this and will start to make a difference.'

She tells me that dynamite fishing is when explosives are used to stun or kill fish. It's a destructive fishing method that causes damage to coral reefs and harms marine ecosystems.

Why have unsustainable fishing practices been allowed to happen? It's a question I've posed to a number of people – a complex question layered in political, economic and food resource issues – and I'm always keen to hear their viewpoint. Beth is keen to answer.

'It's a big-money industry, people high up involved, so it's been allowed to continue. Oceans are also very difficult to police and regulate – there are so many loopholes. Years ago, when there was the issue with Chinese trawlers off the South African coast, they would turn off their radar or throw their catch overboard, so it was difficult to catch them red-handed. If you arrest them, they are replaced the next day or they just pay the fine. They just keep doing it. The ocean is a very difficult place to protect.'

Beth is an accomplished freediver. She holds a national record for freediving 50 metres, constant weight with no fins (CNF) – a technically and physically demanding discipline where the diver descends and ascends on a single breath, with no fins, no pulling on a rope and no changing of weights. The constant weight means the diver carries the same weight throughout the dive and can't drop weights to return to surface. No fins means nothing on the feet, except for a thin layer of protection like socks if the water is cold. Beth does it barefoot, as it feels more natural and there is less drag.

She achieved this in Sodwana Bay, 200 kilometres north of Durban, on the Indian Ocean coast. 'It's a favourite diving spot and those who have been there know how choppy the waters can get. I had the flu on the day and the sea was full of sharks. I was quite nervous. But I did it and when I was in the water, luckily, there were no sharks,' she says slowly in her yoga voice.

'People think that sharks are these man-eating monsters that seek you out and attack you, but when you're freediving you see that they're not. Media has made people fearful of them. You see it in Bermuda where there are no more big fish. There are hardly any sharks, I've been going there for five years and I've never seen one. It's amazing to see a grouper, you never see them and you never see a big one,' she says.

Beth is a fish whisperer, naturally attuned to the sea and its creatures, unafraid of what lives beneath the waves. She tells me, 'Potato bass are protected in South Africa. They all have different personalities. Some want to swim with you, some are terrified.' I hear her smiling.

'Manta rays are extremely intelligent animals. In Sodwana we saw a manta ray and she was definitely hanging out with us. She started to swim away so I spoke to her like I speak to dolphins and she stopped, turned around and then flipped onto her back. You know that when animals show you their belly it's a sign of trust. I was swimming over her and we were looking into each other's eyes and we had this amazing connection. It was so emotional.'

Beth submitted the manta ray's belly identification to the Marine Megafauna Foundation as they do manta ray research and conservation. 'They got back to me and told me the manta had already been documented and it was by me two years ago. I didn't recognise her because in the two years that I hadn't seen her she lost her tail and had a bite out of her wing, so she'd been attacked by a shark. I gave her the nickname Bethany Hamilton, the surfer who had her arm bitten off by a shark. I thought it was a good name because Bethany is still out there surfing and living life to the fullest.'

Beth tells me that she and Miles are planning on breaking the world record for the longest kiss underwater. They're currently living in Umdloti, a small town on a stretch of sandy beach a few kilometres north of Umhlanga, with one entry point, a road that is flanked by dunes covered in lush green sugar cane. The sea breeze moves through it like fingers through hair. I know it so well and can picture the subtropical green against azure sky that gives way to a view of deep blue Indian Ocean. The beach is pocked with rock pools teeming with fish and flora. It is one of my favourite places on Earth and I've spent many childhood holidays sitting waist deep in a rock pool eating mussels with my dad. My conversation with Beth brings back good memories.

A few months pass and I call her again. I haven't spoken to her on the phone since she WhatsApped me to tell me that she was pregnant;

we've just had a few messages back and forth. She answers after two rings: 'Hi, I haven't heard from you in ages.'

I tell her that I was watching a documentary about the sardine run and parts of it had a distinctly Beth Neale quality to them, so I watched the credits and there she was. 'Beautiful footage of the whales and the sharks, by the way,' I tell her.

'Oh, ja, that was the sardine run last year, it was amazing!' Her relaxed South African drawl is still there, and I can hear her smiling. I can see her in a wetsuit, pregnant belly pronounced, blonde hair whipping her face. 'I'm actually at the sardine run now. I was in the water swimming with all these beautiful fish and on the beach it's people with plastic packets shoving as many dead sardines into them as they can.'

Beth is standing barefoot on the sand at Aliwal Shoal. I can hear the excitement in her voice and the clamour around her. 'Baby is already a little mermaid. She's swum with sharks in the Bahamas and the Maldives.' Her yoga voice is even more relaxed than usual. 'I feel great! Even in the first few months, I'm still freediving.'

I picture the bustle on the beach. The nets have been cast and are pulling in millions of sardines as people watch and wait at the water's edge for their turn to pack their containers with the ocean's bounty. A frenzy of activity turns the usually quiet beach into a hubbub of noise. Men in wetsuits, women in colourful sarongs and T-shirts, bright against dark skin, and the sun at its zenith playing on the water's surface. Excited shouts and single-word instructions mingle with the roar of the waves and the low drone of boat engines. Fishermen are waist deep in water and surround the nets, they sway and shift with the mass of sardines caught in them as the ocean pushes and pulls. Anglers are there to pull in apex predators; forming a scraggly line at the water's edge they reel in dusky sharks weighing over 200 kilograms.

Women busy themselves with scooping silvery fish, a moment ago so agile in the water, now choking in grocery bags. I'm 600 kilometres away but in my mind's eye the contrast between alive and dead is startling.

The sardine run is a migration that occurs every year in winter, between May and July, when millions of sardines (*Sardinops sagax*) swim from the Eastern Cape along the KwaZulu-Natal coast and move northwards to Mozambique. They spawn in the cool Agulhas Current, which runs from Agulhas Bank up to Mozambique where it then moves eastwards into the Indian Ocean.

The shoals form enormous dark masses many kilometres long and can be seen from the shore and from the air. It's a feeding frenzy for water, land and air predators.

'My wetsuit is starting to feel really tight and my belly is clearly visible,' says Beth.

I send a message to her a few months later to see how she's doing. She responds: 'Devastatingly, I lost my baby at 10 weeks. I'm doing much better now, but it's been very traumatic and just taking it day by day.'

In the Maldives on 26 February 2023, Beth and Miles break the world record for the longest underwater kiss, setting it at 4 minutes and 6 seconds. I chat to her a few weeks later and she is in high spirits. It contrasts with how she felt in the weeks leading up to the event, while they were training, when she couldn't hold her breath.

'Deep down I knew I could do it, but I didn't want the pressure of it. It's hard to keep your heart rate down when you think about all the people who'll be watching – judges, a representative from Guinness. I had to shift my mind, remind myself that being underwater is what I love. My motivation is my love for the ocean.

'Luckily, when it came down to it, I enjoyed it. We had one opportunity and we made it work. I lost myself in the experience and the next minute Miles was pulling me up.'

It was a good lesson for Beth – this was the first time that she wasn't at one with her breath holding and she had to remember her 'why'.

As we chat, I recall my own breath holding practice, and learning how to do it better under the tutelage of freediver and champion swimmer Peter Marshall, and how deeply mental and meditative it is. The focus teeters on the thin edge between control and letting go, observing sensations but not being part of them.

Jump to 2025 and Beth and Miles have two daughters – four-year-old Neve and four-month-old Nera. 'Neve swims ten times a day. She loves being underwater and just smiles and smiles. The happiness that I feel when she swims up to me and gives me a kiss; these are the greatest moments of my life,' she says with tenderness.

Being a mother has shifted Beth's perspective on freediving and she realises that for her it was never about breaking records. It was always about the connection with the sea and the power it holds.

the black mermaid

The ocean can be a place of worship, a place of ancestors, a place of deep respect.

– Zandile Ndhlovu

It takes months to schedule an interview with Zandile 'Zandi' Ndhlovu as her diary is packed with workshops and travelling. On a Zoom call we chat when the new year is still tender and the anticipation and excitement of new things is high. It is 4 January 2024 and we are both in KwaZulu-Natal, albeit about 400 km from each other. She is visiting her grandmother at her rural hometown of Emantlo, near Vryheid, where cows and goats and people and chickens roam.

The tips of her hair are blue and she has an easy smile. Her nieces run around her as she bites into an apple. She is in South Africa to spend Christmas and New Year with her family, which keeps her mood buoyant and her mental health in check. She has been in São Tomé bridging the space between water and children. For just over a week she worked with 24 children aged between 11 and 16 to make them comfortable in the shallows and the swells of the Atlantic. She was invited by a private school on the island but asked that they expand the privilege to children in a nearby village, making the ocean an equitable space.

'São Tomé is another amazing ocean-facing community where you don't see a lot of black and brown people in the water in a recreational way, but also you don't see them in the water in a way that is linked to even careers. So, I was asked: come do what you do in South Africa with us in São Tomé. I got kids ready for the ocean – we did pool work to understand breath hold training and then it was going out to sea and helping them acclimatise to the ocean and helping them find comfort. I'm going back again now in January to continue the work that we're doing,' she says, as she opens her arms and invites a young girl to sit on her lap.

'The organisation that I'm working with is called Over the Swell, and they're doing work in helping to record whale shark populations. São Tomé didn't know that they have whale sharks, but the fishermen had always seen them and they call them Mapinta. And so, it's this work of helping to understand the species but also have the local community and local kids advocating for the beauty that is in the ocean, protecting the ocean, and thus changing our narrative around the ocean,' she continues.

There is one question that is burning on my lips and I ask it, since Zandi grew up so far from the sea, in Gauteng: 'What drew you to the ocean?'

'What drew me to the ocean?' she repeats the question to herself. 'I was going through a hard time. I end up in Bali in 2016. I go on a snorkel trip. I always go back to that because for me, as someone who feels like an oddball in the world, it was the moment when I found belonging.

'I looked beneath the surface and I just thought, what is going on here? It was a revelation of what I've always believed; that there's no one normative. Like, in our land-based world, we have ideas on what is pretty and what is first and what is … But in the ocean, everything matters, and everything is equally beautiful, and everything exists in a way that says, the ocean is the universal equaliser. Right?'

Zandi falls in love with the ocean and on her return to South Africa she starts scuba diving. It lets her look to the bottom of the ocean without fear – she can breathe while she is exploring. For someone who grew up in inland Soweto, she needed the assurance of breathing apparatus. In 2018 she saw a YouTube video of three women freediving, gracefully swimming underwater without scuba gear, and knew this was what she needed to do. The following year she did a freediving course, and it affirmed her journey thus far: the knowledge that this was all she wanted to do.

Her family thought she was crazy. But, 'I wanted to bring everyone from my community to a place where you're perfect just as you are,' she says, 'a place where the burdens of the world are carried by the biggest body that we've ever seen. And I just found it cleansing. I just knew that I wanted to create change, but I also wanted to change the narrative of how particularly we as black people have held to the water. Whether it is the ocean is a white people thing. Diving is a white people thing. I wanted to change that narrative because in the midst of that narrative, we're missing out on the most beautiful world there is.'

In Sodwana Bay, under the tutelage of Riaan de Waal, Zandi received her freediving instructor certificate. 'I just knew that I was seconds from leaving my job, leaving everything. And so, when Covid came around, it gave me the perfect moment to say, peace. I'm going to go be a mermaid to the world. I realised that my friends were a hard entry, because we're still stuck in the hard narrative. Children are normally more open to these things, right? And I think that's when I started writing the dream of saying, how do we create these moments? Like the moment I had in Bali.'

When Zandi left the successful consultancy that she had built with two other partners, there was a big fight with her family. It wasn't just about her; she had family members who relied on her for financial support. 'My grandmother used to say: what the hell is wrong with you? And the one time I caught her gossiping with her friend and she's like, there's the water one, that one.

'The water has always been such a foreign space, especially the ocean as it's linked to our own belief systems. To be able to be someone who dives in the ocean, dives with sharks, comes back with footage … I think it changed up our family. Now my grandmother's like, she's going to need to go back to the water anytime now, she doesn't belong to us any more, she's not only ours. Which is sweet.'

According to Zulu beliefs, ancestors dwell at the bottom of the ocean. It's a sacred space and thus not a space for the living. There is also the belief that there are snakes in the water. Often, if there's been the drowning of a child, be it in a river or the ocean, if the body is not found, people will say that it was taken by a snake. This is a hard thing that strains against ritual because burial, the retrieval of the physical body, is important.

For Zandi, the internal narrative is about what lives in the water, what takes people, who is taken and who doesn't come back. 'The external narrative,' she says, 'is the entire world telling us that black people aren't water people. It's a cultural belief system that we have taken on as our own, which is not true. Right. For me, it's not about breaking the internal narrative, because whether we believe in mermaids or snakes or ancestors, the ocean is a sacred place. For me, it's incredibly sacred.

'I believe we can hold a duality of narratives. The ocean can be a place of worship, a place of ancestors, a place of deep respect, but it can also be a place where we enjoy and we celebrate. And these waters get to witness our joy when they've witnessed so much of our pain.'

I'm curious about her freediving practice, and I remind her that the last time we spoke, in 2022, her breath hold was three and a half minutes. I ask her if she maintains her freediving fitness when she's away from water. Her answer is a straightforward yes, and she unpacks it for me. 'It's my silent time. It's feeling the source of life move through my body. And I feel like, even in freediving, there's so much work that we do in the water, but a lot of that work is done in dry training, because when you think of prepping your body for depth, it's to understand it on land so that you are able to know the prompts when you're at depth.

'Earlier I went for a run with my nieces. Then you come back and you feel where your body is at, where the breath is at. Sometimes the breath hold is long, sometimes it isn't. It's just being human. My maximum hold is at 4 minutes 45, which is exciting. This year I'm working on consistency because when I travel, training becomes a hot mess,' she laughs.

At two and a half minutes into breath hold, Zandi gets contractions. For her, breath hold and really cold Cape Town water are places of voluntary discomfort. When she's diving, she immerses herself in a place where she has an opportunity to touch the discomfort that lives around the body. When the contractions begin, Zandi manages herself and when they turn into hard thuds, she counts herself down, reassuring her mind that everything is okay. 'Then you just take that suction of air and you're just like, oh, my God, I love the water and I love breath,' she explains, giddy with the mere imagining of it.

Zandi advocates for indigenous knowledge, especially in the face of the need to protect our oceans. Indigenous knowledge has sustained peoples for decades, centuries, millennia. It is those closest to the water and the earth, the fishers and the harvesters, who are the first to know when things change. 'I want indigenous voices to be heard and recognised,' she says, 'to ensure that when we partner and collaborate with western worlds, there's a realisation that no one helicopters in. We collaborate, we bring knowledge from both sides and we co-create.'

I share Zandi's view, and believe that indigenous knowledge will unlock solutions to the climate crisis – which is why I ask my next question: 'What does your grandmother say?'

Zandi's grandmother, Christina Khumalo, is in her nineties. The question is laden with the anguish of things lost.

'We have become monsters,' Zandi replies. 'Of course, the land cannot talk to us. How can we expect it to speak to us when we've become monsters? And I think she's right. Everybody goes to Joburg, and everyone's looking for better opportunities, which is great. But in the migration, in the pursuit of the capitalist end, so much is lost. We're losing our lands, we're losing our waters, we're losing the men, we're losing the children. I feel like it's all interconnected, as everyone says. The climate crisis is so linked to social justice issues in every single way.'

Zandi is the founder of The Black Mermaid foundation and works with under-represented communities. Wherever she travels to do workshops and talks, Zandi asks the locals where to swim, catch fish, dive, as they understand the water. In Madagascar she spoke to a man who told her about the hurricanes, a story that reminded me of my conversations with scientists and environmentalists about how we will experience extreme weather more regularly. 'Their hurricane season has become so hectic that they get four-metre swells that ruin everything, and it's gotten worse every single year,' Zandi says. 'And so, their ability to start from scratch is becoming harder. It's interesting seeing water reclaim land spaces in different ways. We can call that flooding, and we can call it drought in certain forms, but we can see something is off. Everybody can tell that something is off, whether it's migration patterns that aren't the same any more, humpback whales not returning at the same time, sharks acting out of character. Something has changed. Something is changing.' Her expression is serious as she shakes her head, letting the blue ends of her hair smack her face.

It is mid-morning and the day feasts, cooling itself under a thicket of grey sky. Barefoot I walk the asphalt road winding down to the beach. Yellow-billed kites glide over albizias, searching for morsels of dead flesh. Along the edge of a grassy pavement large ants crawl with societal purpose. Ballito is teeming with life. And then I wonder about the lack of insects on the windscreen on our drive down to the coast. Years ago the glass would be splattered with them; this year there was hardly a mark. Even in a country so biodiverse, species are dwindling rapidly.

Waves tumble and roll as I sit cushioned by sand, my gaze fixated on the constant motion of life passing, happening. Of aliveness. I mull over my conversation with Zandi, imagining those who have passed, their spirits mingling with all that is alive and dead on the ocean floor, indistinguishable from the grains of sand and bits of shell. I bury my toes into cool sand, gravelly and old. If I close my eyes I could fall asleep, as I sit under clouds waiting for drizzle, for rain, the rumble of ocean my lullaby. I let it soften me with its touching.

ambitious human nature

When people ask me why I love freediving, I have three words in mind: depth, challenge and excitement.

– Alessia Zecchini

I'm watching a video of Italian freediver Alessia Zecchini in a swimming pool built for depth. She swims down past a concrete diving platform to the bottom of the pool where there is a circular hole leading into a darker, deeper, narrower pool. The camera follows her and I find myself holding my breath for her. Feet first, she stretches her arms above her head, left hand over right in the deep-dive position, and, like a hydrodynamic projectile, floats downwards. The pressure sucks her down; she knows exactly what she is doing, making the tiniest of intentional movements. It is such second nature to her that it would be odd to see her move out of the water, clambering against gravity on land. Down she goes, a lean, svelte figure, the different shades of blue on her swimsuit mingling with the bouncy shadows in the water, giving the impression that her legs are covered in silvery scales. It's only an illusion, one that I want so hard to believe is real.

Aptly named Y-40 The Deep Joy, the indoor swimming pool is the deepest thermal pool in the world. It plunges to a depth of 40 metres, which is like looking down from the top of a 14-storey building, and holds 4 300 cubic metres of water. The water is warm, between 32 and 34 °C, which is a very comfortable temperature for long swims. It isn't built into the ground, as I had initially thought, but above ground, as part of Hotel Terme Millepini near Padua, Italy. Besides its depth, what makes the indoor pool unique is that it contains thermal water from the nearby natural springs, bringing the experience even closer to diving in the natural waters of the seas and oceans.

I was reluctant to contact Alessia at first. The blue-eyed face smiling model-like in various posed photos made her seem – to me, anyway – quite unapproachable. She was, and still is, the women's world champion freediver in various disciplines – another reason to be aloof if she chose to be. I sent her a message on Facebook and to my very pleasant surprise she answered within a day. I had a deluge of questions to send her. Instead, I plotted my list of questions carefully; I didn't want to bombard her and risk putting her off. She agreed to chat on the phone.

Water is second nature to Alessia. After crawling and walking she entered the sea and from the age of 13 began formal training in apnoea. At the age of 11, during training at a swimming school where one of the drills was to do a length in one breath, she discovered she was good at it. In soft Italian, she tells me: 'There I found the joy of breath hold and the urge to always do one metre more. Also, going away every summer to the sea, there too I liked to be underwater.'

Of the course in apnoea at 13, she says, 'I fell in love with it so much that I never missed a training session, which was twice a week, late at night. At 14 I learnt that I couldn't compete until I was 18, but I carried on with my training and with volleyball,' she says.

At 18 she competed in Turin and came away with two silvers. It didn't take long for her to move on to international competitions. 'I knew from the beginning that I had the ability to push myself further in breath hold. First in the pool and then in the sea and the ocean. When I first started, I could hold for 45 seconds. With lots of determination and training, I reached 6 minutes before I turned 18. I kept going and after a few years I reached over 7 minutes. Then I stopped because it's a discipline I don't like any more,' says Alessia.

She lost interest in static breath hold because there is no movement of the body – one stays still and simply holds the breath for as long as it's bearably possible. She turned her attention to depth, a discipline that was far more challenging.

'What I like most about apnoea is definitely the sea. The contact with water, the element itself, feeling it on my skin. It's like flying, being in this element that is so elegant. Admiring the blue beneath me is something that fills me with joy. I love being in that environment,' she says as ambulance sirens and hooters and the quintessential cacophony of Italian city life hums outside, beyond the walls of the indoor swimming pool where she has just finished her training session.

Before a competition, her focus converges to the central point of her performance – the technicalities and the breath hold. When she practises breath hold, her mind is exclusively on her breathing and the silence around her. She observes and tries to stop her thoughts. She prepares with visualisation too. In her mind she sees the entire event, from the beginning, the preparation on the surface, her last breaths, going upside down, every minute sensation and action that she may feel during the dive. More than this, she sees the end, the joy, the protocols for her exit, the satisfaction. This helps her to minimise technical errors, but also to overcome the moments of suffering she experiences during the actual dive.

I ask her if she ever dreams about freediving and she tells me that it rarely happens. 'The few times that I have dreamt about it were very particular.' I can hear her smiling and there is a twitch of laughter as she recalls the memory. I picture her perennially tanned face glowing with bashfulness. 'For example, the last time was during the world championship and I dreamt about the depth that I needed to reach, I was convinced it was real, that it wasn't a dream,' she says. 'So, on the day of the dive I thought the depth was 10 metres more than what was predetermined. I was anticipating 10 metres more than the previous dive, 5 or 7 metres more than the pre-arranged dive, because I had dreamt it and it was so real. So, when I dream of apnoea it is very real!' She sucks in air through her teeth as she shares this intimate detail about her subconscious workings.

My next question is about her first competition. I ask her to describe it for me. 'It was already a dream being at my first Italian championship, my first important competition. It was in Turin and it was a unique joy.

'It was the first time that I could demonstrate my skills; before that I was limited because of my age. The competition was an amazing experience. I was first to dive, calm in my tiny swimming costume, and the emotion was spectacular because I did my best ever, I took it to the maximum and slowly but surely I stacked my adversaries behind me and like that I took two beautiful silver medals, which gave the strength and the encouragement, the incentive, to always do better.' As we converse over the phone, I am travelling with her back to her home, where she lives with her parents. Minutes later, I hear kitchen noises – crockery and cutlery being carried to the sink. I picture her mother clearing the table after dinner.

I'm curious about what she does in her day, so I ask her. 'Besides training, which occupies a large part of my day, I work with my sponsors and take care of other work necessities. But I always try to find a balance and at a certain hour I switch off and make time for friends or spend time with my boyfriend, my parents. In my opinion it's important to always have a balance – maximum concentration and then switch off completely for equilibrium and relaxation. Obviously, it's important to eat, the Mediterranean diet for me is the best that exists.' I hear her smiling as she says this.

'Maybe it's because I'm Italian. The simple things are what I like most. My boyfriend is a cook so my dietary needs are well taken care of. And then if I'm able, I like to watch the sunset.'

Alessia is on the skinny side of lean with a preternatural athlete's metabolism. Some would argue that she needs more muscle mass, but her body holds the grace and the force required for depth. While self-contained and very disciplined, she likes to be in motion, so when her schedule permits it, she partakes in outdoor sports. 'I ride my bicycle, go rollerblading, fly kite, I like doing a bit of everything and anything. I like trying new sports and discovering what I'm good at.' She likes to pick olives during harvest season. On a Facebook post there are photos of her donning a cap back-to-front, tracksuit top sleeves pushed above her elbows, her legs wrapped around the trunk of a tree as she reaches up with one hand to grab the fruit. It is one of her favourite things as it reminds her of childhood when her whole family – parents, cousins, uncles and aunts – would help with the picking.

My next question is what she thinks the biggest problem currently affecting the environment is. She tells me that she doesn't have the expertise to tell me, but what she sees on her travels and in her aquatic experiences is the erosion and destruction that the ocean is causing.

'There is too much water. The waves are eating everything and destroying the beaches in Italy and the world. In Italy in winter it's disconcerting because there is no beach. In Ostia, which is a famous beach near Rome, there are no stretches of beach, only stilt houses. We all need to wake up and stop being stupid. We have to give our oceans a lot more attention and care. We need to take care of what we do on land, because it all goes into the ocean. We need to try to remove and eliminate the waste that we leave on the beaches, this is a small but essential gesture that can help a lot because the amount of refuse that gets offloaded into the ocean is so much that we all need to collaborate in a bigger way. The state needs to get involved to preserve the oceans as much as possible as they are an indispensable resource.'

As I correspond with Alessia, the world is in the thick of the global Covid-19 pandemic, with most sporting events cancelled – even the 2020 Olympic Games, to the dismay of many, both participants and all those spectating. 'With Covid our competitions have been postponed,' Alessia says, 'like Vertical Blue, the world championships in Turkey, and many others. The next objective and the only objective for the year is a competition in Curaçao where I will attempt to reach the maximum depth in the no fins discipline. The Olympics is the dream of every athlete and it is also mine. We were candidates for Paris 2024, but unfortunately no longer, but we're preparing to go to Los Angeles in 2028.'

Months after I chat to her, in July 2021 at Vertical Blue on Long Island, Bahamas, she again won overall and set three world records. At the Confédération Mondiale des Activités Subaquatiques (CMAS) Outdoor World Championship 2021, she set a new world record with a depth of 105 metres, 10 metres more than the previous record. On 27 March 2023, during the Secretblue competition in Moalboal, Philippines, she set a new world record in CWTB (constant weight bifins) of 107 metres. After two days she went deeper, surpassing her record by reaching 109 metres in 3,36 minutes. On 24 May 2023 at AIDA Oceanquest Philippines she took her record to greater depths with 123 metres, setting a new world record in constant weight with monofin. In April 2024, during the Camotes Freediving Challenge in the Philippines, she set a CMAS free immersion (FIM) world record, descending to 104 metres. Free immersion is when a diver descends and ascends along a vertical rope using only their arms; they don't wear fins either, relying entirely on upper body strength. In October 2024, at the CMAS 8th World Championship Freediving Depth in Kalamata, Greece, she achieved depths of 100 metres in CWTB and 109 metres in constant weight with monofin (CWT). For her 2024 CWT record, Alessia fell short of her 2023 record by a few metres. There are so many factors that influence this – environment, water temperature, currents and the diver's physical condition on the day.

Her record attempts have not been without heartache. In 2017 one of Alessia's safety divers and a dear friend, Stephan Keenan, died after assisting her to safety. Alessia was attempting to cross the Arch of Dahab's Blue Hole when she became disorientated. Dahab's Blue Hole on the Red Sea coast is an iconic and notoriously dangerous sinkhole that is over 100 metres deep. The Arch is a 26-metre-long underwater tunnel that begins at 55 metres and connects the Blue Hole to the open sea. Scuba divers and freedivers love it – it is exciting and treacherous, a test of their limitations. But, the test has been fatal for many.

Alessia went through the Arch to the open sea, and Stephan was supposed to meet her at the exit to guide her ascent. Their timing was misaligned, with Stephan descending a few seconds later than scheduled. They missed each other at the juncture and Alessia, unable to locate the ascent line by herself, swam off course. At a depth of 50 metres Alessia was disorientated, but Stephan found her and finned her to the surface. She made it out, but Stephan experienced shallow-water blackout and was found floating face-down some distance away.

His was the first recorded death of a safety diver in action in freediving history. Since then Alessia has dedicated her records to Stephan. In the 2023 Netflix documentary *The Deepest Breath*, which chronicles their journey, Alessia says, 'He will always be in my heart, he will always be with me because I want him by my side for the rest of my days.'

The tragic incident at Blue Hole didn't stop Alessia from freediving and she continues to be just as goal- and success-orientated as any other competitive freediver. Her human nature is to be ambitious; her mammalian nature is to be amphibious, and these two factors combine to make her the best in the world. Alessia outperforms her own records. As I write this book, no other woman has beaten her deepest dive. She is at the very top of her game, plumbing depths where the light fades quickly, a place where many would be afraid. Alessia likes the dark. It's a solitary place where she can let her guard down. I think that being deep in the sea, slipping through water in silence, brings her comfort. As a young teenager she already knew she could do things that others couldn't. Her early success with apnoea has allowed her to be in water in a way that few humans ever could.

I watch eagerly for news of her next competitive attempts.

shaped by the sea

In the struggle for survival, the fittest win out at the expense of their rivals because they succeed in adapting themselves best to their environment.

– Charles Darwin

While present-day humans are not strongly differentiated, vast amounts of genomic data now make it possible to study subtle patterns of genetic variation.

– Melissa Ilardo

I am curious to know how humans have adapted to living near the sea. Charles Darwin's theory of evolution by natural selection describes how species adapt to their environments, making them a better fit for it so that their survival is easier. As he sailed on the HMS *Beagle* as a naturalist observing the world, I imagine that the long, slow days surrounded by open water influenced his thinking and brought with it a perspective of time that is long and multigenerational.

Natural selection happens by chance and not by chance. It is not random, but requires things to happen and change to initiate it. It requires a purpose. It's a natural mechanism by which organisms, be they plants, animals, slugs, insects or bacteria, use the traits that help them survive and breed well and pass those traits on to their offspring.

Natural selection is a process that can lead to evolution. According to yourgenome.org, evolution is 'the change in the characteristics of a species over several generations and relies on the process of natural selection. The theory of evolution is based on the idea that all species are related and gradually change over time'.

Some species change more than others, and only out of necessity. If that amount of time and energy is expended, there needs to be some advantage to a species changing. One of the beautiful things about this process is that we live alongside creatures that for millions of years have been swimming in the same seas that we swim in today. Jellyfish, sharks, turtles, coelacanths, horseshoe crabs and lampreys are some of these prehistoric water-dwellers.

Jellyfish have been around unchanged for the last 500 million years. The exact timeline is difficult to pinpoint because there are no fossil records, but those who study them know from their genetics that they've stayed pretty much exactly as they were. Sharks formed 350 million years ago and have existed for longer than trees and the rings of Saturn.

Sharks were essentially the first major group of organisms that were mobile and reproduced sexually. They haven't changed much over the millennia – they still have the same body shape, cartilage instead of bone, a primitive spinal cord and nerve structure; they still hunt in a similar way and are communal creatures. All those years ago, they hit on a winning formula and all they've done since then is tinker.

There are other creatures that developed more recently. Dolphins, whales, porpoises and dugongs are some of them. These species have gone back to the sea. They left the sea as fish and amphibians, and went through a massive evolution. Fossil evidence shows that dolphins were once long-snouted wolves. Researchers can see a distinct correlation between evolution and brain size; these creatures had to get smart. During the last 30 to 40 million years, they seemed to go back to the ocean after the downfall of the dinosaurs. Over several million years, their back legs disappeared, their front legs became flippers and they transformed into animals perfectly adapted to life in the water. There are traces of their life on land; whales still have tiny hip bones from when they were four-legged mammals.

I'm watching a documentary about the Bajau – a group of people whose spleens are significantly larger than everyone else's. The Bajau are sea nomads who have lived on, and in, the waters of Malaysia, Indonesia and the Philippines for centuries. Their lives are totally dependent on water and when they're not in the sea, they're paddling in boats or sleeping in their floating homes. Their history and their daily movements are intertwined with the western Pacific Ocean. They are able to dive to depths beyond 70 metres on one breath, spearing fish and octopus and collecting the fruits of the sea, including crustaceans and sea cucumbers, by simply using weights and a wooden mask. They've been using the same fishing techniques and tools for centuries. To boot, the many years of diving have shaped their bodies so that they are better at it. This fascinates me. Their interaction with the sea has actually caused them to evolve. The scientist who discovered that they have larger-than-normal spleens is Melissa Ilardo. I contact her via LinkedIn – bless social media – and she responds, happy to share her findings.

Melissa is a geneticist based in Salt Lake City, United States. Her soon-to-be-husband is a percussionist for the Utah Symphony. I wonder what it must be like to have so much science and music in one household, all those ideas and harmonic nuances floating around. It must be amazing.

We meet on a Zoom call. Her eyes flash with intelligence and when she smiles her light-brown bob bounces. Melissa glows with elation; still on a high from all the excitement and publicity about her discovery. I quickly understand that Melissa has an obsessive interest in indigenous people who present unique DNA; for her, the Bajau were a huge missed opportunity. She surmised that there must be something special about them, so she aggressively began seeking out a path for bringing her logic to light.

This led her to doing a PhD and tracing a specific supervisor in Denmark named Eske Willerslev. He told her, 'If you can find a project you're passionate about, I'll support you.'

'I've been a scuba diver for many years and human evolution interests me. When I put together the spleen hypothesis, I was told it sounds interesting but it's risky. Was I betting my PhD on this?'

Melissa's spleen hypothesis was a hunch – she supposed that people who spend a lot of time diving to depths have significantly larger spleens, a result of human adaptation and evolution. Seals that do sustained deep dives, such as the Weddell seals, also have disproportionately large spleens. Part of what prompted Melissa's study was this knowledge. For a geneticist like Melissa, proving this would be groundbreaking.

The spleen is an organ that performs several important functions. It filters old and damaged red blood cells as well as abnormal cells and germs from the blood; it regulates the levels of red blood cells, white blood cells and platelets; and it stores blood for future use. It's part of the body's lymphatic system and helps protect the body from disease and infection. A larger spleen would mean a larger store of oxygenated red blood cells, ready to be released into the bloodstream when needed. In a freediver this would be a perfect physiological adaptation.

She began by using DNA from ancient material from Siberia, sequencing human samples from three cultural and geographic contexts spanning 7 000 years. Then, in 2015, like Darwin she took to the seas in a quest to identify and understand the unique characteristics of the Bajau.

She visited a Bajau community who live very remotely, in Jaya Bakti village on an island connected to the larger island of Sulawesi via a bridge. The best piece of advice Melissa received was to learn Indonesian, which she did. 'The community is remote and quite removed from larger population groups. Their distance from the mainlands also keeps them disconnected from mainstream culture. What is in easy reach from Jaya Bakti is the ocean and the Bajau go on weeks-long excursions. All of this provided an exemplary cohort for research.'

To stick to a tight budget, she chose to get to Jaya Bakti on the back of a scooter driven by Adi Saahi, a local man she'd only just met but who spoke excellent English. At that point, her grasp of Indonesian was still in its early stages. She hadn't realised just how far away the village was – it took four hours to get there. It was hot and humid, insects buzzing, misty jungle everywhere. It was also Ramadan, and it would've been rude to arrive at the village before sunset. She and Adi stopped at a restaurant. The awkwardness between them lengthened, especially because she felt guilty for eating in front of him while he was observing his fast. She would learn afterwards that he didn't want to go to the village because he'd heard unsavoury stories about the villagers and how he'd have his things stolen.

She could see the village across the water. 'At this point I'm getting really excited that we're really close, but still unsure of where we're staying for the night. I don't know if the village is even going to want me to; I'm showing up out of nowhere, just ridden four hours across the island on a scooter and I have no idea what's going to happen.'

At the restaurant they met a woman who lived nearby and offered to go with them to the village to introduce them. They arrived as the chief, his wife and others were breaking their fast. Adi and the woman explained the reason for Melissa's visit, who she was, where she was from. And then the chief's wife got up and walked away. Melissa thought the worst. Had she offended them? Was her attire inappropriate? Were they unhappy with her proposed research? It was none of this: the chief's wife had gone to prepare rooms for them at their house. They told her that they were very excited to have her there. Melissa's first visit could not have gone better.

'There is a lot of stigma around this population and they are highly marginalised. To me they were the most incredibly welcoming people. The chief and his wife took me in. The divers I went with were so open and generous. They were eager to learn about their genetic heritage. On my second visit I brought ultrasound machines and kits to get spit samples. I needed comparison populations so I went to other villages close by. Every person was keen and eager to discover more.'

Melissa continued to stay at the house of the chief and his wife.

'One of the biggest things I noticed was how deeply connected the Bajau are to the sea; this was more striking than in some other diving populations. Food, songs, storytelling, everything comes back to the sea,' she says.

Another thing that struck her was how soft the soles of their feet are. 'They have the softest feet because they hardly walk, they're in the water for most of the day, spending 60 per cent of their waking hours in the water. The closest mammal to the Bajau in terms of underwater working time is the sea otter.'

The Bajau engage with breath hold diving many times a day and they are renowned for this ability. Melissa wanted to find out if their capacity for apnoea was linked to physiological adaptation. Using her portable ultrasound machine, she measured the spleens of 59 Bajau and compared the results to the spleen size of people from the neighbouring village of Koyoan – inhabited by the Saluan people, who do not dive – as well as a European cohort.

The studies confirmed that variants in the PDE10A gene have increased spleen size in the Bajau. What this means is that their spleens are notably larger, by as much as 50 per cent; this was the case in both divers and non-divers, proving that the entire population had adapted through natural selection. With a larger spleen, the Bajau have a bigger reserve of oxygen-rich red blood cells, ready to be pumped into the body during breath hold.

Part of the human diving reflex is a contraction of the spleen, which pushes red blood cells into the bloodstream to boost oxygen. Splenic contraction caused by the diving response was first observed in the Ama, Japanese women who have been diving for seafood and pearls for centuries. Because of their larger spleens, the Bajau have about 10 per cent more red blood cells that can be mobilised in the body. In terms of breath hold, this allows the divers in the community to take less recovery time between dives.

Melissa's research led her to find another gene associated with the mammalian diving reflex. The evidence she uncovered shows that the gene that affects vasoconstriction, known as bradykinin receptor B2 (BDKRB2), has been favoured by natural selection and is a much fitter gene than others in the Bajau population. This gene regulates the cardiovascular system, and in the Bajau this gene constricts peripheral blood vessels very effectively, directing more blood to the brain and the internal organs – and keeping it there – to protect them. This allows for longer breath hold without negative effects. Melissa explains that the vasoconstriction response is important in the diving reflex because it protects the vital organs.

The Bajau have also developed a tolerance for oxygen deficiency. This has happened in other parts of the world, most notably in people living at high altitudes, such as the Tibetans. In a human living at normal altitude, this chronic state would cause medical problems such as blood clots, gout, nosebleeds and bruising.

Through the process of natural selection, the Bajau have become perfectly adapted to their environment and their lifestyle. Time-wise, this process was either a weak selection process over 15 000 years or a strong selection process over 2 000 years or so – Melissa believes it was the latter. The Bajau have been marine hunter-gatherers for millennia, and are akin to other marine mammals in terms of their capacity for being underwater. They are the product of behaviour and lifestyle, and show how humans can evolve physiologically.

Her research was not without issues. At one point in her research Melissa was forced to stop by authorities who believed that her doing research was wrong and inappropriate.

It is November 2023. Over a few short days spring has tipped into summer and Johannesburg is an explosion of green; every tree, bush and flowering stem is expressing greenness. I recall that plants react to environmental stress, such as rising temperature, by becoming greener. It is hotter, by about one or two degrees. I'm amazed at how the Earth becomes more beautiful under pressure.

I'm on my morning walk contemplating the chat I'll be having with Melissa later this evening. The asphalt is strewn with jacaranda flowers, lilac and dying, a contrast to the bursting floral splendour. She's excited about starting her post as associate professor in the Biomedical Informatics department at the University of Utah. Her LinkedIn profile mentions a new research project that explores the evolution of another population that practises breath hold diving in their daily life – the Haenyeo, all-female divers of South Korea. Like the Bajau, the Haenyeo are a unique population that have adapted physiologically through natural selection. It will be interesting to discover whether only the women have evolved, or if the modifications have been passed on to the men.

It's 8 p.m. here and 11 a.m. in Salt Lake City. Melissa is all smiles. She spent a number of years working for pharmaceutical start-ups, and while it was interesting, keeping the funders happy felt restrictive. 'I want to ask questions for research's sake and in academia I can do that. So yes, I am very happy to be back doing what I love.'

'What is your research about?' I ask her.

'That I can't tell you, because it hasn't been published yet, and it's a scoop. But I'm excited to tell you all about it when I can.' Melissa is beaming.

Melissa is fully immersed in the exploration of indigenous humans and part of her work is to recruit students and PhD candidates from these groups as it makes the research so much more eloquent and meaningful. 'There's something special about indigenous people that's worth celebrating. A lot of them have been marginalised. Rewriting this narrative is something that happens because of my work. Someone once said to me, research moves at the speed of trust. And that's true. You have to build trust first before you do anything else. It's important to reach out to these populations because the people themselves, the languages, are disappearing.'

She considers herself lucky to have gone to an Aboriginal conference in Australia. She sat quietly in the back and just listened, aware that it was a privilege to be there. She is pleased to have connected with Krystal Tsosie, a native American researcher, through new colleagues and friends. She seeks out people who can help her bring the superhuman characteristics of indigenous populations to the fore. There is urgency to her work and she tries to bring this across emphatically to her funders.

Melissa and her husband are flying to Copenhagen to celebrate their one-year anniversary and for her husband to meet her supervisor – Raspen Nielsen. 'He's such a character; I really want my husband to meet him.'

Copenhagen is where it began for Melissa, it's where she found the support for her risky research project, and I predict that soon she'll be making world news with another genetic discovery.

On 19 February 2025 Melissa emails with the subject line: *Good News!!!* Her research on the Haenyeo divers, which she hasn't been able to discuss with me, has been approved for publication.

Haenyeo means 'diving women' in Korean. The Haenyeo are all women and they dive on an island called Jeju, which is off the southern coast of the Korean peninsula. Diving is not a recent practice for them – there is mention of them in 17th-century literature. But up until the 18th century, diving was mostly done by Jeju men. They dived daily to harvest seafood and seaweed. This changed when heavy taxes were imposed on them, so the women took over the diving work, becoming the breadwinners. This has continued to this day. With their thin cotton diving attire and adaptation to cold water, in the 1970s and 1980s the Haenyeo caught the attention of researchers curious to discover more about their environmental physiology. The curiosity has not abated, especially because their bodies may hold information about adaptation.

Jeju has a unique culture and language. It's as different from Korean as Norwegian is from Dutch. Melissa tells me this because she knows

I'm interested in language and linguistic nuances, and to demonstrate how isolated this population is from others on the Korean peninsula.

'We had a Korean grad student from Seoul working with us and a Korean grad student who was from Jeju. The one from Seoul couldn't understand what people were saying when they were speaking Jeju dialect. So, there's a movement to call it its own language. That distinction is important because it actually also reflects this genetic separation between Jeju island and mainland Korea that we found in the genetic results,' she explains.

Another fun thing about the language is that it's characteristically much shorter than Korean. Melissa says that the Haenyeo think that one of the reasons for this is that there is a long history of diving, so they need to speak to each other quickly, in shorter sentences, at the surface. 'I don't know if this is true,' says Melissa, 'but it's kind of cool that diving may be so integrated in the culture that it's defined the language.'

For Melissa, the context is important for the science. It tells her that there's a chance that what she's going to see from her research is that everyone in Jeju is genetically related and different from everyone in the rest of Korea. And that's exactly what she saw. 'Genetically, Haenyeo and non-Haenyeo were all part of the same population in Jeju. What we think that means is that, ancestrally, everyone was diving.'

Melissa classified participants as Haenyeo divers and Haenyeo non-divers to distinguish what could be a training effect from a genetic effect. Melissa and her team saw both effects. They saw that Haenyeo divers, through the practice of everyday diving – as this is what they do to make a living, even in their sixties and seventies – have a more pronounced drop in heart rate. When all the participants held their breath and put their faces in a bowl of cold water to stimulate the human diving reflex, their heart rates dropped. This happens when anyone dives but with the Haenyeo it was an even greater drop. Their hearts have been trained to respond to diving with pronounced bradycardia. 'We had one participant whose heart rate dropped about 40 beats per minute in just 15 seconds of holding her breath – really incredible.

You could see the numbers dropping dramatically, which you don't normally see,' says Melissa.

Melissa thinks the big drop in heart rate is a training effect, and not a genetic effect, because they only saw it in the divers of Jeju. Melissa and her team think that the act of diving increases the bradycardia response, which is something that's also been seen in competitive breath hold divers. 'So, it's not new, but it's a nice confirmation. It's interesting because most competitive breath hold divers who have been studied are not in their seventies,' says Melissa.

It was remarkable to discover that you can train bradycardia even into your seventies. But equally significant was a genetic effect that the researchers were able to confirm. There's a genetic variant that's been under selection in the Haenyeo to decrease diastolic blood pressure, particularly while they're diving. Melissa's team saw this in the divers and in the non-divers. All of the women from Jeju whom they tested had this response: their diastolic blood pressure was lower during diving. Diastolic blood pressure, the lower number in a blood pressure reading, measures the pressure in arteries when the heart is at rest between beats and refills with blood. As to how this manifests in the actual lives of non-divers, she tells me that it may influence pregnancy outcomes by reducing the risk of hypertensive disorders of pregnancy, and it may even reduce the risk of other vascular complications, including stroke. 'It's very exciting to think that genetic variation that evolved to protect divers may protect everyone in Jeju, and may be something that we could recreate to protect the rest of the world as well,' she says.

Melissa thinks that this genetic variation is related to the fact that these women dive throughout their pregnancy. They've evolved for diving during pregnancy so that it is safer for them and their unborn child. Researchers know from studies of sleep apnoea (when people stop breathing involuntarily for short periods while sleeping) that it increases the risk of hypertensive disorders during pregnancy. This includes blood pressure related pregnancy complications such as chronic hypertension, gestational hypertension and preeclampsia, which can lead to serious complications for both mother and baby. 'We think that diving throughout their pregnancy, as they all do, would increase the risk of these kinds of complications. And so over many generations of women diving through their pregnancy, they've actually evolved for it to be safer, because of this change in their diastolic blood pressure. It's exciting because we think that this phenotype is driven by women. I talked to many Haenyeo women who dove until the day they gave birth. So, it's pretty special. Once again, women carrying children are driving the change of our entire species,' explains Melissa.

Melissa believes that the same is happening in high-altitude populations: being pregnant at high altitude is hard on the body and on the foetus, and this may be driving selection in those populations.

It was only on her return to Utah that pregnancy as a driver became a point of interest. When Melissa gave a talk about the results, someone in the audience from the maternal health field commented that it was obvious to him that the blood pressure phenotype was related to the fact that the Haenyeo dived throughout pregnancy. He made that connection for Melissa's team.

When Melissa was with the Bajau, she would always ask, 'Did your mom dive?' And they all said yes. When she asked, 'Did she dive when she was pregnant?', they all said yes. 'I think this is universal amongst diving populations, which means that it could be driving the selection that we see in those populations and in ways that we don't really understand yet.' Melissa and her team collected DNA samples and performed simulated dives in Jeju with Haenyeo divers and non-divers, and did the same in Seoul. They created a simulated dive setting so that participants, whose average age was 65, would be comfortable and there was no risk of drowning, alleviating concerns for the non-divers. They put out mattresses and a bucket filled with water at 10 °C, as this is the ideal temperature to trigger the diving response in this kind of setting. In the ocean the response would be different, but Melissa clarifies that as long as there's a 10 °C difference between the air and the water, the response will be triggered.

The Haenyeo are famously closed and have turned away many outsiders wanting to explore their culture and environment, but with the help of researcher Joo-Young Lee – who has been studying them for over a decade, especially their thermoregulatory response and cold adaptation, and who is well-loved by them – Melissa was able to carry out her genetic exploration.

Each participant put their face in the water and the researchers measured heart rate, blood pressure and carbon dioxide levels. Interestingly, when the Haenyeo are in the ocean diving, their bradycardia readings are different. 'Divers who are actively diving for sea urchins are working so hard in terms of swimming that their heart rate doesn't drop, it actually stays the same,' says Melissa.

As we chat, I notice that Melissa is tightly wound. She's trying to upload her findings to a website to share them with other scientists. This is part of how she lets the outside world know about her work. But so far, it's not working and she's unable to talk to a human who can help her with the glitchy website. I tell her about extreme swimming couple Ram Barkai and Samantha Whelpton, how the contrast between air and water temperature probably gives them an edge. Melissa nods in agreement. 'Yes, there's the science to back that.'

Melissa is tuned into the world of the human body, the evolution of it, within the context of the sea. Her revelations are charged with urgency. Her work celebrates what makes people unique and resilient. She wants to show human adaptation to the world and at the same time she wants to conserve the physiological intelligence of the people she studies. I have no doubt that more revelations will follow.

swimming

choppy seas, a mirror for life

As is the wont of the sea, it remains calm and smooth,
but at times it will heave with storms and the waves
will rise like mountains.

– Homer, *The Odyssey*, translated by Samuel Butler, 1614

It's August 2024 and I'm in a gym pool in Joburg. Six weeks ago, in an excited conversation with a friend, I committed to doing an open-water swim in False Bay. It seemed like a tremendously good idea but once the flurry of enthusiasm simmered, I regretted it. What was I thinking? I love being in the sea, breaststroking at my own pace, I'm comfortable freediving, I have a good level of fitness, but proper swimming requires a special set of skills and a different kind of fitness. The mere thought of it made my heart beat faster, but how would I tell my friend I'd decided against it? I couldn't. So, I committed to being all in, spoke to my brother who is an excellent swimmer, took his advice and started doing laps and drills in the gym pool.

As I train in preparation for the swim I come to a realisation: after six weeks of doing laps, swimming is still hard for me. Granted, I'm not tall, so reaching the other side of the pool requires more strokes. Also, everything is calculated, from my breathing to the pace of my stroke and ensuring my body lies straight on the water so that my heels kick air. I have to work on my proprioception. I have to think about the position of my head, how I turn my neck as I take a breath through my mouth, how my shoulders rotate so that I pull my hands and arms through the water. It is a propulsive motion that I still need to think about.

The man in the lane next to me helps by watching my stroke. 'Tilt your head a little more downwards so that you can see two or three tiles in front of you,' he says, referring to the tiles on the floor of the pool. 'It'll take you six weeks and then you won't have to think about it, your body will just do it.' Another six weeks? I think to myself, but I listen keenly to his words and wonder why I never paid more attention to the swimming coach's instructions at school.

I find freediving easy; it's more intuitive for me. Holding my breath is very different from breathing while swimming. I can hold my breath for three and a half minutes, which feels like less of an exertion than swimming. Being underwater feels softer, calmer and more wondrous. It requires less will. Perhaps I find more stillness beneath the waves and swells; the sounds there are different from the surface sounds, and they arrive at my ears differently. Underwater there is peace and I'm distracted by the curiosities of the ocean.

Doing freestyle, especially in a swimming pool, requires a lot more willpower. I think it's the repetition of it. The up and down in the lane until the training is done. I'm trying to compare freediving in the sea to swimming in a gym pool, which is not a fair comparison. Of course lane training will be lacklustre. I think about my swims in the Mediterranean, in the Aegean, in the Adriatic, in the Persian Gulf, nothing organised or competitive but long enough to feel miraculous, long enough to put me in a reverie. I imagine an open-water swim in the ocean to be a vastly different experience. The thought excites me.

I keep swimming and get into a good mental zone as I follow the blue line at the bottom of the pool. The gym sounds are muffled and it's pleasantly echoey – the doof-doof music and beeps from the super circuit far away. I exhale bubbles as I pull my left arm through the water, then my right, propelling myself forward towards the edge. I admit to myself that there is a twinge of fear every time I contemplate the open-water swim. It is still distant, not yet so close as to be real, but it scares me. My inner voice reminds me to trust my body, trust my pumping heart and respiring lungs. I notice that a part of me, somewhere small and deep inside, believes that the open-water swim will be easier than this – other things to think about, things that are different and new. I imagine the sun's silver on the undulating water on a smooth overcast day saturating the different greens of the vegetation. The anticipated newness of the experience excites me and motivates me to up the speed of my stroke. I plough through the water, creating small currents around me.

Moving in a straight line does something to time. It stretches it out and divides it into equal parts. The repetitive forward motion causes my mind to amble to the chat I had with marathon swimmer Carina Bruwer.

I'm always wanting to know what it feels like to be other people. Carina is six feet tall, muscular, an extreme athlete, fit, with skin that tans easily. She's Amazonian. I wonder what it must feel like to be her and I imagine it to be quite awesome. She is a flautist, a celebrated swimmer, an entrepreneur and a mother of three. Being that physically gifted must be grand. But a bay is not always as smooth as a pond, and while Carina has many gifts, she's experienced her fair share of literal and metaphorical choppy waters. Now in her mid-forties, life experience has taught her to swim with the tide.

Carina likes to do 'firsts' – big swims that other people haven't done – and she tells me about her triple-country swim. She swam from Nice in France, along the coast of Monaco to Ventimiglia in Italy, a route that stretches about 21 kilometres. The water was a gorgeous aquamarine, beautifully clear and warm, tropical compared to Cape Town. The swim was a very slow one. 'I was swimming against the current all the way,' Carina says, 'and also it was wild. Usually, on a neutral day, 21 kilometres should take me five and a half hours. This was a slow swim and I finished it just on the seven-hour mark. So yeah, it's also conditions dependent and because often I'm the first person to do a swim, like in this case, you don't necessarily know the currents or the prevailing conditions, and usually I'm just kind of scraping together a team and people who are willing to help me. Unfortunately, the way I've done most of my swims is not very technically savvy. I just go and I swim. So, this swim specifically, I should have gone the other way.'

If Carina had started at Ventimiglia and ended at Nice, she would probably have done it in under five hours. 'But that's open-water swimming. You can't always plan perfectly and it's a bit like a mirror for life. You expect one thing and you get something completely different and you just have to go through it, stroke through it and enjoy the process.'

Carina has learnt that it's not all about the time. When she was younger – 25 years old, to be exact – she swam the English Channel. She really wanted to do it in under ten hours, which she knew she was capable of. In preparation for the swim she trained 8 kilometres daily and upped her calorie intake, putting on 10 kilograms and adding a buffer of fat to her body that would help her stay comfortable in the cold. But she hit the current and she was stuck swimming in place for about three hours.

In the end, she crossed the channel in 12 hours. 'I hated the English Channel and I wouldn't really tell anyone that I did it because, I was like, that's not good enough. But it's just such a good lesson, really, that the ocean teaches you. You can do everything from your side, you can do everything right, but you can't control things outside yourself. Sometimes you can't even control things within yourself. And you just have to let go of those expectations without letting go of your drive or ambition.'

Slowly, through her career, Carina embraced the philosophy of letting go of expectations and embracing the journey. It's better to let things unfold and see what the other side looks like because it's often quite different from what you expect; because of that, it's quite awesome. I ask her how she plans the basics of her swims – the eating and the stops. 'I don't even need to plan, you know,' she answers. 'That's just part of the sport you do. Depending on the distance, you plan your stops, for me a stop equates to a very quick stop where I tread water. I'm not allowed to touch the boat or touch anyone. So, from the boat they'll throw an energy drink or a banana to me, I'll have a quick sip or bite and throw it back. I literally start swimming again unless there's something to discuss with a support crew member. I don't like stopping too long as I get cold and lose focus. If I'm going to swim 20 to 30 kilometres it's a one-way journey and that's what I'm focused on. It's such a mental game.'

Carina doesn't like to eat much while doing a marathon swim but she knows she has to, to replenish her body and maintain her stamina. She's glad for the specifically formulated gels that are available nowadays. Twenty years ago, when she swam the English Channel, she remembers that a man who swam it on the same day had three chickens, drinks, bananas and more on the boat. Carina had forgotten to get food, so they had to stop at a vending machine on the way to the start. Much like life, each person has their own way of getting to the finish line.

Each person also has their own psychological strategy for completing a long-distance swim. Carina usually stops after an hour to eat and reset. Further into the swim she may take it down to 45 minutes and, if she's struggling, she'll stop after 30 minutes to get a little more food into her body. 'So much happens in the mind. I mean, you can be physically trained for it, but if your mind isn't right, then you're gonna fail. I found that when I'm starting to lose it – my strength is going, and it's happened a couple of times – I have to fight really hard to regain it or I'll give up. Frequent stopping and chirping the crew is not a good idea.

'Marathon swimming is an individual sport and no one else is going to do it for you. It all comes down to you. If the conditions are tough or your body's giving up, the crew can't do anything. You've just got to swim through it. You've got to maintain that strength or find it from somewhere if you want to finish.'

Carina is open about the hardships of the sport. There are pain points and it is common for her to get earache, a sore throat and sore shoulders during her swims. Shoulders are a big issue for swimmers. If waters are rough or if the swim requires a wetsuit, there is extra pressure on the shoulders. Carina has nagging shoulder pain that she's never managed to get rid of, so before a long swim she swallows an anti-inflammatory. As her body ages, she finds that after about three hours of swimming she develops a dull ache in her hips that worsens as the kilometres progress. But none of this stops her from doing what she loves, a sport she stumbled upon and that became a calling.

She has learnt how far she can push her body. She understands water temperature and what happens to her when she starts to shiver during her swim. 'It's very seldom that you're going to swim ten hours without any challenges or pain. For me, it's having those conversations with myself. We're so much more capable than we tell ourselves, what the world tells us and what society tells us. And it's often fear that stops us and holds us back. And fear can be so many things – fear of pain, fear of failure, fear of the unknown.'

As a flautist, Carina began swimming at university to increase her lung capacity. She could barely do three laps but soon she was comfortably swimming four kilometres at a time, bunking classes to be in the pool. When she got news of an 11 km open-water swim from Simon's Town to Muizenberg, a distance that was daunting to her, she called the organiser. She was worried about the distance, the cold and the sharks. His words were, 'There are more sharks on the road. Just come, you'll be fine.'

She can still remember standing on the beach in her red costume, terrified, seeing mostly men around her and thinking, *You're a weird bunch.* She told herself that if she didn't like it, she could stop. It took her about twenty minutes to get into her stroke and to feel the beautiful rhythm of the ocean, this different space. She immediately felt at home and had a profound moment: *Wow, this is where I want to be.*

Three hours later, the swim was over – too soon. Carina was on the beach and thought, *I still want to do more of this.*

It sounds dramatic, but for Carina it was life changing. 'That feeling of being in nature, far away from the mess that is the world, was incredibly special and I loved it and I still do.'

She came second overall and first in the female category. Everyone wanted to meet her and some of the swimmers took her under their wing and mentored her. They recognised her potential; from that point, her life became a wild and wonderful adventure. She was encouraged by inspiring people. This, and her own personal drive, were the perfect combination, launching her career in open-water swimming.

Soon afterwards, she swam Robben Island and Cape Point. It was the early 2000s and the sport was still small and niche, and she became this 'crazy girl' in a red costume swimming around the Cape making front-page news, being interviewed by SABC, eTV and international news and sports channels. She accomplished all the big swims in the space of two or three years – Robben Island, Cape Point, the English Channel, the Strait of Gibraltar, False Bay.

It is 2005 and Carina is 25 years old. She's committed to crossing False Bay, a 35 km stretch of open water about 5 to 8 °C warmer than the Atlantic Ocean. The temperature is higher because of the subtropical Agulhas Current that flows into the C-shaped bay. Carina will be the second person to cross it and she's waited patiently for the right conditions. It is summer, so good weather is imminent, yet slow to arrive. As the days and weeks pass, Carina grows impatient. She waits a little longer and then, miraculously, on 5 March, the weather is perfect.

Because Carina has made front-page news, there are cameras ready to capture the event. She even has a sponsor, which in those days was rare for open-water swimmers. It is still semi-dark and Carina, her crew and the camera crew prepare themselves for the crossing. An early start is necessary if she's to finish before sunset.

The water is glassy and smooth. Yet there is a sense of foreboding as mist hangs over its surface like a shadow. Carina has never seen False Bay like this, so eerily beautiful. She enters the water and a few seconds later swears under her breath because it is very cold. Colder than she had expected. In the excitement about the perfect weather, no one has thought to check the water temperature. She starts swimming because she is committed, and because there's a team on a boat, there are cameras. Adrenalin drills through her. After thirty minutes she's shivering. The water is 13 °C and the air temperature even lower. She stops at her first feed and says to the crew, 'Listen, I'm cold.'

'Yes, it's cold, but the fog will lift and the sun will come out and you'll feel better.' Their response is encouraging. She's experienced this before with the weather, so she ploughs on. An hour later there is still no sun. Carina is horribly cold, unpleasantly cold, but she's never given up on anything in her life. She focuses on her strokes, on her breathing, and then makes a firm decision – she'll swim ten, eleven, twelve hours, however long it will take in this temperature. She feels miserable but accepts the suffering that comes with the decision.

She keeps swimming and it all intensifies. Time passes as she fixates on the ghostly underwater world through her narrow goggles. Her extremities become colder and she loses control of her fingers. They become claws; she's clawing her way through the water. In her body there is pain everywhere. She feels the cold going into places where it shouldn't go: deep into her core, into her organs. She says to herself. *This is now hurting me.*

But Carina is driven and won't give up. After about four and a half hours of misery, something unexpected happens. She starts to feel warm – so warm that she reaches for her swimming cap to pull it off. But she can't use her hands. She feels wonderful. She sees galaxies under the water. She watches an animated shark that looks like a character in a cartoon that's just come out in cinemas. She is hallucinating.

Later, she will remember her mentor talking to her from the boat: 'You know, Carina, you can do this on another day.' She will recall talking back to him and saying, 'No, no, don't worry. I just got warm, now I'm fine.' In reality she doesn't say anything because she's unable to speak.

Moments after the warmth multiplies through her body she stops swimming. The boat crew pull her out and onto the boat. She will have no memory of this.

Later, she wakes up covered in blankets to the rumbling of a car engine and the feel of tyres on tar beneath her. She is on the back of a bakkie and her first coherent thought is, *I didn't make it*. She wishes she hadn't woken up because the disappointment hurts. Everything hurts, especially her heart. She is heartbroken.

Later, the crew tell her that on the boat she was fighting to stay alive. It was as basic as that: she was shivering and she didn't have enough oxygen in her bloodstream. She doesn't remember much of it because hypothermia had warped her sense of time. 'Failing was my biggest fear. My biggest mistake that day was to start in that temperature. It was like a death sentence.'

Failing her first attempt to cross False Bay was an invaluable lesson. She realised that in the wake of failure lies continuation; it isn't the end. She learnt how to fail and be okay with it. It reinforced a life lesson – to accept that sometimes you do everything you can, but it's not enough, and that's okay. You wait for the next right time.

Yet, she could not forget about it. Strand was her childhood beach. She grew up in Stellenbosch, and they used to go to Strand. There, she would look across the ocean and see the mountains on the other side, and it gripped her. It was very hard to go back to swimming. But the pull of the water was strong and three days later she was back in the pool.

It was after the False Bay failure that Carina took on the Everest of swimming – the 33-kilometre stretch that is the English Channel. A year after the successful channel swim, she successfully crossed False Bay.

Nowadays, Carina does marathon swims and connects them to raising money for good causes, such as the Little Fighters Cancer Trust. In the past, when she set a record – and there have been many, including the Cape Agulhas swim in 2004 when she broke the previous record by over two hours, she's held the overall record for the 11 km Around Robben Island swim for eight years – there would always be a sense of disappointment, of it not being good enough, of what's next. It was very ego driven. In retrospect she's realised that swimming is a calling.

I ask her how being a swimmer correlates with being a musician. The question stumps her because in her mind they are two separate parts and versions of herself. She enjoys junk food and nibbling on crisps, so swimming keeps her slim for the slinky outfits she wears when she performs with her band – an all-girl instrumental pop group. Then there's rhythm; both activities require a good amount of that.

Carina is refreshingly candid and tells me she doesn't trust herself to make the right decisions if she's not swimming, so she trains on most days and devotes one day a week to a slower recovery swim. She has a number of businesses and is mother to two daughters and a son. I imagine her days are full and her time management extraordinary.

This weekend she'll be swimming about four kilometres from Cape Town out to a rock with some friends. If it's 17 °C and she can enjoy the sun on her back, she'll swim in a costume. If it's colder and overcast, she'll opt for a wetsuit.

Carina doesn't like the cold.

I look up at the expanse of blue sky, sun bright and beaming, not a wisp of cloud. It matches my mood, my weather. It is the day of my first open-water race at a dam called View Point in Midrand. It's not quite the ocean, but I'll be swimming 1,2 km of open water and it will give me an inkling of what wild swimming tastes like. The commentator spews words of encouragement to the last swimmer in the previous race. Under the tarpaulin there is a bustle of people, sitting at wooden tables, adjusting swimming costumes, applying sunblock, catching up with fellow swimmers. It is a sub-culture. I overhear a muscular man talking about his training for Ironman. I spot a woman who looks to be in her eighties, skin wrinkled but her eyes lively with anticipation. A boy who looks to be about nine fusses around his parents.

Barefoot, I stroll down to the tent where numbers are being penned on arms. The band around my ankle that stores the race chip feels secure. I offer my upper arms and feel the looping of the numbers as a woman with a permanent marker writes on my skin. It feels real; I'm doing this. The commentator calls the race participants to the bank of the dam. He describes the proceedings, how and where we are to enter and on which side to swim around each buoy. My mind struggles to attach to the information – it is all so new to me – so I tap the forearm of the man standing next to me and clarify what the commentator has said. On hearing it for the second time, it feels quite simple.

I stand on the red carpet that leads to the start of the race. The child is excitedly tapping his parents' thighs. It's his first race too. I decide to stick with them in the water. The group walks forward slowly and then it opens up and we're all wading in brown water until it's easy to start swimming. I get into a rhythm and quickly realise that besides keeping sight of the first buoy, it's the limbs and tow floats of the other swimmers that I need to be careful of.

The water is elemental, its viscosity different from the salt-chlorinated water of the gym pool. It is harder and colder. But I don't feel the cold. There are so many distractions that swimming is secondary. And yet, I am aware of keeping my body straight, having my head in the right position, feeling the air and the splashes of water against my heels. I breathe and inhale water. I cough hard, continue. I circle the first buoy, navigating it with other swimmers.

Time feels granular, stretched, I can feel its every particle. I'm aware of the people breathing around me. The smell of diesel fumes from the boat shepherding us. One swimmer, a girl with her head down, going fast, loses direction. The shrill note of a whistle. Her head bobs up, astonished as she pauses and redirects. I keep swimming. I've left the family of three behind – they were too slow, breaking my stride.

I'm headed towards the second-last buoy and I remind myself to go around it so that it is at my left shoulder, otherwise my time won't count and I'll be penalised. Navigating this buoy is slow; swimmers are confused about which side to approach it from. The men in the boat tell them where to go. A lot of water is spat out of mouths. It is a cacophony of air and splashing. My goggles and cap still feel secure and I am so grateful as I've had more menacing thoughts about the efficacy of my gear than the efficacy of my body. Neither let me down.

I circle the last buoy and train my eyes on the blue-and-white inflatable arch at the finish. I am nearly there. The last few strokes feel like nothing. I am buoyed by the water. I swim to the point where others have stood up to walk out, and tentatively I feel for ground under my feet. The dam bed feels coarse and muddy. I find traction and scramble out of the water, onto the embankment and under the arch. A woman asks for my Velcro bracelet with chip. I rip it off and hand it to her.

I did it. I pull off my goggles and squint at the glare bouncing off the dam's surface and smile. The sky has turned a deep meaningful blue.

enjoyment

To the joys of the sea, the salt waves, and the freedom of the wind
I give my heart, where no walls confine,
and the sun and moon embrace the tide.

– From *The Seafarer*, translated by Ezra Pound

Open-water swimming has gained popularity all over the world. People gather in the early morning twilight to bathe and entrain to the strokes and breathing of a group, to feel that feeling of being connected through the element of water and sensing the movements of others. They imbibe in the exhilaration and unpredictability of the water.

In South Africa groups of swimmers meet regularly to enjoy the communal, social and fitness aspects of sea swimming. In Durban, in Gqeberha, in various areas of the Western Cape, large and small groups meet to enjoy the softness and the hardness of the waves, and the sheer bliss of the after-swim glow. On the Cape Peninsula, Scott Tait's passion for swimming and for the sea led him to organise open-water swims at Long Beach in Simon's Town. In swimming circles, he is legendary and goes by the name of Scotty. He is a fifty-something triathlete and owner of a swimming school called Swim Cape Town. He is a waterman, taking people into different aquatic environments to teach them how to read them, so that after four weeks they have an understanding of the movements of water, be it ocean, lake or river. He coaches those wanting to succeed in big swims like Robben Island and the English Channel, and he promotes swimming as a recreational sport.

Scotty is committed to the sea and to the ancient sport of swimming. 'I get immense joy from seeing people enjoy themselves in the water,' he confirms. A number of years ago, watching people in the waves from his home in Glencairn saved him from his shadow. He was in a dark place, recovering from an injury, and then he got Covid. The illness progressed into long Covid. In False Bay, where twilight is violet and at midday the sun's rays set fire to the waves, Scotty hoped for a miracle.

He hung his hopes on the people he watched as they splashed about in the sea he loves. He was living vicariously through them. He tells me how ocean swimming has helped many people conquer the darkness. 'It's a quiet, safe space for a lot of people.'

The miracle arrived as an idea to start an open-water swim that would encourage Capetonians – young and old, newbies and veterans – to explore adventure swimming. The Around the Buoy swim, better known as ATB, was born.

ATB happens once a month and brings together all sorts of people to swim along a marked out route that starts and ends at Long Beach in Simon's Town. Scotty is very organised as safety is his top priority. He gets official clearance from the Navy, and there are lifesavers present for the duration of the swim. 'We don't skimp on safety. We want everyone to be safe, and then have a great time.'

The swimming group is still small. It's a social activity designed for those who are new to open water swimming and those who want to train in a safe environment. It's not a race and it's not timed. The location was chosen specifically for its safe waters – there are no rip tides.

Scotty's clear voice brims with excitement. 'If you're a swimmer in Cape Town it is almost a crime if you don't swim in the ocean. ATB is about getting people into the water, where they can swim in the company of magnificent creatures like short-tail stingrays and puffer sharks.'

There is another reason Scotty organises the swims: to change the perception of False Bay. 'When people think of False Bay, they think of great white shark attacks. Yet there hasn't been one for six or seven years. Fish stocks are depleted so great whites are feeding offshore. Orcas are also coming into the bay and taking out the shark population.'

The biodiversity in False Bay is abundant but it is changing. The winds have changed, moving old kelp and rock lobster eastwards. Seabird life is changing. Pelagic fish species are shifting and it is no longer big bad shark territory.

Social swimming, also known as wild swimming and adventure swimming, is becoming trendy. People like Scotty have made it easy and acccessible. Social media has popularised the activity. People want to experience the health benefits and enjoy the rush of endorphins. It feels good. Cool wind on skin, water, sun, the ground beneath – all the elements are present. Scotty's monthly ATB swims are occasions that test and fortify fitness, and also strengthen social fitness. They're not just about the swim. People mingle and catch up on shore. Friendships are made and a level of trust is formed, a tacit promise of 'see you next time'.

People bond over a shared love for the ocean. They bond in the water. There is power in sea swimming – it is epic in its very nature. Scotty reminds me that the ocean will test anyone and it will always win. 'It will challenge your fears because you are out there in the elements – there is wildlife around you, wind, sun and waves, but it is an incredibly rewarding experience. It changes your perception as to what is possible.'

It was not long after he introduced the ATB swims that Scotty became infatuated with another idea: bringing back the Fish Hoek Mile. The swim was last held in the early 2000s and it was a popular one on the calendar – a fundraiser for the Fish Hoek Lifesaving Club. The club is ranked as one of the best surf lifesaving clubs in South Africa, and teaches sea awareness and lifesaving skills to children aged 4 to 14 with its Nipper programme. Scotty started discussions with the club, of which he is a member, to bring it back. Finally, they relented.

On 14 September 2024, swimmers followed the original route, starting at Clovelly Beach and finishing at the lifesaving club at Fish Hoek

Beach. 'We had three rescue boats with 20 lifeguards on board, support staff, lifeguards on the beach, paramedics and lots of people helping with registration and time-keeping.' Scotty is justifiably proud.

The Fish Hoek Mile is a race, it is timed, it is taken seriously, and participants swim their hardest. Scotty tells me that Amica de Jager took first place. This piques my interest because she was chosen to represent South Africa at the 2024 Olympics in open-water swimming, but never went to Paris because of a red tape botch-up. I make a note to contact her.

Not every swim is in glassy waters and a recent women's-only swim happened in challenging conditions. The Simon's Bay Mile Swim is the only all-female swim in the country. Scotty tells me that 180 women swam on the day, but not everyone made it to the finish line. The waters were choppy that morning. Scotty believes that you don't fool around with the element of water; it's better to end a swim if you're feeling unsure, and many of them did. As he says, the sea will always win.

It is for pure pleasure that Oscar Guttierez swims in the sea. Every morning just before six, he makes his way to the water and swims for about forty minutes, regardless of how cold it is. Right now, he wears a silver-grey scarf, the colour of his hair, which he wears mid-length and wild. I want to reach out and touch the scarf, which has the sheen of silk to it, so luxurious, but don't. He strikes me as someone who is so receptive to pleasure that it is mostly what his life is about. His purpose and his pursuit are to enjoy himself. It's an attitude free of worry and I wonder if it's because he's been swimming every day for most of his life; if the flowy sea keeps him in a state of flow.

His hair suits him. His accent is Guatemalan. His body is relaxed. When I ask him how old he is, he deflects the question by closing his eyes, shrugging his shoulders and saying, 'That, I forgot a long time ago.' I put him in his late fifties, possibly sixties; it's hard to tell.

He tells me that swimming has become part of his internal clock. Every morning, in his home in St James, he rises early, puts on his swimming attire, grabs the bag packed the night before and left by the front door and walks two short blocks to St James tidal pool. At 6 a.m. he begins what he poetically describes as his lonely exercise in the cold water. For Oscar, swimming is personal, an intimate experience between him and his surroundings. 'I don't socialise. I may socialise and say hello to some people. I say good morning. Hola. Hello. Welcome. How cold the temperature is, is not part of the exchange.'

Oscar is one of the few regulars who swim between 20 and 40 minutes at a time. Not even the winter solstice deters him. He extends the cold by taking a cold shower afterwards. He tells me, 'I cannot elaborate properly on the benefits but I can tell you that the rest of the day is amazing.'

Oscar started swimming as a child, when he was ten. Born in Guatemala City, he took up swimming while he was at school and trained in the public pool. His father passed when he was five and, with six children, his mother had her hands full. This meant that Oscar could bunk school to go swimming without his mother finding out. He grew up in the US, has lived in Mozambique, spent many years in Johannesburg and then moved to the Cape Peninsula.

Oscar is a photographer and the people at that hour of the morning fascinate him. The seascape and the people inspire him. Sometimes, after his swim, he goes back to his house to get his camera. He has spotted William Kentridge taking a dip, remarking at how interesting it is to see him without his iconic white shirt. 'I took a photo of William Kentridge, the famous artist. I wanted to take it without him knowing. He was looking at the sea. I took a picture of him from the back. People comment and say I always see this guy in a white shirt.'

He tells me about a man who has a swim and then percolates coffee between the rocks. He shares a photo of this – a man, a towel around his waist, leaning towards a moka pot boiling on a small gas stove, the sea in the background. He has captured the nuance of the moment, the juxtaposition of rock and shaped aluminium. I lose myself in the picture and can almost smell the espresso.

There are two ladies who do a fine art interpretation of the sky, the sea and the clouds, but not of people. He has photographed them too.

He tells me that sometimes he doesn't think, he just swims. Then other days his head is full of ideas, visual things. He recalls the happenings of the past week or days. He wonders if he has said anything inappropriate, done anything wrong. He reflects on his immediate past.

On a day, while he was swimming, he watched buses arriving: people were coming to be baptised in the tidal pools. So, Oscar fetched his camera. 'I managed to take a photo I was quite interested in. It made me think about the dynamic of people getting into the pools and those doing the baptising. Jesus coming to your life. You know what I was thinking? They are happy today. The priest is happy, the people are happy. Those people that have been baptised, they're poorer now than they were before being baptised. I'm not criticising, it's just an observation.'

He is not prescriptive about his swims, preferring to be taken by the moment. Sometimes he swims in the tidal pool, along its perimeter, other times it's back and forth. Sometimes he swims in the open water, it depends on the waves. Sometimes he stops to just enjoy the feeling of being in the area, to embrace the moment. 'As a photographer, I love to observe the sky, the silence, the wind – all those beautiful things that the sea brings to you. Like nowadays we've seen a lot of dolphins by the pool. So, we have to be careful because they are quite big.'

Oscar has encountered seals but prefers not to engage with them, getting out of the pool to go swim somewhere else or the next day. 'Sometimes they come into the pool, or you can see them by the rock and they look at you, and sometimes they want to follow you. I move out of the way because yes, it's their place.'

One area where Oscar refuses to swim is at Danger Beach. There, had it not been for two energetic lifesavers who pulled him to the safety of the shore, he would have drowned. 'The waves came in and took me out, inside the sea. It was so fast. I couldn't swim back. I was exhausted, I swallowed so much water and I was in serious crisis. The sea, it swallowed me. And I know how to swim. I raised my hands and the lifesavers came in and just grabbed me out.'

Oscar tells me he was fascinated with how they did it – one lifesaver grabbed him, the other swam about thirty or forty metres away just watching that everyone was okay. They knew exactly what they were doing and understood the currents.

The experience hasn't deterred Oscar. If anything, it has instilled in him more admiration for the vast ocean. Winter, summer, predawn or daybreak, Oscar swims. His devotion to the roaring sea is unshakeable.

I look at a photo of a dead whale that Scotty has posted to the ATB WhatsApp group. I think about Oscar's words about the creatures of the sea, that it is their place, that he will get out of the way of a seal.

Scotty writes that a dead humpback whale has washed ashore on Long Beach in Simon's Town, the area of the ATB swims. He advises against swimming there until the carcass has been removed. I look at the picture for a long time: the whale is huge, lying on its back so that the ridges on its underside are visible. I can see its long left flipper. Its body tapers to where its tail begins: a large triangle semi-immersed in sea foam. The photo was taken at sunrise, a blush of orange visible on the horizon. The whale looks black. I've read that each humpback has a distinct black-grey-white colouration that extends to its flukes. This whale has white markings around its ridged ventral side. Scientists will be taking samples and doing tests. I wonder what they'll find. I've read that a humpback whale can live for 90 years.

The story is in all the main newspapers. The humpback whale was a juvenile female and it seems to have died from natural causes as there are no marks on its body to show that it was attacked by another animal or human. The City of Cape Town will remove it but there are warnings to swimmers to stay out of the water until its body fluids wash well away.

swimming

Investigation by marine scientists shows that the juvenile harboured parasites, which means that she was probably ill before she died – a healthy humpback wouldn't have had those parasites. The Mammal Research Institute Whale Unit identified the whale as an individual previously sighted near Dyer Island off the coast of Gansbaai in June 2024. It was identified by its markings and the use of the Happywhale database, a global citizen science project that engages the public in identifying individual marine mammals.

A few days later I read that the whale's carcass was taken to a landfill site in Vissershok. The ATB photo of the whale haunts me. Not because it is dead, but because it is out of its depths in Vissershok, out of its natural environment. I know that whales die, that whales beach themselves when they are injured. Sometimes there is a mass beaching, like the ones that have happened at Kommetjie and Noordhoek. But there is something sad about a creature of that size being out of the sea.

I think I'm tending towards melodrama. My human emotions are misunderstanding the cycles of life and death. The sea is full of ghosts. Perhaps the whale's song has returned there. The ocean gives life and then takes back what belongs to it and transforms it. In the sea right now, fish swim. On its surface, devoted swimmers enjoy the waves. I bask in the wonder of this.

rip currents

Nothing worthy in life comes for free or is easily obtained. One must dedicate oneself to the process. Hopefully, the journey and all its obstacles will make the destination priceless.

– Amica de Jager

Sometimes in life we get caught in a rip current – the kind that could break our spirit, should we let it. After chatting to Scott Tait, the triathlete who started the Around the Buoy swims at Simon's Town Long Beach, I keep thinking about Amica de Jager, the open-water swimmer who, even though she qualified, was excluded from the South African squad for the 2024 Olympic Games in Paris.

Amica provisionally qualified for the 2024 Paris Olympic Games by securing a continental spot for Africa during the 2024 World Aquatics Championships in Doha. In an interview with *The Herald*, her coach Brian Redelinghuys said that the reasons provided for her exclusion were that she and her teammates were wearing the incorrect kit and had communicated with a former coach without obtaining permission from Swimming South Africa (SSA).

I try, but I cannot wholly imagine the magnitude of the moment when Amica received the news – the small, atomic explosion of it. Hours, days, weeks and years of training all blown away the instant she's told that she's not going to the Olympics.

Being an athlete at this level comes with a glut of external challenges that add to the personal ones. The physical endurance is intertwined with the psychological, and on a bigger scale it is all entrained with the coach, the team, the inner-circle supporters, the fans and the broader expectation of the entire world. I've read about the performance metrics, the anxiety, the difficulty in maintaining iron-clad confidence, and the mental fortitude required to be the best. Topping these are the emotional challenges athletes face when administrative decisions impact their aspirations.

How do you go through something so monumentally devastating and not feel defeated? How do you define yourself after such a life-changing decision is made for you? This is what plays on my mind as I wait for Amica to answer my WhatsApp message asking if we could chat.

A few days later I'm chatting to Amica. She fizzes with the vigour of youth and there is the economy in her movements that I've seen in many high-performance athletes, conserving their energy for training and competing. The blue of her blouse and beaded necklace contrast with her shoulder-length blonde hair, emphasising its lustre.

As we discuss 'the big moment', it's as though she's moved beyond the devastation of it. Her focus is squarely on her work, her training and the 2028 Olympic Games. She is disappointed, but she's not crestfallen. She provides a different angle to her exclusion and tells me that what occurred was this: because of changes in the process of selection, she could not compete and she chose not to appeal as she didn't want to ruin her chances for the next games. She doesn't seem despondent; instead, she exudes the quiet determination and discipline of someone who knows herself and trusts her body. Like other high-performance athletes, she implicitly knows what each ache and pain means and how far she can push her limbs. She also has a deep Christian faith and this, she says, keeps her hopeful.

Amica grew up in Gqeberha and began her water journey as a pool swimmer. A few of her friends were part of the Nippers, where they learnt lifesaving and, of course, to swim in the sea while contending with all sorts of currents and weather conditions. The day that Amica went to King's Beach to join the Nippers at the age of 12, she was petrified of the ocean as she had never done any swimming in the sea. 'When I tried out for the Nippers, I stayed at hip depth and wouldn't go out any further,' she says. She had done a few river swims before that – the Redhouse River Mile, the Sundays River Mile – and always kept her head out of the water. With a nervous laugh she tells me that she never wanted to know what big fish were underneath her, even in a river. She feels the same way today.

For the initial sessions with the Nippers, she had a coach on either side of her and every time they took her out a little further. The more she discovered about the ocean, the more her fear transformed into enjoyment. 'Somewhere along the line I lost that fear,' she says. It was going through the whole process of Nippers that made her brave, made her put her head down and swim open water properly.

We get onto the topic of rip currents and riptides because on every beach I've ever been on there is a sign that explains where the rips pull and how to swim out if you're caught. Rip currents are wave-driven and common at surf spots; while riptides are tide-driven and found near river mouths and channels. She tells me that you can learn how rip currents behave. 'With more time in the ocean I began understanding rip currents and how they can actually help you swim. Time in the ocean got me to learn that it's not something to fear, but actually something to enjoy,' she says. 'I started absolutely loving it and learning the currents.'

Many people panic – or worse, drown – in rip currents. For Amica, this is more a consequence of their not knowing how to act in those situations. 'Having learnt from a lifesaving standpoint, I use the rip current, it helps you to get out behind the waves faster.' It was a total switch for Amica when she became comfortable with the seemingly unpredictable movements of the water. 'It was really useful for me to learn how a current acts and behaves. It takes away the element of fear because you know how to get out of it and how to use it, how to react in that situation,' she says. 'During lifesaving competitions, especially when the ocean is rough, you actually look for the rip currents and, in a race, if it's really rough and there are big waves, you actually run to the rip current to use it to get out to open sea.'

Open-water swimming became her new crazy discipline.

When Amica was in high school, she and her family moved from Gqeberha to St Francis Bay. It was a small town with a big culture of surfing and Amica found herself at home. She tried it all – surf skiing, paddling, body surfing – and continued swimming in the sea. She began training under the guidance of Hayden Holmes, who wholly embodies the concept of 'waterman'. 'He is a well-rounded ocean man and he taught me and my sister to be well-rounded ocean athletes.' This is where Amica matured in her love of open-water swimming and water sport. If it was surfing conditions, she'd surf. If there were great downwind opportunities, she'd go for a surf ski paddle. If she didn't have any equipment, she'd bodyboard. Through Hayden, Amica learnt to vary her sports and have fun in the water no matter the weather. In 2015, when Amica was 15 years old, she took part in her first National Open Water race in a dam in Grabouw, as part of the Eastern Province team.

She remembers her first experience of deep ocean swimming – it was the Bell Buoy race in Gqeberha. They started on Pollock Beach in Summerstrand and swam two and a half kilometres to a buoy. When she looked back to shore, all she could see was the Radisson Blu, just the tip of the hotel, and nothing else. 'That race was the epitome of that tricky balance of being afraid of marine life, such as sharks, and conquering that fear,' she recalls.

The race scenario helped her overcome that fear because, as a competitive person, she focused on the race and the swimmers around her – instead of wondering what was underneath her. She did do a freediving course at one stage, with John McCarthy – a highly regarded surfer, swimmer, freediver and environmentalist based in Durban and founder of Ocean Child, a sea wilderness adventures company. His perspective on sharks changed her approach. He told her that the sea is their habitat and we are encroaching on their environment. It reassured her when he said that sharks aren't naturally aggressive.

He described his experiences of freediving with sharks and how calm they were. Controlling your reactions to them and staying calm makes them feel calm. The moment you start to panic you set off a commotion and sharks respond to that because they're sensitive to your state of mind. 'I can't say I'm good at that in practice. I think if I had to see a shark, I'd probably panic. From an open-water swimming standpoint, you're always on top of the water, you're not really, like, in the water.'

What Amica loves about open-water swimming are the variables. There's a lot to take into account. She enjoys the tactical thinking behind an open-water race that takes in the ocean conditions, the winds, currents and the pace of the other swimmers. 'If there's presence of onshore winds, then it's super choppy and you've got to deal with that. You've got to adjust for currents and think, okay, if the current's pulling this way, then I need to account for that and swim this way to make the buoy.'

There's the element of swimming in a pack of swimmers. Just like marathon running or cycling, marathon swimmers work off a slipstream. 'You're all swimming together in a pack and by doing so you're conserving energy. So, you're dealing with a pack mentality,' she explains.

If she's been pulling too much, she pulls back and rests a little because everyone is on her tail. At other times she makes a break for it and tries to get the others off her slip. 'There's a lot going on and I love the thinking that's involved in a race. No two races are the same.'

The environmental conditions of every race differ, which is why open-water swimming doesn't have time-based records.

Her most difficult race was the Olympic qualifier at the World Championships in Doha in 2024. It was the 10-kilometer race and because it was the Olympic qualifier, the competition was extremely intense. 'I've never raced as hard as I did in that race. That was my best race. It was my hardest, but also my best,' she says.

Part of her not going to the 2024 Olympics, despite qualifying at that race, was that World Aquatics changed its qualification criteria and South Africa did not update its internal criteria to match these. In previous years there'd been two qualifiers, with the first round being an elimination round. In 2024, the elimination round was removed. The top three athletes from the first round competed in the second round, whereas before they wouldn't have. Amica came 27th in the qualifier, split seconds from making South Africa's internal top 20 criteria. According to World Aquatics, she qualified for the continental spot and was awarded the African continental quota spot, but South Africa declined that spot and it was given to Peru. So, there was no African representation either. 'It was a tough pill to swallow because you have these facts and at the end of the day you can't do anything about it,' Amica says.

In open-water swimming races, the measure of performance is 'time behind the winner'. Amica swam her best race, completing it in 1 hour, 58 minutes and 38 seconds. To compare, the winner – the Netherlands' Sharon van Rouwendaal – had a time of 1 hour, 57 minutes and 26 seconds.

Amica decided not to contest the decision because she has bigger plans for her swimming career. I tell her that I think her decision will help extend her career and she thanks me because it's something she still battles with. 'What keeps me going is believing that God has greater plans for me, and that it's going to work out for the better,' she says.

Amica is aiming for the next Olympics in 2028.

She is pleased to be living close to the ocean again because for the two years leading up to the 2024 Olympics, she was living in Pretoria to train at altitude under the guidance of coach Rocco Meiring and his Olympic squad. Rocco is respected for his contributions to the country's swimming success, and for nurturing emerging swimmers and several elite swimmers, including Tatjana Schoenmaker. Being away from the sea was Amica's sacrifice to qualify for the Olympic Games. At the same time, she was doing her master's degree in computer science. 'Since moving to Cape Town, I've been trying to get involved in as many fun ocean races as possible.'

Amica's week is heavily scheduled. She works as a software engineer and trains nine sessions per week, Monday to Saturday, before and after work. She swims for 18 hours and tops that up with 3 hours of gym training. There isn't much time for socialising, except on weekends. Swimming is all about consistency and every training session is like putting a coin in the bank.

Each session is different, with a focus on an area of conditioning. She'll do vertical kicking, drills, dives, starts, race pace and lactate sets. The lactate sets help improve her ability to tolerate and clear lactic acid, especially during a race. It's a high-intensity workout that for Amica brings on nausea and shakiness; she pushes through that, ensuring that her time isn't dropping. It requires tremendous focus. 'Every time it hits it feels bad, and that's the purpose – to get it feeling so bad in training that when you're racing, you're used to it and you don't even realise it. Racing should be easy because the hard stuff should've already been done in training,' she says.

Two hours of racing ends up in a touch photo finish, so Amica also trains the fast-twitch muscles. She adds that each athlete is different – each body reacts differently to different stimuli – and that's part of the process of learning what works and what doesn't. She applies trial and error to her feeds and tests them during training. Her mother is her feeder during races. At her first 10-kilometre race, Amica took half a banana. As she was swimming, she realised that she couldn't chew and breathe at the same time, so that wasn't going to work. She now feeds on a liquid nutrition range.

Her post-race recovery includes an ice bath – which, for now, she tells me jokingly, is the extent of her tolerance for cold-water immersion. She's used to the warm waters of the Eastern Cape, so prefers to plunge into the Atlantic wearing a wetsuit. She also includes a lot of stretching and hyperbaric oxygen therapy, which helps improve her recovery, especially when she has a 10-kilometre race on one day followed by a 5-kilometre race the following day. Food is part of regaining strength and she forces herself to eat substantially, even if after a race she has no appetite.

swimming

In terms of support, it takes a tribe. Her mom is the anchor that keeps her grounded. 'I don't think her nerves can handle watching me race for two hours but she does it, so I've actually got the easy part because when I'm racing I'm not stressed.'

Then there's her family, her friends, her coach and her training buddies. People having her back is paramount to her success. She knows that endurance is not just about the body – it's about the people who carry you when your own strength falters. Every training session, every swim against an unrelenting tide, is buoyed by the force of those who believe in her. It's about faith.

cold immersion, chief mermaids and pleasure seekers

The sea, once it casts its spell, holds one in its net of wonder forever.
— Jacques Cousteau

I'm in an outdoor pool during a cold front in spring. The water is cold, maybe 13 °C. I search for a warm spot inside my body and find it just below my heart, just below the sternum, where the ribcage opens. Pain flashes along the inside of my arms – my veins and capillaries are constricting and the sensation is a more expanded version of how my pupils feel when light suddenly becomes bright.

I'm aware of my body in the water, but not. My mind has to hold on to the awareness of my body and it's like my mind now has the freedom to float away – a helium balloon pulling upwards. The idea of it floating into the sky, out of the atmosphere, out of sight, all thought and cognition far away, is surprisingly thrilling. With the mind released there is a different awareness – more primal, more present – like there only ever was a now, with no past or future. Time dissolves and becomes meaningless. I am aware of my extremities; it's my pinkie fingers and toes that are turning cold and numb. They're colder than the rest of my body.

My teeth start to chatter and my mind jumps back into my body. An icy wind stirs leaves and dust, whipping the debris along the paving. I exhale, squeezing as much air out of my lungs with my abdominal muscles as I can. I sink slowly and am completely immersed. I have an inkling of why people submerge themselves in cold water: perhaps it's a way of reclaiming one's animalness.

As I change into dry clothes, I notice that my mood is even, my thoughts have a calmer rhythm and I feel good. My skin is buzzing.

Cold-water immersion has become an extremely popular practice and pastime. On any given morning along beaches and on the banks of rivers and lakes, one can spot people, either on their own or in groups, enjoying the invigorating chill. Cold plunging elicits a dopamine rush, and those who dip regularly say that they feel more alert and are less stressed; their skin is more toned, and they notice weight loss. They also say that it's highly addictive.

While some people swim, dive, snorkel, surf, paddle or boogie board, others dip. Everyone has a different reason for being in the water. Anne Taylor is both a swimmer and a dipper. Every Sunday, come rain or shine, she meets with friends at Muizenberg to swim. Gleefully, she says: 'Me and the other ladies swim in old Speedos, but our chief mermaid swims in a leopard-print bikini.'

The mermaids, as Anne and her friends call themselves, don't like to swim in the tidal pool where there's a meditative Wim Hof vibe going on. Rather, they go into the waves with the wind and the exhilaration. The feeling that it's good to be alive has a different quality in the sea. There is an undertone of vulnerability; it's not safe: 'It's that thing: it feels so good, so you have to be careful, but you push a little and you find that space that hits the buttons.'

When Anne's friend from Johannesburg came to visit, they stayed on the Atlantic seaboard. They rose early and made their way to Saunders' Rock Tidal Pool, at the southern end of the promenade where Sea Point meets Bantry Bay. At 11 °C, Cape Town water is cold and all the rage for people chasing the health benefits it provides. Everyone was very quiet and very serious in their immersion. Anne likes to complain about the temperature – it's part of her process: 'A man looked at me all Zen and said, "Just breathe".' In certain circles and at particular pools, cold water exposure is taken very seriously.

cold immersion, chief mermaids and pleasure seekers

For Anne, the water is a life line. She has just returned from hiking the Whale Trail and says, 'When we got to Noetzie, where there's the sea, every single thing in me just opened. I felt like I could breathe. I find it absolutely compelling, I never feel better than when I'm near the sea.'

Anne and her husband used to live in Gauteng. The decision to move to the coast happened while they were on holiday, on one of those perfect summer days when the air is still and the sea calm. They were both in the water when her husband said to her, 'Why do we live in Johannesburg when we can live here?'

Her husband believes that there are sea people and there are mountain people. Anne is a sea person. 'One significant swim for me happened in 2018. I always swim on New Year's morning at sunrise and I pull my mountain husband with me, even though he's a reluctant swimmer. The ice-cold water of the Atlantic is very exhilarating and very alive. Every cell in your body is activated. On New Year's Day in 2018 my nephew had been badly injured in a car accident. My brother called to say my nephew had died. It's the saddest thing to ever happen to our family. It was a key thing for me to come out of the ocean and get that phone call. The swim, since then, is in honour of Calvin. The ocean is very affirming for me, it makes me feel alive. I remember the absolute tragedy and absolute joy of that day. It's a weird crying, a necessary alchemy.'

Swimming and the weather have a particular rhythm. Athambile Masola arrives home in Muizenberg after a week of travelling. She's a writer, poet and blogger, and lectures in the Department of Historical Studies at the University of Cape Town. She travels a lot for her work and her research. She has missed the ocean and her swims. The weather is good so she fires a WhatsApp message to her swimming group to see if anyone would like to join her for a swim from Simon's Town harbour towards Glencairn and back. Communicated times get confused and the woman who said yes can no longer meet up with her.

Athambile sets off on her own. Her swimming is rhythmic and she basks in the pure pleasure of being in the water. The wind is mild. She knows that each section of beach has its own personality, where the wind and the waves do something unique. She tells herself nothing will happen, while also knowing that anything can happen. She holds the paradox in balance. She is acutely aware of seals and anticipates worst-case scenarios. She is comfortable and decides to swim a little further past the electricity substation. It's the first long swim on her own. At the white houses the current changes, as it always does, but she decides she can do a little more and continues. It's quite weird, and she can feel her brain doing a leap of 'yay'. She can see the wreck. She swims a bit further and only then does she turn around to go back to where she started.

She tells me that she ponders the psychological effects of swimming in a group. Her search for the right clique was akin to looking for the right church or hair salon; it was like shopping around for a therapist in whose company you are completely comfortable. It took about a year of trial and error until she sent a WhatsApp to a community, along the lines of: *I'm looking for a group with diverse swimmers, I'm tired of all the mlungus.*

Someone DMed her and from there she became part of a handful of women who swim on Tuesdays, Thursdays and weekends. 'We are all ladies and we all keep up – two in front, one in the middle and two at the back. It's a rush of endorphins, we're simulating dolphins. I am mentally and emotionally fit in that formation – because I'm a slow swimmer – there are other swimmers around me.'

Swimming is a vulnerable space for Athambile, not for the potential dangers that the ocean presents but because of other people. She tells me that in some groups she feels overweight. And yet, she has been swimming, breathing, swimming since she was at school in Gqeberha.

Now, swimming is her thing, her morning thing. She swam throughout winter, the rainy season, which for her was a massive feat of discipline and endurance. Discipline, growing up, was her mother's realm; she held tight to it and doled it out with a wag of her finger. It came with hardness.

Discipline is different now: it's a good thing. Pursuing passions requires allotted time and planning – packing your swimming gear into a kitbag, putting a naartjie or a banana on the kitchen counter as a pre-exercise snack and going to sleep early the night before to increase the pleasure factor.

Athambile has never had aspirations beyond the things that she can do – get a master's, complete a PhD, write. But for her 40th birthday – she's 37 as I write this – she's contemplating the Robben Island swim. A neighbour who is in her fifties and has swum Robben Island demystified it for her. In Athambile's voice, there's resolve: 'It's not a triathlon, it's within reach.'

What attracts her to the Robben Island swim is also its history. Things happened there long before the treason trials of the 1990s. It's been a penal colony for ever and ever, a place of exile and imprisonment for four hundred years. The leader of the Strandlopers – Khoikhoi Autshumato, who was the intermediary between his community and Jan van Riebeeck, together with his companions Jan Cou and Boubo – were imprisoned there. A slave called Eva, supposedly from Madagascar, was jailed on the island, as were other women. In the 1700s Muslim leaders deemed to have too much influence were chained on the island. Lepers, lunatics and people with chronic illnesses were sent to its hospital in the 1800s and early 1900s with the promise of fresh air, keeping them far from Cape Town society. In 1819 Xhosa leader Makhanda Nxele attempted to escape by boat with other prisoners. Many of them drowned, including Makhanda.

Besides the comfortable fit, what Athambile likes about the women in her swimming group is their age, which brings with it fewer body hang-ups – or none at all. No one is self-conscious in a swimming costume. I tell her that the good thing about being middle-aged and older is that you appreciate your body for what it can do, for accomplishing a physical task, for having no pain. It's a realisation that arrives with age, at about fifty.

Athambile has observed the politics of the body in swimming groups. Where everyone is scantily attired, people size you up, follow the curve of bum and thigh. A slim, muscular body becomes currency. Speed becomes currency. A hierarchy forms of fastest to slowest.

She wants to enjoy the pleasures of the water in a different way, and she does.

From her house, a little inland from the coastline, another female sea worshipper articulates her love. Catherine Corder tells me that after our chat she'll be venturing out for a swim. She's just been in the Cederberg and needs to balance mountain with sea, she says, moving her hands up and down like a scale. Like Anne Taylor she is a sea person – a mermaid, if you like.

Catherine is surrounded by women – hydrofeminists – who contemplate the meaning of water, the space and territory of it. Hydrofeminism is a global movement that explores our bodily connection to water, emphasising that we are all fluid, interconnected beings, challenging the rigid boundaries between human and non-human, between land and sea. She tells me that hydrofeminists, and many others, believe that the waters are haunted by ghosts, historical trauma, political decisions. Who didn't have access, who has fishing rights, who gives them, who decides on Marine Protected Areas (MPAs) is all part of this rich field of enquiry that is complicated and heartsore. It's about experiencing wild water and theorising it at the same time. 'The women around us swim and then meet up and talk about it, write about it, share their academic practice and then publish papers.'

Catherine grew up in Muizenberg, where she surfed and windsurfed a lot. With her own children she did the same and for years they surfed as a family. In 2019 she went to the launch of Craig Foster's book *Sea Change*. 'He described the ocean with such deep emotion that

I decided we should go buy mask and snorkel and put our heads in the water.'

For the first time ever, they saw what was in the water and it was a 3D experience of home: 'We had always been interacting with the surface and waves and boating and sailing and suddenly we realised that this place had an astounding depth. Being in the water was a big explosion of learning.'

Catherine signed up for an online course given by the Two Oceans Aquarium. She joined full moon beach clean-ups in Muizenberg. She went every month. People talked about marine life and what they saw among the rocks. Mesmerised, Catherine eagerly put her ear to their descriptions of crustaceans and nudibranchs. At all these community initiatives, the women were knowledgeable about ocean life and very welcoming. Most importantly, in all of their words there was utter love for the ocean. Beach clean-ups were a gateway to this newly discovered wild world.

Catherine encountered Lisa Beasley, who was obsessed with nudibranchs and made it her mission to stop the periodic cleaning of St James Tidal Pool. Every six months, the pool was drained of water and the walls scraped clean, destroying the habitat of numerous marine creatures, especially the small, colourful nudibranchs. Lisa and her co-operative of volunteers convinced the City of Cape Town to clean the pool in a different way, without chemicals and without killing thousands of animals. St James and Dalebrook became flagship pools for testing the new cleaning process.

False Bay is dotted with tidal pools. A tidal pool challenge, where you start at daybreak and swim in ten pools between St James and Cape Point, has become popular. It spans a range of pools – popular, ratty, never been cleaned and flourishing, remote.

'False Bay is warm and mostly safe. You can walk off some of the beaches into the most amazing kelp forests. It's accessible and you can quickly find out where other people are diving.' Swimming, freediving and exploring rock pools are social and communal activities.

WhatsApp groups have been knocked together to share visibility, water temperature, wind and weather information for the Cape Peninsula, making it easy for ocean lovers to decide where to go, and which side of the peninsula to dip into – False Bay or the Atlantic.

Catherine was drawn to other women with whom she shared a similar lifestyle and life stage. Feroza Salie is one of them. 'I have a grandchild, Feroza has retired from teaching and we're in the life stage of being free to play with our friends,' says Catherine.

Their friendship is based entirely on the ocean. Being in awe is the first pull – the delightedness and physicality of being in the water. One of the ladies doesn't wear a wetsuit so that she can feel the kelp against her skin. Catherine and Feroza wear wetsuits so that they can stay in the water for longer, honing in on the creatures and taking photos of them. Photography is the second pull. Marine biologists and divemasters help identify the water creatures and impart knowledge about their environment and behaviour. For Catherine, every single thing is new and incredible. 'It's an intense experience that develops our sense of home and community. Our horizons have expanded.'

They meet up two or three times a week, and dive mainly in MPAs, which means that there are no spearfishermen about so the fish don't feel threatened and are hanging out. I like to think that the fish are as curious about humans as we are of them. The women don't scuba, which means they can come to the surface to talk and look at the sky.

Catherine and her friends always have six items with them: costume, wetsuit, mask and snorkel, weight belt, long fins and camera. Each part of the Cape Peninsula supports different life forms. One day they discovered a monkfish, a deep-sea fish that had come up into the Kelp Forest. It was with nerdy delight that they observed life as if they had never seen it before. 'The collective discovery is so bonding. Afterwards we drink tea, huddled in the back of a car. It's not philosophical, but we're definitely appreciating life.'

holiday vibes

Dance with the waves, move with the sea, let the rhythm of the water set your soul free.

– Christy Ann Martine

It's New Year's Day and I'm walking on Salt Rock Beach with my husband Franco. The beach is thrumming with people high on celebration. At the designated swimming area, between the red and yellow flags, we stop at the water's edge. A man holds the hands of his small children as they squeal in terror and delight every time the sea tickles their legs. They run away from the sea and then run back towards it.

I look around, taking it all in: the couple with a Staffie and a poodle on leads, the dogs panting, tongues hanging loose, too hot to do anything, a group of women in matching white T-shirts and black cycling shorts laughing underneath a beach gazebo, teenage girls in neon bikinis and matching overshirts photographing each other with the sea as background, a girl and her dad throwing a ball to each other, a row of women, arms and legs covered, wearing matching hats in different pastel shades, pointing at something or someone in the water. Further along the beach, just outside of the designated swimming area, a man and three young children dig a hole in the sand.

From the street there is hooting and music with a heavy bass. On the beach the ding-a-ling of an ice cream vendor's cow bell, the sharp prrrt of a lifeguard's whistle. On the beach there are people sitting, standing, lying, laughing, shouting, talking and chiming with the rolling waves.

Those who haven't dozed off under umbrellas are all smiling. I turn again to the sea where people are bobbing, running, rolling, diving, floating and swimming. Happiness is everywhere.

I turn my gaze to the six lifeguards sitting on their high chairs, exactly in the middle between the flags. None of them talking, all of them fixated on the swimmers in the water, their bodies tense and ready for action. Today is a big day for them – they have to contend with drunken throw-caution-to-the-wind attitudes and people who go in too deep but don't know how to swim, and those who drift beyond the designated swimming area or too far out. Their responsibility is huge.

I start making chit-chat with a woman next to me. She tells me that she lives in Shakaskraal and that she's here today with her brothers and nieces and nephews to have fun. They don't come to the beach often but on public holidays, and especially on New Year's Day, they do. She swims in a dress over a swimming costume and gym shorts. The swimming attire on South African beaches fascinates me – it is both so cultural and so personal. The woman takes my hand and shakes it, 'Pleased to meet you, I'm going back to have fun now,' she says and then runs into the water to join her family.

My husband finds a patch of dry sand and sits down – he gazes out and loses himself in the horizon. I let him be. I go into the sea until I'm thigh deep and feel the pleasant slap of water against my middle. I go in further until my toes no longer feel sand and I'm bobbing along with the others. It feels so communal – we are all in this together, literally.

On the walk back to the holiday apartment, we pass a man threading bait onto a hook. 'What you catching?' I ask casually. 'Dorado and blacktail,' he tells me, cigarette dangling from his lip, 'but I haven't caught anything yet.'

I'm in Charlie's Pool at Thompson's Bay in Ballito. (On the sign it says that the tidal pool was built in 1962 by a Mauritian immigrant named Charles de Charmoy, hence the name.) I spot a man who is also wearing swimming goggles and, like me, is swimming laps. It's 3 January; the new year is in its infancy and there is the fresh energy of new hope. With months of training behind me, I feel ready for the open-water swim I'll be doing at Simon's Town Long Beach later this month. My 15-year-old daughter is swimming alongside me. Mid-lap she stops and tells me, 'I'm good, you carry on.' She drifts away to float and frolic, preferring to listen to the chirps and conversations happening in the groups of people around her – families enjoying the holidays. They remind me of how mussels and anemones grow and live in clusters. There are about thirty people in the tidal pool, so plenty of space to feel free.

The water is limpid and clear. Beneath me angelfish swim and flutter around the anemones. A large school of transparent grey fish swim along the wall, unperturbed by human limbs. It's been overcast but today the sky is crystalline and the Indian Ocean a deep blue. I look beyond the tidal pool to the beach, which is covered in colourful umbrellas all leaning in the same direction against the slight breeze. They are orderly and staggered and if I squint they could be scales on a giant fish.

This is such fun. I hear Afrikaans, Chinese, isiZulu and the slurs and accents particular to this part of South Africa. Everyone is happy. I wave at my daughter on the other side of the tidal pool, checking in on her: she's fine, perfectly in her element. She lies on her back and with arms and legs in the shape of a star, she floats, letting the water carry her. Even as a teenager she returns to that childhood joy that is the sea.

I get into a rhythm. As I swim seawards, I watch people as they walk along a concrete area that hugs a rocky cliff and then pass through a hole in the rock that takes them to the next beach. I turn around and watch the goings-on on the beach and watch people swimming in the waves, rising and dipping with the swells. It's just past 9 a.m. and already the beach is full.

I change from crawl to breaststroke, just for variety, just to get a different feel in my limbs. I see the man in swimming goggles has turned onto his back and is doing backstroke. Somehow he manages not to bump into anyone. He clearly does this regularly, swimming slowly and evenly in a perfectly straight line. He has the relaxed confidence of someone who needn't worry about disturbing others as they will get out of his way.

My training complete, I lie on my back with my ears underwater for that muffled sound that is so peaceful. I stay like this for a while, feeling the sun on my face and the tiny prickles of salt on my skin as it dries. I enjoy the bobbing sensation as the water moves in tiny waves. Unless it's in a bucket, ocean water is never still. This enormous system is constantly moving.

I remember reading in a *National Geographic* magazine that currents move water around four major ocean basins, cycling cold and warm water between the poles and the tropics. This movement is caused by tides, which are affected by the gravitational pull of the moon and the sun, but mainly the moon as it's closer, as well as winds on the ocean's surface that move the top layer of water. There are also deep-water currents that move with the fluctuations of salinity and temperature. The Coriolis effect – caused by the rotation of Earth – is what gives direction to ocean currents so that water moves clockwise in the northern hemisphere and anti-clockwise in the southern hemisphere. Layers of currents journey around the globe.

I tread water and look towards the horizon to the open sea. It is unimaginably vast to me. If I had to swim in a straight line for months, I'd reach the shores of Dongara in Australia, about 4 600 km away. If I swam 20 kilometres per day and had a few rest days in between, it would take me eight months. If I continued my swim from Coffs Harbour, on Australia's east coast, I would circumvent a few Polynesian islands and then reach La Serena in Chile. The 11 830 kilometres of ocean would take me about 21 months to swim. Those are large distances and yet humans have managed intercontinental swims. French-American long-distance swimmer Benoît Lecomte swam a number of sections of the Atlantic Ocean, one of which was a stretch of 5 980 km from Hyannis, Massachusetts to Quiberon, France in 1998. He was accompanied by a sailboat with an electromagnetic field to ward off sharks. He swam for 73 days over 6 months. On the days in between swims he was on the boat, and also spent a week in the Azores – a Portuguese archipelago. In 2018 he attempted to swim across the Atlantic, every kilometre of it. He left Choshi, Japan, hoping to make it to California, but after swimming 2 735 km of the 8 900 km journey he aborted the swim because the mainsail of the assistance boat was repeatedly torn by heavy winds. On the first cross-ocean swim, Benoît raised money for a cancer charity. On the second swim, he wanted to raise awareness of the impact of human waste on our oceans. During his swims he saw many types of fish, but also plenty of plastic.

I think back to my conversation with palaeo-oceanographer Robyn Granger, how she told me that the oceanic system regulates weather and climate, absorbs and transfers heat, and spreads nutrients and gases around the planet. It takes about a thousand years for an ocean current to complete a cycle and return to its starting point. It is such a perfect system. Benoît has experienced swathes of this system with his own skin.

I wonder if the ocean brings the precariousness of our existence into sharp focus. That each of us is but a drop in the grand scheme. Experiencing the ocean as Benoît has must bring you face to face with the potential of death – every stroke and every moment in the water is one where you are living on the edge of what happens next, the good and the fatal.

Still treading water, I look up at the sky, which billows and blusters like Benoît's broken sail, above the wind.

protection

the changing migratory patterns of southern right whales

Here on earth, blue whales come to the ocean surface mostly at night, their hearts pumping a torpid four to eight beats a minute. Their songs are composed of a handful of notes, but we usually hear only about half of them, the tones dropping into frequencies too low, too deep for us.

– Achy Obejas

From a conservation perspective humans should do what is in their power to create as little impact on the planet as possible.

– Matthew Germishuizen

Matthew Germishuizen remembers clearly the first day he went out to sea to tag a southern right whale. 'We were on the boat in the waters of Hermanus heading towards a southern right with her calf. We got close and I thought we would stop the boat there, but we just kept going until we were on top of her. She was lying on her back and all I saw was the white of her stomach. I became anxious as I realised how many things could go wrong. We were on top of a 15-metre-long whale weighing 50 tonnes and anything could happen.

'For these encounters we rely on the element of surprise, otherwise the whales do swim away. She could easily tip the boat. Our tagger Amy Kennedy shot a tag into her and she turned upright and sank a few metres. We followed her for about half an hour to check that she was okay, and she was.

'They usually recover after about ten minutes. The torpedo is 30 cm long, which is quite long, but they have such a thick layer of blubber on them that they don't really feel it. It's the initial shock that upsets them,' Matthew explains.

Matthew is doing his PhD on the migratory patterns of southern right whales. I chat to him via Zoom on a hot day in Johannesburg and a cool, drizzly day in Hermanus, where he is based. The love for his work is immediately apparent. 'I can't believe this is what I do every day,' he says, grinning, green eyes glinting under a mop of dark hair.

Growing up in Pietermaritzburg he was obsessed with the weather – severe thunderstorms, maps, pressure systems were scintillating pastimes for him. He began birdwatching and was fascinated with biology. In his twenties he found a doctoral degree at the boundary between biology and oceanography; following whales was perfect.

He gives me a brief rundown of what happened to southern right whale numbers in the 20th century. First, he tells me that the Southern Ocean is a complex scenario, quite resilient to climate change because it is insulated – the Antarctic Circumpolar Current acts as a buffer. Strong upwelling and downwelling driven by this current circulate cold, deep water to the surface where it absorbs carbon dioxide and heat from the atmosphere, then carries them back down into the deep ocean. This ocean is a massive carbon sink, absorbing and storing enormous amounts of heat and carbon dioxide.

Matthew goes on. After the 1920s, southern right whales were recovering from extensive whaling. There were only 300 individuals left in the world but the species was growing in number. Then, during the 1960s, the Soviets slaughtered thousands of whales. The USSR expanded its whaling operations by adding large factory ships to its fleet. In the North Pacific, total whale catches rose from 3 970 in 1961 to just under 13 000 in 1964. Whaling dramatically affected southern right whale populations and in the 1970s the count was only in the hundreds. Since then, recovery has been substantial, with the population growing into the tens of thousands. The population count reached 6 000 in the Southern Ocean, and there was a steady increase until 2009, at which point its growth became stunted.

Matthew tells me about colleague and tagger Amy Kennedy – her work calls her to the Galapagos, South Africa, the Philippines, any location where marine mammals are being tracked. For tagging whales she uses an air rifle with a probe. The signal on the tag lasts 12 months, after which the scientists can no longer track the individual. But 12 months is long enough to get an idea of where these mammals of the deep roam.

Matthew is part of a team at the Mammal Research Institute (MRI) and travels to specific areas in pursuit of these torpid creatures. From July to October, the team is in Walker Bay, and then moves to the West Coast of South Africa, all along the Cape Peninsula up to Cape Columbine, Paternoster, to tag the supergroups of humpback and Bryde's whales from September to January. Their trips have been successful. In 2021 they tagged four whales, in 2022 11 whales and in 2023 14 whales.

Matthew agrees that there has been a human effect on our oceans. The western Antarctic peninsula has been warming because of anthropogenic climate change – in the past seven years or so it's seen an alarming decrease in sea ice. It's a source region for krill, which are small, shrimplike, planktonic crustaceans and an important food source for whales. Krill rely on sea ice for protection when they are young.

Changes in the environment are measured with a roundabout yet effective method. The colour of oceans is becoming greener due to changes in algae abundance and type. Increasing temperatures are part of what creates this shift. Orbiting Earth are satellites that detect colour. Each one gives a different approximate calculation of ocean colour, depending on its algorithms.

'With satellite we get an estimate of how much chlorophyll is in the ocean by light reflected back. It is green and the pigment gives a spectrum. It provides a rough estimate of how much algae is in the ocean. Copepods, krill, jellyfish and salps [small marine invertebrates] feed on algae. It's a way of establishing how much prey is available to whales.

'The data is pretty useful and a large part of my work is how best we can use chlorophyll to indicate suitable feeding grounds. We don't know about trends in the prey of southern right whales, we don't know how much there is and where it's distributed, so if we can use chlorophyll to quantify feeding grounds it can be useful,' explains Matthew.

I imagine what it would look like if our marine waters turned green, the kind of coruscating green that only planet Earth could manufacture, turning oceans into floating forests.

In the Southern Ocean there has been an increase in chlorophyll concentration in the past 20 years and the reasons for this are varied and region dependent. Some areas have become windier, leading to an increase of mixing of nutrient-rich waters; other areas are experiencing warming, decreasing the amount of sea ice, which impacts other things.

Less sea ice means more sun penetration and photosynthesis, and the proliferation of algae. Also, the less sea ice there is, the less habitat for Antarctic krill. In their larval and juvenile phases, krill graze on algae under the sea ice, so if the krill move away to a more habitable zone, the area they've left will have more algae. Krill don't need more algae – they need sea ice to protect them from predation when they are young.

This is how environmental change happens; it's a domino effect in which one thing affects many other things. Matthew points out that this is neither good nor bad, but rather systemic, the whole system working together to keep the balance, which Earth is very good at. Once fully grown, krill enter a pelagic stage, living on algae that is floating about.

Decreasing sea ice and rising water temperature have caused the krill to move, changing the foraging journey of southern right whales. The tracking tags show that the whales are foraging further north. Each individual swims thousands of kilometres in a year – one of the whales travelled 15 200 km in 367 days – and swimming from Hermanus to Argentina is not uncommon for them.

Matthew thinks the whales are adapting to decreasing krill availability by shifting their foraging behaviour – moving to the mid-latitudes and feeding on other prey sources. This is what the track data reveals of the whales tagged in 2021 and 2022, compared to data from a tagging study in 2001 and 2002.

'They seem to be using the Bouvet Island feeding grounds, situated in the Southern Ocean at the southern end of the mid-Atlantic ridge, which are likely the closest source of krill to our coast, and have shifted their focus to feeding more north on copepods [small crustacean forms of animal plankton] or having to travel further to find krill. This is the hypothesis we've come up with.'

The breeding females have also become skinnier, dropping 23 per cent in body weight since the late 1980s because of the reduction and fluctuation in krill populations in their feeding areas. This has affected how often they calve – every four to five years, instead of every three. If a female doesn't have the right body conditions, it's difficult for her to conceive.

The southern rights engage in mating behaviour on the South African coast, but conception happens somewhere in the Southern Ocean – Matthew says they don't know exactly where. The gestation period is more than a year, between 12 and 16 months, during which time the pregnant females continue to feed and gain as much fat as possible. 'They spend three months without feeding, and lose up to 25 per cent of body weight, which is a huge cost, so it's really important that they get the right nutrition before they can reproduce. They come to our coast to give birth, then rear and lactate the calf. This occurs from September until late November, then they move offshore to start feeding. The calf stays with the mother for another year or so, until she's pregnant again,' explains Matthew.

Southern rights are one of the fastest-growing creatures in the animal world. Each day, the calves grow a few centimetres and gain 10 to 20 kilograms. By about seven months, the juveniles already weigh 10 tonnes – impressive. Their lifespan is anywhere between 80 and over 100 years. To give an idea of longevity, in May 2007 a marine biologist found a living bowhead whale off the coast of Alaska with an old harpoon fragment embedded in its neck. It was from the whaling era and dated to 145 years ago. The harpoon was identified as a bomb lance manufactured between 1879 and 1885 – the whale had survived a hunting attempt from that era. The discovery shed insight into the longevity of bowhead whales, which are now known to live for over 200 years.

There is no trace or record of cancers in whales. They have a low-stress life, are large and have slow metabolic rates, and by proxy of body weight and lifestyle they're able to live very long.

Els Vermeulen, Matthew's colleague and supervisor, runs annual aerial surveys in which mothers and their calves are photographed from a gyrocopter and a helicopter. This gives perspective about the numbers. In 2016, the annual October aerial count from Plettenberg Bay to Muizenberg revealed 55 mothers with calves (110 whales), the lowest count in 54 years. Then in 2018 it went up to 702 mothers with calves (1 404 whales), and in 2020 the count went down again to 80 (160 whales). An aerial survey of the bays along the southern Cape coast on 28 August 2023 revealed 556 mothers with calves, a total of 1 112 whales, between Hermanus and Witsand. A good reproductive year, but whether the females will calve again in three years' time is yet to be seen – to conceive, the whales need to get their fill of krill.

While there are differing points of view on the growth of the southern African coast's whale populations, Matthew believes the numbers are up. In December 2023 the MRI Whale Unit team observed orcas killing a humpback whale off Cape Columbine. The team spotted another pod of orcas in that area too, and since then it's something they've seen more often – if predator numbers are increasing, it means the whale population is doing well.

Chatting to Matthew, it occurs to me that so much about whales is a mystery. They've always been travellers, charting paths across oceans, following currents and instinct. We know that their migrations are shifting. Warming waters, melting ice, new feeding grounds, the encroachment of human noise and other forces are reshaping their routes. But still they find waters that are rich in nutrition. With a rapidly changing climate, the ocean is telling a different story, and the whales are adapting, redrawing their maps as they go.

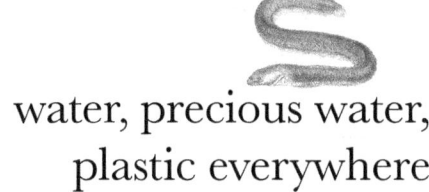water, precious water, plastic everywhere

We're more woke to pollutants but we need to make that link between our behaviour and our footprint.

– Anusha Rajkaran

What we have loved,
others will love, and we will teach them how:
The sea, too vast to conquer, too deep to exhaust,
is ours to treasure, not to destroy.

– William Wordsworth, *The Prelude*

Beaches the world over are strewn with litter. Some are overrun with it. Oceans are soaked with human-made waste. Sewage and run-off from agriculture and industry spread their tragedy into aquatic environments. In Mogadishu, Somalia, bits of plastic cover the beach; in some areas no sand is visible. In South Africa, sewage spilling into the Indian and Atlantic oceans is causing *E. coli* to bloom and spread disease.

As I walk along Umhlanga Beach, there is plastic everywhere. There is worse, of course. On an island off Cuba, the islanders have collected so many shoes that have been swept to shore that they've made a mountain of them.

In the North Pacific Ocean between the west coast of North America and Japan, a soup of plastic and marine debris has formed. Also known as the Great Pacific Garbage Patch or the Pacific trash vortex, it is two distinct masses of debris collected by the massive North Pacific Subtropical Gyre – a large system of swirling ocean currents. The accumulated trash is made up almost entirely of microplastics mixed with fishing gear and shoes. The water looks like a cloudy soup of inedible croutons.

Microplastics and nanoplastics are the most prevalent solid waste in the aquatic environment. It is estimated that approximately 5,25 trillion plastic particles are present in the world's oceans. Plastic pollution on Earth – in both terrestrial and aquatic environments – is predicted to grow by an additional 710 million metric tons by 2040, even if immediate action is taken to reduce waste. The questions that pound in my mind are: How did we get to this? How did we let the pollution problem get this bad?

In the Eastern Cape, Anusha Rajkaran looks for microplastics in estuarine environments. Anusha is an associate professor in the Department of Biodiversity and Conservation Biology at the University of the Western Cape. She fell in love with estuaries in 2001, when she worked among the mangroves of Mngazana Estuary in the Eastern Cape, immersed in the lush vegetation and gliding on the slow-moving water of the winding creeks.

It was the magic of the mangroves that compelled her to focus her research on estuaries. Mangroves are made up of trees and shrubs that thrive in water with high salinity and flourish in soil that is waterlogged and has low oxygen levels. In South Africa, mangroves are only found in predominantly open estuaries on the east coast as the estuaries there create an environment that allows them to grow. The water moves slower here than in the sea, and the rivers bring in fresh water, lowering the salinity. The slow passage of water makes estuaries an ideal nursery for fish and a place where organisms flourish.

Anusha remembers enjoying the beauty of mangroves at high tide when she and fellow researchers were on a boat moving through the creeks on crystal water, watching the fish stir, gazing at forests, looking at the branches of trees mottled with lichen and marvelling at the shade dappling the water. Mangroves buzz with life. There are fish among roots, crabs crawling on branches, birds flitting from tree to tree. In the early morning the mangroves showed a different beauty: what Anusha saw above the water she saw mirrored on the water.

From 2002 until 2020 Anusha went to Mngazana every year, first as a student and then as a supervisor, as there was lots of work being done there. Anusha witnessed the estuaries and the forests changing. More houses were built along the hill adjacent to the estuary. The illegal sand mining towards the mouth increased over time. The channels changed in depth and direction because of sand deposition. There is a large delta: sometimes there are channels through the delta and at other times there aren't because the channels move with the flow of water. Creek mouths move. Tidal currents and river flow shift sand. High tides push sand inland, depositing it on the estuary floor and along its banks. The outgoing flow of low tide carries sediment back towards the ocean. Floods wash sand downstream and out to sea. Strong waves at the estuary mouth push marine sand into the system. There is constant movement and reshaping.

Mngazana became the birthplace of Anusha's research and it is where she wants her ashes to be scattered. Her research aims to quantify the microplastics in estuaries so that the problem can be understood and from there a solution can be extrapolated. The objective is to see which plastics are unique to a particular estuary so that a change, an impact, can be made. A component of the doctoral degree of one of her students, Rosemary Eager, was interacting with schools and learners to make this generation more conscious of their climate and pollution footprint, something she wishes would be part of the curriculum for all learners.

Back from some fieldwork, she describes something she once saw that has stuck with her. 'We were in Tyolomnqa Estuary, which is south of East London, and the last estuary where we find mangroves in South Africa. We were finding high levels of plastic coming from oceanside. You want to pick up everything but you can't make an impact. I saw a bird's nest with blue fishing gut that the bird had woven through it. It was depressing. But you have to make peace with it, the fact that plastic is everywhere.'

Anusha's research extends to documenting how animals in mangroves live with plastic. 'Plastic interacts with all facets of the biosphere – what is already out there will be out there for a very long time. It's our task to start finding ways to reduce what leaves the land and finds its way into the ocean and vice versa.' One of her newest studies is in the Nahoon Estuary in East London, looking at microphytobenthos species and how they establish themselves on plastic. The team is watching the succession of the species from 24 hours to 30 days.

Microphytobenthos is the collective name for microscopic algae and cyanobacteria that live on the surfaces of sediments in aquatic environments, especially shallow marine, estuarine and freshwater ecosystems. Phytoplankton are distinct from microphytobenthos in that they are free-floating in the water, whereas microphytobenthos live on the seafloor or sediment surfaces. Microphytobenthos also live on plastic. Imagine a boat that has been bobbing in the harbour for a long while, its underside coated with slimy green and brown stuff – those are microphytobenthos and phytoplankton. These microscopic plant-like organisms attach easily to rocks and other materials, both natural and unnatural. Diatoms are unicellular organisms, found in both microphytobenthos and phytoplankton. They can photosynthesise, and have silica cell walls that give them a glassy appearance.

Phumlile Cotiyane-Pondo, who heads the new study, explains that anything that floats in the ocean can attach itself to plastic. Phumlile was born and grew up in Gqeberha, where his proximity to the coastline indelibly marked his interests and career journey. He has travelled the entire coast of South Africa, from Kosi Bay to Gqeberha, and from there to Port Nolloth and back to Gqeberha, looking at the diatom microalgae that live on the rocks. He started studying diatoms as part of his PhD. He found these microorganisms fascinating with their beautiful ornamentation and ecological importance. Observing diatoms and how they live on artificial material such as plastic is being investigated all over the world, and Phumlile studies how they attach to and live on plastic in estuaries specifically.

'Biofilm accumulation occurs on anything that can submerge in water. Bacteria will attach, followed by diatom microalgae. After that you'll have larvae of different animals in that system. Diatoms secrete a mucilage that allows them to move about on the plastic, or another substrate, and this makes it possible for other things to attach, trapping them in a sense.'

Phumlile is curious about the dynamics of biofilm accumulation in an estuarine environment, where the water moves differently from how it moves on a rocky shoreline. 'In a coastal environment I looked at the diatoms that live in the crevices of rocks. But with any scientific research there are unanswered questions and assumptions. There are tides that pull back from the rocky shore, exposing them to the sun, which causes the plant cells to desiccate. Or the cells run away from grazers. An estuary is different, and plastic is different to rocks.'

Plastics are a novel habitat in estuaries. All kinds of flora and fauna can attach and be moved to new places as the water moves the plastic around the estuary and out to sea. This means plastics could introduce invasive species to new places just like ships do, along with other vectors that move on the oceans across the planet.

Plastic pollution in aquatic environments is one of the most pressing environmental challenges across the globe. The results of the collective research will better prepare us for a world that may change drastically because of plastic pollution.

I tell Phumlile that it saddens and scares me that the world has changed so radically that we're having to make plans to accommodate plastic. He simply shrugs his shoulders.

Many animals are already ingesting plastics and time will tell how it will influence the health of food chains. Microplastics are found in crabs, mussels, oysters and fish destined for human consumption, in addition to table salt, seaweed, honey, tea, beer, and tap and bottled water. Once ingested, these tiny bits of pollution hang about in lung tissue, the bloodstream and even placenta in the womb.

A friend and colleague of Anusha, Trishan Naidoo, did a study on the amount and types of plastics swallowed by fish. Close to two hundred juvenile fish from four species living in mangroves along South Africa's east coast were sampled – Mozambique tilapia, Malabar glassy perchlet, crescent grunter and mullet. Over half of the fish contained microplastic particles. The main plastic types were rayon, polyester, nylon and PVC – fibres that come mostly from clothing.

Why are marine biologists interested in microplastics ingested by fish? Overarchingly, their presence has devastating consequences for fish health and reproduction. What has been observed is that it decreases growth and causes weight loss; there is transfer to organs, inflammation, liver toxicity, endocrine disruption and decrease in rates of reproduction. This results in lower fish stock, which has detrimental consequences for communities that rely on that trade. It changes the oceanic biosphere because the larger fish preying on these fish move due to lack of food. It has a knock-on effect on the entire system. Like the changing sandbanks and water pathways in estuarine environments, change is inevitable, but when it is affected by human-made waste, it takes away from the inherent self-regulating beauty of the system.

A few years before Trishan's published findings, in other parts of the world a group of ten scientists under the leadership of Lucy C Woodall conducted a wider study to check for microplastic debris in deeper areas of the sea. Titled 'The deep sea is a major sink for microplastic debris', the research took place in multiple locations, including the Northeast Atlantic Ocean, Mediterranean Sea and the Southwest Indian Ocean, to assess the abundance and composition of microplastic fibres in deep-sea sediments across various oceanic regions. The study was conducted in 2014 and is considered a pioneer in this ambit of research. It brought to light how human-made debris is so extensive that it's even found in remote marine environments.

Plastic is everywhere: in the sea, in rivers, our urban waterways, in the stems of plants, in the bodies of animals. How it will affect the systems on Earth is yet to be seen. I wonder how the Earth will cope, how it will balance itself.

I'm pushing a trolley in the fruit and vegetable section of my local grocery store. I think about the life of a trolley, where it ends up when it breaks, whether the plastic is transformed into another item or if it's discarded in a landfill to break down over hundreds, thousands, of years into bits of nanoplastic. It astounds me how fresh produce is still packaged on a polystyrene tray wrapped in clingwrap. I find all this talk about plastic in our aquatic environments distressing. The inevitability of all of us, every living creature, living on a planet where plastic is everywhere and inside everything is quite depressing. That the situation is likely irreversible is even more distressing. I am hyperaware of how I use plastic. I try to buy products that are packaged in less of it. For many years now, I've sought out clothes made from natural fibres, as so much synthetic fibre lands up in the planet's water and soil. I stay away from single-use plastic. I know it's not enough to make an impact, but I try.

I meet Chris Krauss on a gusty day in January 2025, when the southeaster blows hard across the Cape Peninsula. Chris is a founding partner of Sea the Bigger Picture, an organisation that encourages children to respect and enjoy the sea through an educational programme that takes them to the water.

He can only meet me now because earlier he was at the hospital helping a man he'd been snorkelling with that morning. They'd been attacked by a seal and his companion had been bitten on his calf and on his foot. 'The seal kept coming for us; I held it back with my GoPro stick, which is now full of bite marks. It was going for anything that moved, it was even biting the kelp,' he describes.

He tells me that he's in the kelp forest every day taking people out to snorkel and showing them the diverse creatures that live there. He loves the kelp forest because it's such a calm contrast to the chaos of the world. He shows me a video on his phone of a giant short-tail stingray. It is enormous as its wing-like fins undulate through the water. He takes a bite of the biscuit that accompanies his hot chocolate and becomes animated as he describes the animals he has seen underwater. 'Seals are incredible. Last week I was swimming with one for a long time. I've seen a sevengill cow shark off Miller's Point. They're so majestic. They're the Yodas of the sea world; they're so chilled. I also see shy sharks and pyjama sharks a lot.'

On his arm is a tattoo that reads 'anything is possible' and it becomes clear as we talk that this is his guiding light. He tells me that they no longer do beach clean-ups because it led all of them, on the team and the volunteers, to suffer environmental burnout, which he describes as 'incredibly demotivating'.

'We would do a beach clean-up every month where we would choose a location and then clean it. The next day you'd go back and there was just more plastic. We did a clean-up in Black River on Paarden Eiland – we collected 8 500 plastic bottles and 800 kg of polystyrene, it was frightening. Two and a half tons of plastic goes out of that river into the sea every day. It got to a point where we just couldn't clean another beach,' he explains.

They decided to refocus. They were preaching to their own staff because in terms of plastic pollution the numbers weren't diminishing. They began a programme called Defenders of the Blue, which changed attitudes – for Chris, this has increased impact a hundred-fold. This approach helps to prevent litter from reaching the ocean, effecting change before litter is thrown onto streets, into waterways or left on beaches. The programme introduces children from previously disadvantaged communities to the sea and along the way they learn to swim, to feel safe in the water, to respect the ocean and its marine life. In South Africa, a lot of plastic pollution comes from communities that are underserviced.

'These kids who are chosen for the programme, their parents didn't have the opportunity to go to the beach. We teach them how to swim and do citizen science over four Saturdays. When we take them to Windmill Beach and they're confident in the water, actually thriving in the environment, the joy that I see in them for me is even bigger than seeing their attitude change. Working with these kids is so rewarding.'

For Chris, the top factors that contribute to plastic pollution in the sea are lack of education, lack of waste management and infrastructure, and the standpoint of *it's not me* and *out of sight out of mind* – in other words *if I can't see it, it's not my problem.* There are socioeconomic reasons for people's attitudes. Sea the Bigger Picture aims to change these attitudes, and it's working. The children who've been through the programme have created recycling programmes at schools, sparked plastic awareness campaigns, started eco clubs, and are changing the mindset of friends and family.

There are numerous citizen groups and NGOs that regularly clean the sea and the beaches. Zoë Prinsloo began picking litter off the beach when she was ten years old as part of a Girl Guide initiative. Seeing all the rubbish everywhere made her want to preserve marine environments. At 16 she established the non-profit organisation Save a Fishie.

She's now 22, and over the years she's organised 260 beach clean-ups, visiting 11 beaches across South Africa, collecting 20 tons of litter. Her marine conservation efforts have garnered international recognition. In 2019 she attended the United Nations Youth Climate Summit in New York City. She was named one of the Top 100 African Youth Conservation Leaders in 2021. In December 2023, she set a world record for the longest continuous beach clean-up, spending 27 hours cleaning Milnerton Lagoon Beach in Cape Town. When I chat to her briefly on the phone, she's in the car having just driven out of Athlone, Cape Town, where she and volunteers from Green Riders picked up rubbish in parts of the area. 'Beach clean-ups begin inland because it all ends up in the ocean,' she says. It's a practised turn of phrase she uses to make people aware that every effort helps.

protection

I ask her what happens to the litter that is collected and her mood shifts; suddenly she sounds tired. 'Some of it gets recycled, but the rest goes to landfills, unfortunately. We have a good relationship with the City of Cape Town and they arrive soon after we leave to collect the bags of rubbish. We do the best we can to get it out of the environment and off the beach.' She explains that while some plastic is viable for the recycling process, the rest is too degraded or too dangerous – like syringes – or can't be recycled – like nappies.

Like Sea the Bigger Picture, for her, education is a key to changing how people view litter and the natural environment. They take school groups to their beach clean-ups. 'When kids pick up lollipop sticks or chips packets, things that they use, it hits home much stronger.'

Zoë is preparing for a major beach clean-up that will happen from 17 May until 5 July 2025. She, her sister and her operations manager will set off across the country to clean beaches for seven weeks straight.

Sharon Lee Martin is another trash collector. As part of her free-diving excursions, she decided to start picking up the trash that she saw in the sea and encouraged her freediving acquaintances to join her. They use floating bins made of a brightly coloured mesh material so that sand and small animals can fall through and back into the water. The bright colour also helps the divers to be visible. Some of the most difficult clean-up dives have been in Hout Bay Harbour and at the Royal Cape Yacht Club, where the water is murky and the ocean floor is heaped with rubbish. They've found a welding helmet, a case of 24 still-sealed beers, discarded nets, bottles, fishing gut wire and lots of clothes.

There are many people across the country helping to keep beaches and waters clean. In KwaZulu-Natal, One Planet SA educates children about plastic pollution – one of the participating schools has become totally plastic free. Along the Indian Ocean coast other groups and initiatives get together on weekends to keep beaches clean. It makes me feel good that people are being part of the solution.

Environmental consultant and founding member of Frack Free South Africa, Judy Bell, drives thousands of kilometres around South Africa observing nature, chatting to people in remote communities and playing her part in environmental justice. 'I do a lot of trips, I meander, I get into my bakkie and do about four trips a year, about 5 000 kilometres each. That's why I had to unretire and go back to work, the diesel cost was getting too high.'

These trips are her last chance to see what is happening with climate change – or, as she calls it, global change. 'We've abstracted from the planet to the point that what we're doing, how we are living, is no longer sustainable. Everything's changing and changing really quickly. I've seen it in the last 30 years, happening slowly and, now, all of a sudden, the last two, three years, I've seen massive changes. One of the things I first noticed was that I wasn't seeing raptors in the sky. The skies were empty and in a lot of places you suddenly see raptors and you think, wow, this is what it used to look like. And then you realise there's a chicken hatchery that's throwing out the dead chickens, and the raptors are feeding on them.

'It's amazing. Birds to me have been incredibly good tools to point to. Are we sustainable or not? Have we reached tipping points? I think we have reached a tipping point with birds.' Judy has observed that the ocean has also changed very fast. 'We used to see no whales and now we see a lot of whales, but we also see a lot of strandings. I was around the Agulhas coast and there were a lot of dead seals. I was seeing them everywhere, dead seals and gannets. We've seen gannet colonies collapse, we've seen cormorants collapse, and it's because we've disrupted everything and we've taken out too much and not put back.'

Judy speaks to me on her return to her home in Howick, KwaZulu-Natal, after a week in Ponta Malongane in southern Mozambique. For her, the most telling thing was that the beautiful, tropical beaches had little in the way of stuff being washed up that was natural. It was mostly plastic and toothbrushes thrown over from the fishing boats out at sea.

She saw tourists along the beach at restaurants. With an environmentalist's eye she watched them, their behaviour, their expectations. She questioned their lifestyle paradigm. 'They want LM prawns. And you think, well, where did the LM prawns come from? But there's no fresh milk, they say. But Mozambique doesn't have grassland, so where are the cows going to be? It's this thing of: *I must have what I believe are the most important things in my life, and they should be transported wherever I go.* It's this excessiveness that is driving our climate crisis further into the ground.'

By joining the dots of everything she witnesses, Judy predicts that conservation may come down to this: the only way we're going to make conservation work is if it pays, conservation tourism through high-end lodges being one of the ways this model could thrive.

Deeply disturbing for Judy are South Africa's problematic wastewater treatment facilities and the raw sewage that flows into our waterways. Many of the wastewater treatment facilities are deteriorating because of old infrastructure and insufficient maintenance. Many are not properly managed, leading to untreated or inadequately treated sewage running into rivers and oceans. Sewage is part of what will make health issues worse.

Judy explains that the Department of Water and Sanitation is now starting to wake up. 'When Senzo Mchunu came in as Minister of Water and Sanitation, it looked as though they were starting to get rid of some of the corruption, and do monitoring and enforcement. Not enough, but they were starting. People in municipalities should go to jail because over half of our sewage works are not functioning. That's just the works, not the pump stations that get it to the works. So, when you've got raw sewage being pumped and the electricity goes off, where does it go?'

In June 2024 Senzo Mchunu was replaced by Pemmy Majodina, who has initiated several infrastructure and upgrade projects to the wastewater management system. She has also started other projects to ensure the future of the country's water security. There is a global standard for how much water is needed per person and under her leadership the aim is to align the country's water consumption to that standard. Per capita water consumption varies worldwide as it's influenced by factors such as climate, economic development and lifestyle. While there isn't a universally mandated international standard for daily water use, several benchmarks and averages provide context. The World Health Organization recommends a minimum of 20 to 50 litres per person daily for essential health and hygiene needs. In the United States, water consumption exceeds 500 litres per person per day. So, needs, standards and access vary hugely. For South Africa, aligning with international standards would involve assessing current per capita consumption and implementing conservation measures to ensure the type of water usage that is sustainable.

Pemmy has a long way to go as timely maintenance is still an issue and extending services to all communities is going to take time and money. She has to contend with water leaks and water shortages, and the water crisis in Gauteng.

An eternal optimist, Judy sounds exasperated as she faces the reality of water pollution daily. She shakes her head at the hail that fell in Johannesburg a few days ago. 'These extremes – I saw pictures of that hail. Crazy. It wasn't hail; it looked like somebody had got a pickaxe and broke up bits of an ice block. No, it didn't look like hail any more. It looked like an extreme weather event.'

The climate crisis brings concerns about water, food and health. Judy predicts that in South Africa, health is going to be a challenge. 'I work with Groundwork on the Global Green and Healthy Hospitals Initiative by way of motivating and inspiring health professionals to become more sustainably aware, to become ambassadors and advocates for a better way of greening health care.'

Years ago, activists, including Judy, predicted an imminent nexus, a crisis that was going to be huge. The first one was energy, water and food. Health should have been added to that. 'It's happened. The dominoes have fallen quicker than I thought.'

Judy foresees that there isn't a country in the world that will escape the climate crisis issues.

In essence, this is a water issue. Water is finite. The amount of water on the planet was here from the beginning and it still is. The problems have arisen because we've been polluting it, abusing it, battering its resources.

Judy's tone is grave. 'The only thing that has saved us is that we are always one rainy season away from a drought. That has been our saving grace. So, we've been able to irrigate and grow food. Our dams have been full. Watch the next few years.

'When food becomes more expensive, even more expensive than it is now, and water has to be bought as opposed to coming from a tap, that's when the problems are going to come.'

As I listen to Judy, I worry about my children. A friend who is a water activist says that there is nothing more we can do to curb the water crisis and that we should just enjoy our lives. In an era of contentious politics, I think we are losing sight of the fact that the water crisis – the problem of polluted water and the lack of access – is not about politics but about our common humanity and the planet on which we live. I've read a lot of doomsday journalism. Things like 'Global water crisis leaves half of world food production at risk in next 25 years' make good headlines. This particular article, which appeared in *The Guardian* in October 2024, urged for action to be taken 'to conserve water resources and end the destruction of the ecosystems on which our fresh water depends'.

There is enormous stress on our water system and half the world's population already faces water scarcity. Our water, our soil, our air needs to be pristine for us to continue as a species. The basis of this is so simple, yet it is so hard for government systems, industry, education and consumption to change. If only they were as mutable as water.

I've noticed how dirty the sea is in Durban. It wasn't like this when I was a child, 40 years ago. Granted, the world has changed and there are now eight billion humans walking, eating and excreting on the planet. I am aware that my efforts are but a drop. But like raindrops pocking the surface of the ocean, I continue in the hope that one day the storm that we create will shape a better future.

I come across a piece of news that causes me to smile spontaneously. In the Polish city of Warsaw, the water and sanitation department – Warsaw Waterworks – is using sharp-edged river mussels to prevent contaminated water from reaching taps. They call the process bio-processing. Eight mussels with sensors glued to their shells monitor and automatically shut off the city water supply if the quality of the water drops. Mussels are sensitive to chemical toxins and pollutants, and will close their shells to protect themselves. As they close their shells, they set off a sensor that alerts the system's computers. If four of the eight mussels close their shells, the entire water supply is shut down. The mussels are put into retirement after three months when they are returned to the lakes of Wielkopolska. More than fifty water plants around Poland employ this technique. I think this is a brilliant and simple way of monitoring water pollution for the sake of citizens' health.

If only it would extend to the health of everything.

jellyfish and goby fish

Drifting through the tide,
translucent dreams in water,
time's soft tentacles.

– Traditional Japanese haiku, author unknown

Jellyfish are among the most ancient creatures on earth. Also known as medusae, jellyfish have no hard parts, so fossils of these creatures are rare. They have been mythologised and revered for their beauty and grace. They are also feared for their painful, often paralysing and sometimes fatal stings. Marine biologist Mark Gibbons knows an inordinate amount about jellyfish. As he chats to me from his home office, his colourful shirt reminds me of a fairy tale captain of a ship in a tumultuous sea. He has a pleasing make-believe eccentricity about him.

He tells me that the life cycle of the jellyfish has two phases. The first is when they are minute polyps resembling sea anemones, hiding in the rocks. The second is as medusae, when they eat the same food as pelagic fish. Pelagic fish, especially sardines, anchovies and red-eye round herrings, eat the medusae babies and the medusae eat the fish babies. There is equivalence in this ecosystem.

Historically, when there are large populations of fish, the jellyfish populations will be held relatively low because there is pressure on the jellyfish. They persist regardless of what's happening in the ocean, because of their resilient polyp phase. Jellyfish have roamed the oceans for 500 million years and predate dinosaurs, insects and even trees.

But if the fish population plummets, as has happened because of overfishing, there are no longer controls on the jellyfish numbers, so these populations expand, and in turn keep the fish population down by eating both their grub and their spawn. In a healthy system, there are jellyfish and pelagic fish, but if there is pressure on the fish, the jellyfish numbers grow tremendously.

In a 9 000-square-kilometre region off the Namibian coast, over-zealous fishing during the 1960s and 1970s caused the demise of the sardine population. The region is the site of the northern Benguela upwelling, where deeper, nutrient-rich water flows coastwards. The pelagic fish population has never recovered. So, the system looks fundamentally different today – dominated by medusae and goby fish.

Before the demise of the sardines in the area, filter-feeding sardines fed on the plankton and kept it under control, but as overfishing depleted the stocks, dying plankton descended to the bottom and decayed, and in the process used up nearly all the oxygen in the water – creating a 'dead zone'. Filter feeders are vital for nutrient cycling and controlling phytoplankton communities: as they take in large mouthfuls of water and then filter it through their gills, phytoplankton and small organisms stay behind and are ingested.

Filter feeders play a major role in trophic cascades, an ecological phenomenon in which changes at the top of the food chain – such as the addition or removal of a predator – cause a ripple effect through lower levels, ultimately altering entire ecosystems.

Mark explains how something almost miraculous happened that caused a new food cycle to emerge. 'Sunlight to phytoplankton to zooplankton to fish to seabird, but now there are fewer fish, so a lot of the seabirds have gone from Namibia because there is nothing for them to eat. Now it's sun to phytoplankton to zooplankton to seafloor because it's not getting eaten. Some zooplankton is going to jellyfish, a lot is settling on the seabed and rotting, decomposing and contributing to bottom, low-oxygen water.

'But the goby thrives in that situation and its population has protection

increased. Hake has miraculously stayed alive even though its main food source, anchovies, are gone, because now it eats the gobies – it has managed to take advantage of this new situation.'

Mark and his colleagues at the University of the Western Cape were curious about how the bearded goby was able to thrive in this ecosystem. With the help of two goby experts – Anne Utne-Palm and Anne GV Salvanes – from the University of Bergen, and a group of students, they performed a series of studies on this fish's habits and habitat. They looked at the water column and assessed the oxygen and hydrogen sulphide content at various depths.

The sea bottom in the area is covered by a thick mud rich in hydrogen sulphide and the bacteria that thrives on this toxic gas. In the bottom 20 to 60 metres of ocean, oxygen levels are very low – this is where the gobies spend their days, where their predators can't survive. They effectively hold their breaths, until they can swim further up at night when they can replenish their oxygen, giving them the ability to survive while cleverly avoiding predators. At night, they mingle with jellyfish and other organisms. Gobies have thick, slimy skins that are immune to the stings of jellyfish, so they hang out on their tentacles and their bells, which gives them added protection from being eaten.

When the researchers looked inside their stomachs, they found that most of the contents was jellyfish and the rest was mud-living organisms and bacteria from the sea floor. Through their diet, the gobies are bringing dead-end products back into the ecosystem.

'Nobody could've predicted how a little fish could bloom a food web that is stable and productive,' marvels Mark.

As Mark unravels the story about the gobies, my respect for them deepens. They possess the kind of biological characteristics that many freedivers would dream of – an ability to stay for hours at the bottom of the sea without breathing, and with no damage to their bodies.

But for every unexpected adaptation like the goby's, there are countless other stories that don't end so well. For every unlikely survivor, like the goby drifting between jellyfish bells, there are many silences where once there was life. When a system collapses or reroutes, it's often the most adaptable – or the most opportunistic – that survive. The goby may have found a way to thrive in murky, oxygen-poor waters, but the seabirds have vanished. It's a reminder that ecological change is rarely neutral.

agreeing to protect the oceans: the high seas treaty

The ocean, Earth's blue lungs, underpins human life and healthy ecosystems. Protecting it is protecting ourselves.

– Lewis Pugh

In December 2022 at COP15 in Montréal, Canada, many of the nations in attendance made a noteworthy commitment – to protect 30 per cent of the Earth's land, water and indigenous peoples by the year 2030. This was an enormous victory for every single person fighting to salvage and safeguard what pristine natural areas we have left and preserve even more of it from agriculture and urbanisation. It is a lofty goal that requires commitment and actions from everyone involved, the results of which may need to be seen and experienced before they are believed.

There is a massive body of research that shows that humankind and life on Earth as we know it is running out of time. A number of factors continue to erode life on Earth – methane gas created by agriculture, carbon emissions caused by industry and the use of fossil fuels, deforestation, pollution and plastic pollution.

The fact that there are eight billion humans, and counting, on the planet has further accelerated climate change and a loss of biodiversity. I've mentioned before that the Earth is a beautifully balancing system and that, to stay in equilibrium, if there is more of one thing, something else has to be subtracted. It is simple mathematics. More humans mean less of other things. The irony is, the more humans are birthed, the less we change our behaviour, the closer we get to the death of biodiversity and our own suicide as a species. It sounds dramatic, but we are on a course of destruction.

What would it take for us to limit our negative effects on the planet? It would take education, religious leaders changing the mindset of their followers, the preaching of a new paradigm. Industry would need to change, human rights would need rewriting, government systems would need to transform radically.

Change is happening too slowly. There is excessive red tape and not enough alteration of our daily lives and economic systems. Nature is bountiful but it doesn't wait for humans to make up their minds – it changes as it needs to. Extreme events – earthquakes, floods, drought, fires – are already upon us and are predicted to become more prevalent. More humans will be displaced. Local economies will be affected. The global economy will be impacted. It doesn't paint a pretty seascape. Yet if we are to redesign this picture from one of desolation to one brushed in blues and greens and vibrant colours, every person needs to consciously do their bit. It is actually that simple.

Thankfully, action to mitigate the stress of anthropogenic climate change on the planet is taking place.

In March 2023, the High Seas Treaty, also known as the Agreement on Biodiversity Beyond National Jurisdiction (BBNJ), was finalised. The United Nations viewed it as a victory for global efforts to counter the destructive trends challenging the health of oceans. It was a vital step for tackling the triple planetary crisis of climate change, biodiversity loss and pollution.

After years of talks and stalled agreements, over 190 countries decided on a common framework to better protect the world's oceans. The treaty would enable the protection and regulation of marine areas beyond national jurisdiction – that is, waters lying beyond 200 nautical miles from a country's coastline, commonly known as the high seas.

The high seas make up two-thirds of earth's ocean surface. Anybody can do whatever they want in these waters, anything goes – there is rampant overfishing, the hijacking of vessels, illegal deep-sea mining, the dumping of waste, and only those who dare to venture there know what else. What the treaty aims to do is curb the threats to our planet's largest habitat.

The treaty will allow for new Marine Protected Areas (MPAs) to be established in the high seas, through the common governance of about half the Earth's surface and 95 per cent of the ocean's volume. While it addresses the triple planetary crisis, it also aims to promote equity and fairness when it comes to the sharing of marine genetic resources and knowledge, especially around deep-sea organisms found in remote waters that could be of value for medical, and other, purposes. How the bounty of scientific discoveries will be shared may cause some sticky situations, and while it looks good on paper, it will be interesting to see how it unfolds.

The High Seas Treaty has been eagerly embraced, yet the reality is that it may take years for it to be formally approved. For it to enter into force, there need to be 60 ratifications, and many countries are notoriously slow to approve environmental treaties, if they ever approve them at all. On 21 September 2023, in 24 hours 66 countries had already signed the High Seas Treaty. Now each country must ratify the treaty under its own domestic process. The treaty will come into force 120 days after 60 countries ratify it. The hope of those who have already signed is that it is ratified swiftly before the June 2025 UN Ocean Conference in Nice, France. Once the treaty takes legal effect, nations can begin outlining new MPAs. Among the biodiversity hotspots in which conservationists want to implement protections are the Sargasso Sea in the Atlantic, the Costa Rica Thermal Dome in the Pacific and the Walvis Ridge in the Atlantic. By February 2025, 107 nations had signed the treaty, but only 13 nations had completed the ratification process.

The Protected Planet Report 2024 shows that 17,6 per cent of land and 8,4 per cent of marine areas are under protection, which is not a lot given the amount of money and effort that has gone into the target of 30 per cent by 2030. For various reasons – political instability, wars, relocation of funds and a cascade of other pressing matters – progress is stagnating. The world is not on track to meet the target. Significant expansion of protected areas, especially in international waters, is essential if the world is to meet its biodiversity goals.

It would probably take a drastic series of events for the High Seas Treaty to be properly ratified, or for the ratification process to be eliminated in favour of speedier progress. The safeguarding of marine ecosystems and ensuring the sustainable use of ocean resources is so important to the survival of everything.

It makes me feel better that other organisations, including the Bezos Earth Fund and Blue Nature Alliance, formed a consortium and pledged $51,7 million during the 16th Conference of the Parties to the Convention on Biological Diversity (COP16) held in Cali, Colombia, in October 2024. The funding aims to accelerate progress in the development of MPAs and advance the treaty's objectives.

The Walvis Ridge runs from Namibia to Tristan da Cunha and the Gough Islands. The 3 000-kilometre-long ridge has an interesting typography of seamounts, abyssal plains and guyots (undersea mountains with flat tops) supporting an abundance of species in both the water and the sky. In some areas, it plumbs to 4 000 metres, and I can only imagine the fascinating marine fauna that lives in these dark depths. Bottom trawling and gill netting are still happening in the area and while the overall fishing footprint is small, if these fishing methods are not reined in, there is the risk of it becoming significantly wider and more threatening. Another concern is drilling for offshore oil and gas, which is already happening in Namibia's exclusive economic zone and will probably be extended.

The Walvis Ridge is a rare linkage of a seamount chain formed by underwater volcanoes to continental flood basalts – in other words, it is a string of underwater mountains and valleys. If it becomes a MPA, it would give marine life a chance to thrive. What this means is that downstream in Namibia there would be more fish, leading to socioeconomic benefits. The area is in the high seas, so it is a global common. The only way it can be protected is under the High Seas Treaty. But even then, I imagine that policing and enforcement will remain a challenge.

The problem with protecting areas under law is that it can disregard the human rights element. In Indonesia, people fish in the high seas and they rely on it for their livelihood. If a MPA is extended in a fishing hotspot, the impact that it will have on the fishers needs to be taken into account. While South Africa attempted to implement policies post-1994 that differentiated between large commercial and traditional fishing practices, the outcomes have been mixed, filled with complexities and challenges. What is needed is for people to address protection from all directions, balancing conservation efforts with communities' socioeconomic needs.

South Africa has established 42 MPAs, which cover about 15,5 per cent of the country's exclusive economic zone. In these areas commercial fishing activities are restricted or prohibited, allowing the ecosystem to recover and flourish. The Department of Forestry, Fisheries and the Environment has also put various measures in place to regulate commercial fishing, including fishing rights allocations, total allowable catch (TAC) and effort (TAE), gear and vessel regulations, and monitoring and enforcement. But these measures aren't properly put into action. Enforcement officials tend to turn a blind eye to the unlawful activities of larger commercial fishing vessels and pick on small-scale fishers who are easier to catch. This is my generalised view, but I've spoken to many people who tell this story.

The High Seas Treaty is part of a broader approach. There are international instruments that oversee laws that are enforced globally. The intention of these instruments is to ensure that laws are interpreted, implemented and adhered to according to a framework. This ensures that knowledge is properly shared and made accessible, and that processes are applied consistently. It basically makes sure that everyone knows what is going on.

The High Seas Treaty falls under the UN Convention on the Law of the Sea. It fits into the Convention on Biological Diversity (CBD) framework. It also falls within the structure of the UN Framework Convention on Climate Change (UNFCCC). The conventions are multilateral, working with other conventions to reach the same goal: protecting the biodiversity and natural environments of planet Earth.

Within these actionable intentions there is place for both citizens and government – people who force governments to make changes, and people in government who commit to nationalising laws. Both stakeholders make an impact. Think of Greta Thunberg, an activist highlighting the interconnectedness between climate justice and human rights. In 2015 Lewis Pugh shook hands with Sergei Shoigu, Russia's then-Minister of Defence and head of the Russian Geographical Society, to protect Antarctica's Ross Sea. It is currently the world's largest MPA, and remains protected even with geopolitical instability as the Russia–Ukraine War continues.

However rife with complexities, the High Seas Treaty is the beginning of a greater awareness of the issues affecting this vital resource. The healthier our marine environment, the better it can absorb carbon dioxide, which in turn can diminish global warming. The greater our biodiversity, the more nourishing our food and the bigger our enjoyment of life on planet Earth.

From my cynical point of view, what the treaty confirms is that institutionalised bureaucracy has finally woken up to the fact that humankind is sadly a threat. To ourselves, especially. The ocean has an immense capacity to restore itself. It is a natural system that knows how to return to equilibrium. Maybe, hopefully, all is not lost and there is time still to save what wild beauty we have left.

In South Africa many people do their part in conserving and protecting the oceans. In 2021 and 2022, when Shell planned to conduct seismic surveys along the Wild Coast to explore for oil and gas reserves, local communities and environmental activists opposed them and won. The win was based on the grounds that there was lack of proper consultation with indigenous populations. The argument was that the seismic testing was a threat to marine ecosystems and infringed on the cultural and spiritual rights of the Mpondo, because to them, as to many others, the ocean is sacred and their ancestors live in the deep. This was the first time that South Africans invoked their cultural rights in climate litigation.

In 2024 Shell again wanted to pursue oil and gas exploration along the Wild Coast. Fortunately, the South African Supreme Court of Appeal dismissed Shell's appeal against a ruling that had halted its seismic exploration activities. The activism against Shell continues because the court allowed for the possibility of Shell renewing its exploration rights if a comprehensive public participation process were consulted. Sinegugu Zukulu, director of Sustaining the Wild Coast, told me that the fight against Shell was far from over. For him, extractive activities threaten the environment, cultural heritage and livelihoods. He reminds me that 'a safe and healthy environment is our constitutional right'. This means an environment free from the effects of fossil fuel exploration and exploitation – an environment in which nature itself has certain rights.

Writing the Rights of Nature into countries' constitutions could revolutionise our lives. In 2008, Ecuador became the first country to do so. That nature needs the legal right to be protected is sad, as it shows how far removed we are from it and how emancipated we've become in our pursuit of so-called advancement. Yet, recognising the Rights of Nature gives an enormous foothold to environmental activists and indigenous communities. It is a tool to protect wild spaces.

Nature as property versus nature as nature is an ongoing fight. The Amazon is a huge green lung for the planet, the biggest tropical rainforest, and yet the protection of it, for the continuation of our own species and others, is not going well. The mining of crude petroleum in Ecuador has caused vast deforestation of the Amazon and contamination of water. Its effects on people living in this rainforest have been ruinous.

I wonder what our predecessors would think.

the human polar bear

There is nothing more powerful than the made-up mind.
— Lewis Pugh

I meet Lewis Pugh in 2009 at Athlone Girls High School in Cyrildene, a suburb in an old part of Johannesburg. He is in the hall preparing for a talk he is about to deliver to the learners. Clear blue eyes against tanned skin, he is tall with bulk on his frame. He looks dapper in his beige chinos and light-blue shirt. He radiates stamina. He looks older than his 39 years, and he has a gravitational pull about him. It's not just his athleticism, it's that his purpose feels magnanimous. His life focus is so steadfast, it is palpable.

The moment he begins, he has his audience riveted. Besides the sound of his voice and the ambient noise beyond the walls of the school hall, there is only the shuffle of limbs being shifted into more comfortable positions.

He talks about long-distance swimming. He describes his swim in the North Pole in 2007 where he was petrified of encountering a hungry polar bear. He tells of his swim around Robben Island where he had others swimming alongside him to limit his exposure to being eaten by a shark. His humour is accessible and there is laughter from the audience. Lewis has already ticked off more swims around famous landmarks than any other swimmer in history. He is also giving a thousand schoolgirls a firsthand account of the effects of global warming, the rapidity at which the ice at the poles is melting.

While he is well built, he is not lean and explains that he keeps some fat on his body to protect him from the cold. At one point he takes off his shoes, rolls up his chinos, sits on a chair and lowers his legs, up to his shins, into a tub of ice and water. He continues talking. After a few minutes he is still comfortable, unfazed by the cold chewing at his limbs, and asks: 'Do you know which part of my body feels the cold the most? It's not what you think.'

This solicits a few guffaws and cross-legged girls shift on the floor, pulling the hems of their dresses further down their thighs.

'My fingers,' he says, dissolving the awkward silence.

He is in South Africa as part of a schools programme to spread the word about global warming and what can be done to diminish the crisis. He was born in Plymouth, England, and while he was a child his family emigrated to South Africa, coating his English accent with a South African one. After completing his tertiary education at the University of Cape Town he moved back to England where he read international law at Jesus College, Cambridge. He then worked as a maritime lawyer and served as a reservist in the British Special Air Service.

After the talk, Lewis and I sit outside in the bright March sunshine. The learners have gone back to their classrooms and it is quiet in the school garden. My mind goes to my belly where a child I am yet to meet is growing in amniotic fluid. The similarities between the composition of the water my foetus swims in and the ocean are not lost on me. The human connection to water begins very early in life.

The sun is in Lewis's eyes, but he doesn't mind – enjoys it, even. From his nursery school in Plymouth, he could see ships coming and going in The Sound. As a four-year-old he dreamt of being on one of those ships, going somewhere. At Camp's Bay High School in Cape Town, he was always close to the ocean.

His first long swim was at the age of 17, from Robben Island to Cape Town. Six years later, in 1992, he swam the English Channel. In 2002, he swam around Robben Island and broke the record for the fastest time. He swam 100 km from Cape Town to Muizenberg. He swam across Lake Malawi. By 2003, Lewis had swum hundreds of kilometres in open water. He wanted to take it further.

'I pictured my life ahead of me and then looked at the life behind me and I decided that I wanted to bring the realities of global warming to people everywhere and I was going to do this by being the first person to complete a long-distance swim at the North Pole.'

I ask him about his training but he is vague; this is a private man who fiercely protects the details of his daily life. About his North Pole swim he says, 'It took many years of training and I stayed focused. I worked towards the goal.'

He can raise his core temperature by 1,4 °C through anticipatory thermogenesis. The term was coined by sports physiologist Tim Noakes to describe Lewis's response to cold-water immersion. Tim Noakes was part of the team that accompanied him to the North Pole. Lewis's body temperature shoots up to about 38,4 °C, a mild fever, before he gets into the icy water. This ability allows him to survive in an environment that would be fatal to most humans. When I ask him how he does it, he smiles almost bashfully and says, 'By listening to rap music.' It's the aggressive rhythm of it that gets his temperature pumped up, alongside years of training and acclimatising.

'As soon as I enter cold water my body shunts all my warm blood to my core to protect my vital organs. It then generates incredible heat,' he explains.

In July 2007 he swam 1 kilometre in an open section of sea across the Geographic North Pole in under 19 minutes. Wearing only a Speedo, swimming cap and goggles, he swam in water that was colder than 0 °C and stepped out without losing so much as a fingertip. What he did experience is pain in his fingers for four months afterwards because the cells in his fingertips had burst.

Lewis has played a major role in effecting positive change for the marine environment. He is the UN Patron of the Oceans. In 2016, his swims in Antarctica and visits to the US and Russia helped finalise the agreement to make the Ross Sea a Marine Protected Area. The Lewis

Pugh Foundation was created in 2016 to ensure that many more Marine Protected Areas were created across more seas and oceans. To date, the foundation has helped to legally protect over 2 million square kilometres of ocean.

Lewis's most recent and most gigantic physical endeavour was in 2023, when he swam the Hudson River from its source – Lake Tear of the Clouds, in the Adirondack Mountains – to New York City, where the river finds its way to the Atlantic Ocean. He swam about 16 kilometres a day over 32 consecutive days and completed 507 kilometres in total. He took on the swim as a personal challenge and, on a broader scale, to emphasise the importance of healthy rivers, unpolluted by industrial waste, sewage and plastics. In an article he states, 'If we want healthy oceans, we also need healthy rivers – it's that simple.'

Every major swim for Lewis is a way to inspire people to protect and preserve the Earth's oceans and all that live in them. Like Amber Fillary, Ram Barkai, Samantha Whelpton, Kiki Bosch and many others who have a superhuman ability to swim long distances in cold temperatures, he sees places that few people have seen. The icy landscapes of the poles are not just the backdrop to his swims – they are the message. In bearing witness, he reminds us that even the most remote waters are affected by anthropogenic climate change, and that our choices now ripple far into the future.

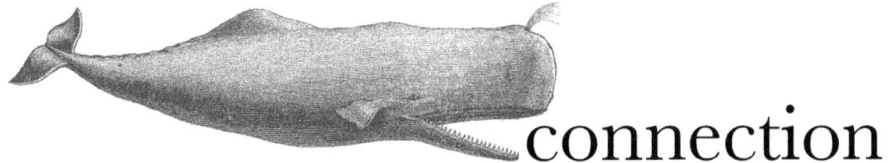connection

our golden kelp forests

We know that globally there's a lot of decline in kelp forests. We're quite lucky in South Africa. We don't know why. For me, this is the caution. This is the reason that we need to up our endeavours to ensure that it's well protected.

– Loyiso Dunga

Along the coast of South Africa, kelp forests are thriving. A large seaweed that forms the basis for one of the planet's most productive and biodiverse ecosystems, kelp has been part of people's livelihoods for millennia. This is what I hear from those who work closely with the flora. Coastal people use the leaves, stems and roots of this prolific marine alga. Historically, in many communities, kelp has been used as fertiliser, animal feed, even as building and packing material. Traditional relationships with kelp go deep, woven into the resourcefulness of people who've lived alongside the sea for generations. Kelp forests are found in both hemispheres and are the dominant biomass in nearshore, rocky, shallow areas. They thrive in cooler waters, being less resilient in warm waters. Exposure to wave action and storms also affects their profusion.

Albertus J Smit – AJ, an ocean scientist at the University of the Western Cape – has been studying kelp forests for the past ten years with a focus on how they are being affected by climate change. He chats to me from his office in Bellville, a suburb of Cape Town, glad to be back from his travels in France where he was attending workshops and sharing ideas with other researchers.

connection

What AJ has seen is that kelp forests globally are coping quite well. Locally, the oceans around South Africa are cooling and kelp loves this. The climate system has changed, with an increase in southeasterly winds, resulting in more waviness and storminess. The waves remove the density of the old kelp, which is eventually replaced by new kelp. 'What we are seeing now is that kelp populations tend to be more dominated by younger, more rapidly growing kelp plants. There is more kelp floating around on the ocean surface and this is to be expected. Storm surges result in the removal of kelp plants and these get deposited on beaches 400 km east in Gqeberha, providing food for intertidal species,' he says, his gaze even and friendly.

As old kelp washes ashore and decomposes, it releases nutrients into the coastal environment, supporting diverse microbial communities. The kelp detritus provides habitat and food for various invertebrates. The areas where new kelp proliferates are also being affected as there is less habitat and food for creatures that live on old kelp. The ecosystems change.

AJ has a keen interest in how coastal ecology is affected by climate change. A shadow of weariness crosses his brow, then his expression recovers and he explains how the crisis is human driven. 'Climate-active gases – carbon dioxide and methane – are a direct result of agriculture. Cattle are a major source of methane gas. Rice cultivation in China and Brazil is harmful. Carbon dioxide released into the atmosphere is directly linked to the way we consume energy through coal and gas, and the burning of biomass and fossil fuels.

'This is not new; we have known this since the late 1800s. In 1920 there was an article about climate change in a New Zealand newspaper. We have known about this for the past one hundred and fifty years and it is very well understood.'

When I ask him what we need to do about it, he tells me succinctly that we need a change in human behaviours. 'In Norway there has been a complete transition to solar energy; there is a lot more reluctance to do this in Australia and the US. Changes need to be political; they hinge on public goodwill and various larger-scale infrastructure and agronomy adaptations.'

Extreme events will become normal. 'Where we were experiencing devastating floods once in a hundred years, these are happening more frequently. They will become part of our daily lives. Malaria is moving further south. Water shortage will be more frequent, which will affect crops. Landscapes will change – the KwaZulu-Natal grasslands will become increasingly dominated by trees. On the west side of the country, certain tree species will take over some landscapes.

'Vulnerable societies, the poor, will feel more pressure because of poor economies. Less access to water will exacerbate problems. In the Pacific Ocean, the small island states at low altitude will become displaced because the land will be underwater, and we'll see climate change refugees.'

With their swaying fronds that seem to trap the sun's rays in their waters, it is understandable why kelp is said to create golden forests. Akshata Mehta is a marine social scientist who talks to people about their relationship to kelp. She tells me that kelp is harvested for abalone farming. It has also been used for generations as fertiliser. 'People tell me that they take the kelp fronds and lay them on their vegetable patch and that it makes the plants grow really well. While this is anecdotal evidence of how people use kelp, it is telling that the practice began centuries ago.'

Akshata dives every weekend, so she has a direct view of kelp forests. She was born in Mumbai but met a South African and settled with him in his home country. She says that the ocean is very accessible in the Western Cape and she takes advantage of this. 'In Betty's Bay there are fronds everywhere. Kelp is increasing because of the nutrients being carried in from the Benguela Current. The canopy is so thick now.'

The forest is flourishing for another reason – one of its main grazers is dying out. Abalone will only grow in kelp forests, but it is disappearing because it's not maturing to maximum size. It takes 14 years for it to get to that stage, but it's in huge demand and poachers are paid thousands of rands for the mollusc. 'It's a huge crime to poach abalone. One of the guys told me that kelp keeps him from getting caught because he hides in it when Cape Nature are checking for poachers. The forest is that thick that he can hide.'

The seaweed revolution is big right now. Akshata has created a video showing the different ways that people make use of kelp. There is a chef who cooks dishes with the seaweed. In the Soetwater Environmental Education Centre near Kommetjie, Phil Mansergh has opened the Kelp Shack, an upcycled kitchen where he prepares ravioli, spaghetti and other culinary delicacies made from these large algae.

In Gansbaai, a company called Taurus Cape Kelp harvests the fronds and collects the stipes (stalks) that are stranded on the beach. The kelp is then processed for use in aquaculture and plant fertiliser. In Australia, the stipe is used to make water vessels, and the fronds are used to make kelp leather.

Kelp forests are changing – the delicate balance that sustains this underwater world is tilting, causing some species to flourish, others to move and some to die out. This watery forest has always been a place of movement – blades swaying in the surge, creatures weaving through their shifting shadows – but in some areas, this lush wilderness has become barren seafloor. While these golden canopies are thriving in Cape waters, persistent ocean warming has reduced kelp along the US coast. Kelp species are sensitive to temperature fluctuations and don't like warm water. Between 2014 and 2016, there was a massive reduction in kelp along California's north coast. A few things caused this: the area was afflicted by a marine heatwave known as 'The Blob'; and a mass die-off of sea stars – the main predators of purple sea urchins – caused an explosion of urchin numbers, which led to the overgrazing of bull kelp forests. Most of the lush forests disappeared. This is a dramatic example of how the loss of a single thread in the delicate tapestry of marine ecosystems can unravel entire species.

South Africa's kelp forests are resilient, with some areas even expanding due to changing ocean conditions. The shifting dynamics underscore the complex interplay between marine life and climate change. These narratives from opposite hemispheres remind me of nature's fragility and the profound influence of climate fluctuations on marine biodiversity. All of me wants to dive through these forests and enjoy their splendour before they collapse. As I write this, I make a plan to do that with my daughters.

around the buoy

When you swim, you feel your body for what it mostly is – water – and it begins to move with the water around it.

– Roger Deakin

I wake up in an Airbnb loft room in Tico's Way in Noordhoek on the Cape Peninsula. Hadedas shriek outside. A rooster crows, a duck makes a guttural quack as it flies overhead. It's just gone 5.30 a.m. and outside there is sunlight against Noordhoek Peak. It's the day of the Around the Buoy swim that I signed up for yesterday. I have a vomit feeling in the pit of my stomach. I'm more worried about the details than I am about the swim. Finding my way there, parking, what to do with my bag. Do I wear the wetsuit I've borrowed? The training is done and I know the pool swimming will stand me in good stead.

I check that my goggles and swim cap are in my bag, chuck it in the boot of the rental car and set off. It feels like a big adventure. Coming over the mountain I see False Bay and my body instinctively relaxes. My mind softens and my thoughts slow. The light is heavenly – thick fingers of sunlight angle out from a thicket of clouds, reaching the water and painting it yellow-gold. Excitement blooms in me and I find that I'm smiling.

I'm making good time and I should be at Long Beach parking lot just before 7 a.m. As I enter Simon's Town my eyes are distracted by a submarine submerging. *Wow*, I think to myself. Simon's Town is after all the beating heart of the South African Navy. Established as a Royal Navy base in the 18th century, it was later, in 1957, handed over to the South African government. Its docks hold the country's frigates, submarines and patrol vessels. When I get to the parking lot it's already full so I make a U-turn and park about half a kilometre down the road next to Pisces Divers. I thought I was early, but this is clearly a popular swim on the calendar.

As I walk, groups of cyclists whizz past, their red lights flickering. On the beach there are groups of people, some in hooded towels, some with wetsuits pulled up to their waists, some with swimming caps on their heads and goggles dangling from their necks. There's a gabble of chatter and I manage to snatch some of it. 'The wind is coming up,' someone says, and the reply, 'Well, it'll make you stronger.'

I amble to the water as I'm eager to check the temperature. It's warm and there's no need for a wetsuit, thankfully. I spot Scotty, Scott Tait – he's under the gazebo, greeting people with a smile as they give their names to be ticked off the entry list. He looks everyone in the eye, making them feel important, me included. I leave my bag under the gazebo next to a few others. I spot Carina Bruwer and call her name. It's the first time I've seen her in the flesh. A slight breeze riffles hair into her face as she walks towards me, lean and catlike. There is a forward propulsion about her, as if her entire body, and not just her mind, is completely focused on what she is about to do. She hugs me, all hard muscle, saying, 'Looking forward to seeing you in the water.'

There are more people on the beach and most are moving closer to the water's edge, readying themselves for the swim. The chatter and laughter have turned to low, serious muttering. Carina is surrounded by a group of men; she's like a whale shark with its prodigal sons.

Scotty calls everyone towards the spot in front of the two orange start flags. He explains the route and then asks, 'Who's doing it for the first time?'

A show of hands and everybody claps. A group of people sing happy birthday to their friend. Happiness and high spirits abound. The water feels wonderful, there's a little wind, the sky is almost perfectly clear.

connection

Scotty tells us, 'Bronze sharks have been spotted in the bay so if you hear a whistle don't ignore it. Get out the water. Don't be like Carina and her crowd – they just carried on swimming.'

I walk into the water until I'm waist deep. It is clear and small waves move towards shore with the current. Three boats are anchored in the swimming area. Along with the group, I start swimming towards the middle boat, the turquoise one, like we're supposed to. Around me are bright pink, yellow and orange tow floats. We swim crawl, I hear breathing, the sharp, O-shaped intake of air that reminds me of when I swam close to dolphins in Kosi Bay. Humans inhaling sound the same as dolphins inhaling.

There's something about moving through the sea with others – the synchronisation of strokes, the shared exhilaration of water against skin – that transforms swimming from an individual pursuit into something communal, something greater. In a group, the sea feels less vast, the fear less biting. There's a rhythm to it, a sense of unspoken connection that comes from navigating the same currents. In a shared experience we move better and feel stronger. The mental lift is undeniable. With every stroke and kick, I am totally in the present moment.

The water is clear and I can see small long silvery fish swimming beneath me. They don't flutter away, they are used to seeing humans and they are also curious. The current shifts and I turn into it, which makes swimming a little easier. The mountains on the other side of the bay are hazy, the sun has not yet burnt the salt off the air. I'm getting closer to the boat; ahead of me about fifteen swimmers have already circled it. They're fast and want to make good times.

I go around the boat and notice its name squiggled in cursive across the starboard hull: *African Queen*. The smell of coconut sunscreen wafts from it. Having circled the boat, I head towards the grey concrete palisade fence as Scotty instructed. I brush against a kelp stem and then put my hand around it to feel its smooth muscular consistency. The lifesaver in the kayak tells me that there are 40 minutes left and

I decide to do another loop. Fast swimmers come past me, arms and hands slapping the water. I wonder about our place in the water.

We are land creatures, but the water calls to something deeper in us, to a memory written into our bones. On my next breath I slip beneath the surface and pull myself with breaststrokes to better feel the ocean, the release from gravity, and the edges of the world soften. Sounds become muffled, there is a quiet here that doesn't exist on land, a fluid suspension that reminds me that humans were never meant to be so rigid, so fixed in place. In the sea, we are both vulnerable and free, small against the vastness but somehow belonging to it. I feel like I need to take a breath and lift my head. The swimmers move around me, as does the current, unbothered by my presence, and I'm reminded that we've never really owned this space, this vastness we call sea.

I'm close to the boat again, a little too close, and I experience a momentary twinge of fear. Being close to big things in the water is scary because I can be easily mown over. On the boat is a man chatting on his phone. He looks at me and says hello. He's eyeing swimmers curiously. Again, I swim towards the palisade fence. The loop feels different this time around. I'm getting a feel for the currents and accustomed to the other swimmers around me.

At the fence I decide to end my swim and I hang out a bit in the shallows. A woman peels off her cap and sinks into the water to wet her hair. 'The water's lovely,' I quip. She tells me that she once swam in Clifton when the water was 9 °C. Her throat got sore from keeping her neck stretched out the water. 'I was okay but my friend got hypothermia. It was hard for her to move her body and she got confused. Not nice. This is much nicer,' she says.

A man joins the conversation. 'Are you doing the Roman Rock swim?' he asks. There are mumbles of *gosh* and *no*. The Roman Rock swim is an annual, premier event. Participants are taken by boat to the vicinity of the Roman Rock Lighthouse, an iconic structure that was built 160 years ago. The man points to it as he speaks, a white rod in the far distance. From there, they swim back to shore, covering about

5 kilometres. Besides the distance, what makes the race a challenge are the bay's dynamic waters. Swimmers need to be fit, and also able to quell the sense of panic should it arise.

Others have joined the conversation, and we're now a small circle of people dipping in the unusually warm waters of False Bay. 'My brother, Justin Hardcastle, swam 32 kilometres in 12 hours when he was 64 years old. He's the oldest swimmer to cross False Bay from Miller's Point to Rooi Els. He's in the Guinness Book of Records,' says a woman to all of us as we listen in awe. 'The guy doing it with him did it in 14 hours. When they were finished, they were so swollen from all the salt, you know,' she demonstrates pushing her lips out and making her arms wide.

The group breaks up and people make their way to the sand. The air is cooler than the water, so I wade and bob a little longer, taking in the scenery around me. The woman whose brother holds a record says, 'It could almost be Greece.' I agree with her.

The hubbub has moved to the food truck – an attractive matte-grey caravan with wooden finishes. I stand in line and look at the menu – on offer is literally every type of coffee conceivable, made with any type of milk desired. There are also snacks in the form of vegan cookies and toasted sandwiches. My mouth is watering – another anticipatory reflex, much like core body temperature rising and shivering in anticipation of cold.

I spark conversation with Robyn. She's holding a reusable coffee mug and I tell her I think it's great. 'I wish more people would do the same.'

She tells me she went around four times. I tell her I did two. She says, 'I saw you in the water, you were taking it easy but you looked very comfortable.' I take easy to mean slow, and she's not wrong. In the line, people comment about the sharks and the sharp rocks. I wasn't worried about either.

I reach the front of the queue. There are vegan almond croissants, which are apparently addictive. Other pastries are sold out. I order a toasted cheese sandwich and an almond milk decaf cappuccino. While I wait, I chat to two women who've also just done the swim. They're part of the divas group. 'Are you in the divas group?'

I tell them no because I live in Joburg. One of them takes my number and fires a WhatsApp to the administrator to put me on the group. The one named Lisa, tells me they're swimming at Silvermine Dam on Tuesday because there'll be wind, and here at Long Beach on Thursday, should I wish to join them. 'But just come in the morning and you'll see others swimming. Just ask them if you can join.'

The topic of hypothermia comes up again – it seems that it's happened to many swimmers in these parts. This time it's Robyn telling her story. During a swim in the Atlantic, she started feeling really cold and someone said to her, 'Get out now, before you get worse,' and she did. They tell me that you have to get used to cold water. Lisa says that through the winter she and a group of others conditioned themselves to the cold. 'It didn't matter what the weather or the temperature of the water was, we went every day and bobbed for 30 minutes. I even put my head in. People don't usually do that because you get an ice cream headache,' she says.

I asked her if it goes away and she says that she pushed through and it did. 'My body got totally conditioned to the cold water,' she says, smacking the padding of adipose fat on her upper arm. 'That sensation of numbness is beautiful, even your thoughts go numb.'

Lisa shivered for about two hours afterwards and would have a nap in the afternoon. 'Cold water makes you feel really tired, your body works hard,' she says.

They ask me why I live in Joburg. I tell them it's because my whole family lives there, but that I'm deeply pulled to the sea. I tell them about my dad who is a good swimmer and his swims from island to island in Sicily. Lisa reckons that the pull of water is genetic and I agree with her.

We say our goodbyes and I make my way to the mobile sauna. On its side are the words Hot Huts. The door opens and out step six people in swimming costumes glistening with sweat. 'Oh, that was hot!' exclaims

connection

one of them. The mobile sauna is popular. Outside the door is a wooden bucket, like a small wine barrel, filled with water for people to wash their feet in before entering. Clad in white linen, the Hot Huts manager Vanessa tells me that the sauna also goes to St James and Dalebrook tidal pools. They also do full moon evenings, where there is a sound bath.

 Bathing is not limited to dipping in the ocean. There are different ways of loving the sea.

kalk bay

With every drop of water you drink, every breath you take, you're connected to the sea. No matter where on Earth you live.

– Sylvia Earle

I've just parked in a narrow road, next to a wall made of stones, in the shade of a dark-pink bougainvillea. I get out the car, wrap my towel around my waist, pull my goggles over my head and leave my flip flops in the driver's footwell. I walk down to Main Road in St James and, on the way, I greet a woman who's clearly just had a swim. Her hair and costume are wet and post-swim bliss rests calmly across her face. As she moves her arms rhythmically with her gait, her movements are soft. Behind her, the ocean is soft. She is an echo of the sea. Being in water softens us. Its fluid nature flows when it is contained. As a river it flows along the veins of the earth both wide and narrow and erodes pathways for itself so that it can meet the sea. Tidal pools offer containment both for water and humans.

It's a perfect day in January when the air is just right – not humid and not dry, but that comfortable place in between. Along Main Road there is pedestrian and motor traffic. Cafés are buzzing with people, food, waiters, chatter, music. At a zebra crossing I cross to the ocean-side. I see Vanessa and her Hot Huts sauna, and people waiting their turn to sweat. She shows me the way to Dalebrook Tidal Pool, a place that so many people have told me so much about and where photographer and recreational swimmer Oscar Guttierez swims regularly.

connection

There is a short tunnel under the railway tracks – painted white, it echoes with the footsteps and chatter of people coming and going. In the tunnel I pause for a moment to look at a small intricately rendered mural of mermaids.

The tunnel opens to a rocky shore and the ocean beyond. A group of twenty-something-year-olds lie on towels, their faces turned to the sun like sunflowers. A middle-aged man pokes between the rocks with a stick. I wonder what he's looking for or if he's lost something. There is another mural on the wall that supports the train tracks – a big heart symbol with the words *Our hearts belong to the ocean* painted in its centre.

To the left is Dalebrook Tidal Pool. There are groups of people hanging out, some are tanning, others are sipping on frozen coffees from a café across the road. A naked baby, barely a toddler, cries at the cool contrast of the water as his mother, holding him under the arms, dips him carefully. At the edge of the pool, a woman sits and dangles her feet in the water – head down, she's contemplating life, absorbed in her own dilemma. It's a safe place for her – surrounded by people, by the sea, but left alone to just be. Three teenagers lean against the oceanside wall looking out at the sea. One laughs at something his friend says – the sound peals through the air, louder than the rumble of traffic.

The scene could be a painting. The composition of people and inanimate objects – bags, towels, clothing, folding chairs – is balanced and artistic. The area is smaller than I imagined, and clearly popular, but I manage to find space for my towel on a rock. I enter the water and it's not as cold as I thought it would be – that, or my body is getting used to cooler temperatures. Goggles on, I go under and join another world. Red seaweed covers rocky surfaces, swaying with the undulating subsurface current. I follow a shoal of small silvery fish – they are used to the arms and legs and sounds of humans, and their movements aren't urgent. Bigger fish catch my eye and I want to point and say *look!*

I lift my head to take a new breath. 'How big are the fish?' asks a man who is in hip deep.

'Quite big, actually.' I show him with my hands, a foot apart.

'Ah, you remembered your goggles. I didn't,' he replies. I love the small talk and banter: being at a tidal pool, a public area, gives everyone common ground and makes you feel like you're part of a subculture. I point out the fish to him.

I take a breath and put my face in again. I hear conversations around me but my focus is on the fish. I've just overheard someone saying they're mullets. I observe their travels as they flutter in between rocks and poke their mouths into tiny holes, biting on microalgae and detritus. My ears are above the meniscus and I follow the commentary, learning that mullets also feed on small invertebrates like worms, larvae and crustaceans.

I feel the need to inhale and again I lift my head. 'Yoh, it's cold,' someone remarks. To me it's still comfortable. The tidal pool offers access to seawater while protecting swimmers and dippers from the unpredictability of the open sea. I'm here on my own, but I don't feel lonely. Here, I don't feel separate from nature. The fish observe me as just another creature in their environment. I'm part of the bigger element of water, and it feels like most of the people around me are experiencing it like they are part of it, too. People look happy and purposeful – their burdens and worries made lighter by the sea.

Across the road is the community centre, which dates back to 1908. Behind it and other buildings are the mountains – steep and covered in fynbos. Dalebrook Tidal Pool was constructed in 1907, a year prior to the community centre, making it one of Cape Town's oldest tidal pools. A number of them were built on the ruins of Khoisan fish traps, like the nearby St James Tidal Pool.

The sea is interwoven in local and colonised histories. It bears witness to the changing patterns of human society. It means something different to everyone. Both the presence and the absence of it is built into our histories. The water in our bodies is fully replaced about seventeen times every year. Somewhere along this flow of water, the sea makes its way into our bodies. If one lives in the same place that one's ancestors lived in, I imagine this would fortify one's connection to place, especially if that place is coastal.

Many times, while walking on a beach in South Africa – in the Western Cape in particular, as I'm the first person in my family to walk on these beaches – it's so apparent to me that I am creating footsteps in a place where my ancestors have never set foot. It's a strange sensation – it feels like displacement, like I am somewhere I am not supposed to be. For a long time, I lived with one figurative foot in Sicily and the other in South Africa, my country of birth. It is only with immersing myself in a place, in the oceans of South Africa, that I feel a part of it, that I feel it is part of my story.

As I look around, I see traces of Khoisan and Indonesian in the faces of some of the people at the tidal pool. We carry our stories and histories on our bodies, just as the sea holds our histories, and the stories of everything on this planet.

Chris Krauss of Sea the Bigger Picture suggested I visit Olympia Café to look at a photo exhibition curated by Traci Kwaai – a sixth-generation fisher child from Kalk Bay and an activist who leads the 'walk of remembrance' tour that recounts the history of her community. I go there. On a wall are photographs of families who've lived in the area for several generations and have lived off the ocean. The exhibition is titled 'The Sea is in our Blood'. Under the apartheid government's Group Areas Act, many of the fishing families were forcibly moved to the Cape Flats and Traci's exhibition wants to remind people that Kalk Bay was a fishing community. She doesn't want her heritage to be erased.

I'm curious about the history of the area, so I drive down Main Road, still congested with traffic, to Simon's Town and park near the white church adjacent to the museum. Inside, there is a video playing of Shamier Magmoet in his well-known documentary *Rise from the Cape Flats*. On one of the walls is a large poster explaining how tidal pools were once used by coastal hunter-gatherers as fish traps. For thousands of years these communities, especially Khoisan groups, gathered stones and built walls in intertidal zones to trap fish that were brought in by high tide. The intertidal zones are the areas where ocean meets land, that are exposed during low tide and covered in water during high tide. It was easy then to grab fish by hand, or to spear or club them. Some of the oldest fish traps in South Africa, dating back 2 000 years, are along the coast of Stilbaai. Remnants of ancient fish traps also mark the coastlines of Agulhas and Arniston.

Water connects us across time and across generations. It is in our blood and in the rest of the trillions of cells that make up a human body. We need water to stay alive. Our skin is waterproof but also porous, which means air and fluids can pass through it. As I look at the artist's rendition of hunter-gatherers, I imagine legs in water and hands open, ready to pounce on a fat fish, the skins of both creatures sensing movement. Hands fast, grabbing onto the fish, holding tight against its flapping body, its scales simultaneously rough and smooth. Hands lifting the fish out the water, its mouth opening and closing, gills straining for air.

I chat to the young woman at the front desk. She tells me she's doing her doctorate on bones – the remains of British colonists, to be precise. 'I'm tired of Europeans looking at the bones of my people, so I'm looking at theirs,' she explains.

I ask her if she could tell me about the history of the fishers and the hunter-gatherers, and she directs me to another museum down the road – Amlay House Heritage Museum. At ground level the house is a museum, and upstairs it is home to Sheribeen Amlay's aunt. Each room of the museum holds a fascination of objects – antique everyday crockery, embroidered tablecloths, a pedal sewing machine, furniture from the early 1900s, and newspaper clippings and photographs on the walls. Sheribeen is eager to tell me about the history of his people. 'Many of our forefathers came from Indonesia, so they understood how to read the sea and knew the life cycles of the fish – depending on the season they knew which fish to catch, and which fish spawned where. This is why the brown people of Simon's Town are such good fishers,' he tells me.

I tell him about what I've learnt from Melissa Ilardo, the geneticist who found that the spleens of the Bajau of Indonesia were much bigger than those of other human populations. A result of genetic adaptation over a few thousand years, the Bajaus' physiology has adapted to prolonged exposure to diving, their ease in the ocean influenced by culture and necessity. We discuss and wonder if, centuries ago, a few Bajau made their way to the Cape, and to Simon's Town in particular, and if Melissa would find the same larger-than-most spleens in their descendants here. I'm guessing she probably would.

History is contentious. What we choose to forget is as important as what we choose to remember. South Africa's colonised history makes the narrative even more antagonistic. The sea has seen the movement of slaves across its currents, the demarcation of borders and boundaries, gentrification, and the shaping of cultural and individual identities.

Sheribeen's stories stick to me. They are heavy and angry. I need to breathe. Outside, the wide neutral sky offers respite. The shrill of insects and the tweeting of birds reminds me that nature doesn't care about our histories.

inheriting the ocean

In the depths of the sea,
the spirits of the ancient ones sing,
their songs rising with the foam
to touch the living with their wisdom.
— From *The Kalevala*, translated by John Martin Crawford

Charlotte Scott is grateful for the sea. It has always been central to her life. As a child, she would holiday on its shores with her family. It is central to her work. It has helped her heal. The sea holds the wisdom to heal. Many people know this. If only more of us would listen.

As I go deeper into researching the effects of climate change on our aquatic environments, I see that there are many points of view. There are denialists who believe that climate change is taking its natural course and that its fast progression is not because of industrialisation or the number of cows releasing gases into the air, that humans have not accelerated it, that we have less impact on the planetary system than we think, that the natural disasters we are experiencing on Earth are caused by changes in the orbit of Saturn around the sun. But largely, there is consensus among scientists that the climate crisis is self-inflicted.

For Charlotte, natural change as the Earth goes through its cycles is good. But the changes linked to human action are detrimental. She feels this as she snorkels in the pristine seascapes of Marine Protected Areas (MPAs). She sees the changes in fish populations especially.

Charlotte works for an NGO based in Cape Town called South-SouthNorth. She is a programme manager and the Global Engagement and Learning lead for the NGO in the Voices for Just Climate Action Alliance. She is also working on a PhD exploring the ways in which amplifying the local knowledge and voices of fishers can shape better policy and ocean governance.

She talks to fishers and communities whose livelihoods depend on the ocean. She sees firsthand how the changes in the sea affect everyone. Every day she delves further into the cumulative impact of climate change, oil and gas exploration, deep-sea mining and overfishing. In her work she supports activists and NGOs advocating for climate justice and locally led climate action as part of an alliance that sweeps across seven countries – Tunisia, Kenya, Zambia, Indonesia, Brazil, Paraguay and Bolivia.

Charlotte was born in Cape Town and grew up camping along its coastline. She has always been close to the sea, both physically and metaphorically. It is little wonder that she pursued a path in the environmental economics of the ocean. She is in the sea often, either swimming in its velvet waves or snorkelling. The experience of being in water is wonderful but also bittersweet. 'I often have the feeling of who knows how long we'll have all these beautiful creatures. I feel like we should really appreciate what we've got while we've got it – take it in, this lovely biome, because a future generation may not see it,' she tells me.

Her reverence for the ocean grew when she was a student at the University of Cape Town. She joined the university's Underwater Club. What she experienced the first time she went below the surface was magic. 'It may sound corny, but it was me seeing a fish and a fish seeing me. There was a sense of being in their world and them seeing us. One species knowing another.'

It's human nature to take things for granted when they feel so plentiful, when fridges in supermarkets are filled with boxed fish, when you don't deal with the reality of a situation firsthand. And yet all over the world, each fishing and sea foraging community is facing a unique blow to their livelihood because of a decrease in fish populations and increasing bureaucratic regulations.

Charlotte is matter of fact. Small-scale fishers and fishing communities have often been excluded from the ocean, despite fishing being a part of their cultural heritage and a key source of livelihood for many. She believes that communities can integrate a different approach that is sustainable and lower-impact, and run with it quite quickly – whether it's catching a different fish species and making it attractive for restaurants and local markets, or locally determined fishing closures, or something else. But integrating that into the bureaucratic government processes that have largely been designed for commercial export markets is difficult.

'Bureaucracy doesn't allow for quick, flexible change. With changes in climate and fish stocks, regulation needs to adapt and adjust quickly for good results, and this is not happening,' says Charlotte.

Charlotte would love to see the design of a better governance system that can navigate and integrate these changes. A system that, instead of being top-down, takes into account what is happening on the ground and at sea and gives local communities a voice. 'Regulations come out as they come out and communities have to live with that.'

Ill-fitting regulations affect everything from legal trade to safety when out at sea. As fish stock reduces, small-scale fishers go out even further, putting themselves at risk. Fewer fish to sell means that there is less money for safety gear. As fishing seasons shift, there is more pressure to go out to sea on days when the seas are rough, something that would not have happened as often in the past.

The Earth's landscapes are varied, coastlines and their biomes adapt to their particular weather patterns; people have relationships with the sea and the food it provides. There is profound beauty in all of this. But the ocean has been politicised. It is rife with historical trauma. Issues of ownership and access are plentiful. There is no one-size-fits-all solution. This is where Charlotte's expertise enters the picture.

Her work centres on localised climate adaptation, blending science and research with local knowledge and locally led approaches. Adapting fishing practices in ways that are more tailored to place work better for all elements of the ecosystem, humans included. Examples of this are the fishing communities in Indonesia that are trying to maintain traditional methods, such as setting their own fishing closure times, to protect the fish they rely on.

MPAs are highly contentious. The clash between customary rights and protecting resources under law is ongoing. Integrating fishers and sea harvesters within MPA governance is challenging. The legitimacy of the MPAs rests on the ability to engage with the community. Historically, relationships have been adversarial and bad blood prevails. For Charlotte, the question is: how do you repair trust?

'In 2019 there was a big push for newly declared MPAs with a focus on biomes in open water. Near the border of Namibia there is a fossilised yellowwood forest in the Atlantic Ocean, which is now protected in a new MPA. It's important that we are able to protect vulnerable and unique ecosystems like these. But the narrative at the time was that these new MPAs were selected with the aim of not creating conflicts with industry. But for genuine resilience, we can't rely on setting aside a tiny portion of the ocean, while continuing business as usual in the rest.' Charlotte holds my gaze for a beat longer, letting this sink in.

MPAs allow sea life to flourish. Fish become resilient, growing fatter, more fertile and having more females in shoals – the 3Fs necessary for healthy populations. For Charlotte, snorkelling in an MPA versus in an unprotected area is chalk and cheese.

'I dive in a site in Castle Rock, which is part of a no-take zone. I see whole schools of stumpnose, whereas in other areas I may see one. I've been diving since 2011 and I've definitely seen a decline in certain species. What has changed is the diversity of fish, there's a lot less diversity now.'

The sea runs in Charlotte's veins. Like the fishers she communes with, her days fall into rhythm with the tides. She can't be away from the coast for long; it affects her mood and her outlook. She too benefits from the water – the sea heals her. At a time in her life when work and life were not in balance, she developed chronic pain. She began swimming in the cold waves of Clifton Beach. The pain subsided and eventually disappeared. 'It gave me a new appreciation for how the sea is really healing. It was the whole experience of it – leaving the city, being immersed in a totally water-based environment and being transported for a moment to another universe where there are no emails and you can't be reached by anyone. You can't think about other things, your response is to survive, so you are very, very present.'

She tends not to talk about the experience, perhaps because it changed her life. She's still trying to figure it out. After going from doctor to doctor and taking anti-inflammatories, it was the sea that healed her. Her physiotherapist has applied the theory that the body remembers pain; it becomes etched into nerve memory, so you feel it over and over.

As Charlotte swam in the frigid water, her whole body experienced pain, moving the focus away from the chronic ache and resetting the pain receptors in her brain. Cold water was a way of cleansing her nervous system of pain debris.

Now she only swims in the Atlantic Ocean as she finds the water of False Bay 'not cold enough'. Laughing, she refers to it as an addiction. She's a strong swimmer and so is her mother. In 2022 they both completed the Robben Island swim.

'Being in nature affects our brain and how we experience life. Life feels different and we process things differently. Being underwater is like being in a science fiction world with creatures that are beautiful and super-weird and colourful,' Charlotte muses.

The way we regulate and protect the ocean doesn't always allow for these complex relationships we have with it. The way we measure the ocean is often in the number of fish available, barrels of oil to be exploited or the square kilometers protected. MPAs protect nature but at the same time limit access and disempower communities who rely on these ocean spaces. They take the sea away from some people and give it to others.

Charlotte's work helps to facilitate communication between communities and bureaucracy. 'I hope we're able to build a system that sees us as intimately connected to the ocean, and gives local communities a say in how they want to care for it, as they know it deeply.'

What Charlotte aims for through her work and her ocean swims is balance, and evolution. Nature evolves, and we should too.

Loyiso Dunga is in Dar es Salaam for the Marine Regions Forum, a conference for marine conservationists to discuss how best to navigate ocean sustainability. He is young, passionate, outspoken, fierce in his opinions; his face open and strong. His short dreadlocks remind me of branching coral.

The word 'sustainability' has been bandied around for years, picked up by beauty brands and celebrities, and I do wonder how it all ties together, how every person's actions are contributing to sustainability or not. How widespread is awareness? Who is more at risk? Who is more at fault? This is the thought process swirling around my head as I wait for Loyiso to answer the door of his hotel room before he returns to the Zoom frame.

'I'm just an ocean lover; that's the heart of it. I'm deeply inspired by the ocean, I revere it, I'm curious about it.' Loyiso is compelled to protect what he calls a powerful and inspiring environment.

As we converse, he from a neutral-toned room and me in rainy Umhlanga, Loyiso explains that he's a marine biologist whose love for the sea was ignited when, over eight months, he mapped the kelp forests on the west and southern coasts of South Africa. It was an opportunity to spend large amounts of time taking in and contemplating the tall kelp plants swaying in the currents. The lush underwater forests reminded him of the forest where he grew up, in the village of Nqabara Ntubeni in the Eastern Cape. Curious, he started snorkelling just to see what was below the surface. He joined groups and snorkelled with other people. He did field trip work in False Bay. 'The experience completely changed my journey,' says Loyiso, who refers to himself as 'the kelp hugger'. He went from being afraid of the ocean to wanting to protect it.

He found himself enchanted by the ocean and he was compelled to stay in that blue space. Passionate about his purpose of directing marine education and outreach programmes, his body language is intentional, shoulders square and back upright. He strikes me as being a protector and a warrior, a man who has his entire ancestral lineage behind him, encouraging him. As he delved deeper into his exploration, he was drawn to the lack of community intervention in MPAs. 'The community link interested me a lot. Ocean protection is without my community, and if I focus on changing this, I know I'm going to be fulfilled even more. If we design and monitor and manage MPAs with communities, they will be more effective.

'The very clear thing is that my community has a relationship with the ocean, has been sustained by it – they fish, mussels and food comes from the ocean. It is this big garden that sustains us. It provides different animals for healing and medicinal value. We use the sea for ritual and traditional activities. It has healing and cleansing properties. The ocean has the ability to spit out anything that is dirty, that it doesn't want.

'The stark difference is that my people can't do this now. This resonates with all the coastal communities I'm meeting. The way of life with the ocean has been severed.'

Based in Khayelitsha, Loyiso meets with small-scale fishing groups between St Helena Bay and Betty's Bay to find solutions that suit everyone. 'The communities want to be a part of the creation of Marine Protected Areas. They say: let's talk, let's sit around a table and see how best we can do this.'

At the conference, he is representing the South African National Biodiversity Institute (SANBI). 'We only have one ocean. You cannot erect fences and walls. Whatever happens upstream comes downstream. The ocean connects us immensely, we need to be coordinated.'

connection

What Loyiso wants to see is dialogue between scientists and indigenous people. 'Africans particularly, they have developed customary principles, norms and traditions. Ubuntu is about I am because we are. If I take care of my neighbour, my neighbour takes care of me. When you cut a tree it's like cutting a patch of your hair, it's like scarring a part of your body. By damaging the sea, we are choking ourselves. We need that wisdom to guide us if we are to develop effective strategies.'

Loyiso wants to understand the forests of the oceans as a promise to his ancestors and to future generations. In marine environments in many parts of the world, kelp forests are changing and some are degrading. He wants to keep the ocean pristine and maintain ecological balance. His ancestors understood the rhythm of nature and the seasons, understood that it was not necessary to take more than was needed. The paradigm was one of abundance for everyone.

I want to further understand what binds us to the sea, so I chat to Zolani Mahola, a performer, producer and singer who goes by the name of 'The One Who Sings'. 'I've just had a swim at Cosy Bay, which is in Oudekraal. I swam to Seal Island, which is a good little swim – nice and playful,' she tells me as she brushes her hands nimbly through her short hair.

Cosy Bay is also known as Sandy Cove, a secluded beach on Victoria Road on Cape Town's Atlantic Seaboard. Zolani loves to swim and she tells me that she took to the water with surprising ease. From her home in Cape Town, Oudekraal is easy to get to and it's cold enough to give her a buzz. It's become her habitual swimming spot. I ask her if she swims regularly and she tells me that she uses it as a barometer for her health and her headspace. If she's in good swing, she'll swim three times a week. If she's not doing well, she's generally not spending time in the sea. On the shelves behind her are photos of her young sons.

Zolani is fresh faced and petite with alert eyes. She was the lead singer of Afro-fusion band Freshlyground for 17 years and is the producer of the podcast 'Back to the Water'. She created the podcast with her friend Pippa Ehrlich and it won them the Independent Nonfiction Audio Storytelling Award at the Tribeca Film Festival in 2024. The podcast showcases the relationship that people in South Africa have with the ocean. One of the first things she tells me is that she sees kelp as an embodiment of her ancestors.

In 2020, Craig Foster of the Sea Change Project commissioned her to capture the song of the sea, asking her to produce a sea forest anthem with renowned French–American cellist Yo-Yo Ma. Yo-Yo Ma has been a United Nations Messenger of Peace since 2006, and he uses his music to link culture to nature, promoting unity and environmental awareness. Through his musical projects and performances, he highlights our common responsibility in protecting the planet. 'The whole reason Craig took me on that first dive was for me to really listen and open myself to the underwater environment and catch the song.'

Zolani remembers it as a clear day with the sun shining when Craig took her and Aron Halevi, her collaborator from Freshlyground, to the kelp forest off Miller's Point. The water was remarkably clear. Before entering they did a small ritual – they prayed to all the ancestors asking permission to enter the underwater environment, and thanked the ocean. The way Craig opened the experience with ceremony paved the way for Zolani's reverence for the sea, as a place that both humbles her and gives her sanctity. Zolani's first wandering through the kelp forest set the stage for what would become the nature of her relationship with the aquatic environment. 'It felt like a welcome home, it was so familiar and yet at the same time so new. That first immersion had a massive impact on me,' she says.

Craig taught her to open to the natural world and to listen with her whole body, not just her ears. So, she listened with the fundamental idea that we are not separate from nature. The idea was to create a composition that embodied the spirit and sounds of the sea forest. The song was, quite aptly, to be titled 'Song of the Silent Forest'.

During that first dive, melodies came to her and she was catching songs. It fascinates me how human creativity is piqued when there is newness and the skin feels something unfamiliar but pleasant. Zolani was in the sea, floating, her feet not touching ground, flying through the kelp forest vertically when music came to her. 'I remember the feeling of coming out of the water and feeling that giddy, cold, drunk feeling that people talk about. I had to keep getting back into the water.'

For the recording of the song, she and the other collaborators collected things from the sea that could be used as instruments – abalone shells, dried kelp and shark eggs for their rattling sound.

On his visit to South Africa, Yo-Yo Ma arrived at Craig Foster's house where Zolani and the others working on the project were eagerly waiting. 'Yo-Yo Ma came and we all performed the song. The late traditional Xhosa musician Madosini played with us, it was extraordinary and very potent,' describes Zolani.

Madosini played her bows, which are traditional instruments, and they had a conversation with Yo-Yo as to how the bows are a precursor to the cello. They could imagine someone hundreds of years ago beginning to play with the gut or the hair of an animal and making music. For Zolani the connection between Madosini's ancient wisdom and what Yo-Yo Ma was bringing with his stringed instrument drew a beautiful continuum.

Yo-Yo then played the song live on his cello, accompanied by the recorded track, for the United Nations' 75th anniversary celebrations in October 2020. The livestreamed concert was broadcast from the GBH Fraser Performance Studio in Boston in the US.

Zolani reconnected with her Xhosa roots and the rituals and beliefs that she had been privy to as a child when her father returned to the lore of his Xhosa heritage. 'That wildness is our birthright and it's our heritage and it's in our DNA. It's something so deeply ancestral, like it's in my pores and in my genes.'

As an adult she didn't have a personal connection with ancestry until she found it in the sea. It opened that channel again, and all the knowledge that her father passed down to her came back to her.

As she interacted with the sea, particularly when she was by herself, the connection deepened.

Now, before Zolani enters the water, she calls the lineage of her ancestors. She describes this as part of being informed by those who came before her, and it informs who she is. The ocean also informs her of where we are as people and as a species, as a collective. She hopes that we can treat it with sanctity so that we don't abuse, pollute or harm it.

But so many children live in conditions of squalor with no guidance from parental figures. The urgency is survival, so there's little or no sense of 'I need to take care of my world' when you're struggling to take care of yourself. 'They grow up in a township where there's sewage in the streets and rubbish dumps at every corner. The more we can expose our children to big natural spaces like the sea, the better,' urges Zolani.

'The song, where can I listen to it?' I ask.

'We have it, it exists, but we haven't released it yet.'

Stefaan Braam, an abalone poacher turned commercial diver, was born in Hout Bay and grew up with his grandparents. His grandfather was a fisherman so from him he gathered the moods of the sea. Stefaan learnt to freedive when he was 13 years old to catch abalone – to help himself, his family and whomever he could. 'With the money I earned I could buy myself clothes and food, and help my grandmother. I had a wetsuit, flippers and goggles, me and a couple of friends went after school to see if we could get some crayfish, limpets, off the rocks. At that time there was a market for abalone and me and my friends made money from it. When I was 14, I got caught by a police helicopter, we paid a fine.'

Stefaan continued to dive on weekends and public holidays to make some money when he was not at school. 'One of my grandma's wishes for me was to finish my matric. I honoured the wish and stopped diving for a year to focus on my matric certificate.

'Then when a guy turns 18, he thinks he's big, a grown up. I went full blast into black operation. I was making R5 000 to R35 000 a night, and using it to build my house. We went to Slangkop. Most of the coastline from Miller's Point, Cape Point, I was there. It's an easy shore entry at low tide. You look for a nice spot and see what you can find. Sometimes we went a little bit longer, a bakkie would pick us up and we'd go out in a rubber duck. Diving down and coming up with abalone would take a minute or two, you don't need a lot of breath if you know what you're doing. There were a few of us who knew about diving; line fishermen who knew where to find stuff.

'White people asked about abalone because there was a lot of it. We'd get abalone for them, and they gave crayfish to us. They knew the value, not us. We figured our own way. This was happening before apartheid, the whites were already busy a long time ago. They were busy taking abalone and my people would help them. They would chase a guy like me all over the place but then took for themselves,' says Stefaan.

The harvesting of abalone (*Haliotis miladae*), also known as perlemoen, in South Africa has a long history. At Blombos Cave, which is located near Stilbaai and has been an archaeological site for many years, excavations in 2008 revealed two abalone shells that date back to 100 000 years ago. They were part of an ochre processing workshop and researchers speculate that the abalone shells were used as containers for an ochre-rich, liquefied pigment that was probably used as skin protection and decoration. Along with ochre, bone, charcoal, grindstones and hammerstones were also found. This tells us that abalone has been harvested, used and probably eaten by people in South Africa for millennia. This finding in particular tells us that these molluscs, which are highly desirable today, were used for purposes beyond consumption.

Abalone shells have also been found in shell middens. Middens are large accumulations of shellfish debris, some dating back thousands and others hundreds of years. At the Klasies River Caves near Nature's Valley, between Humansdorp and Tsitsikamma, where the river winds its way into the Indian Ocean of the Eastern Cape, researchers have discovered shell middens dating back to approximately 120 000 years ago. Those at Klasies River Caves are among the oldest known in the world, and provide interesting insights into the resources that these anatomically modern *Homo sapiens* utilised. In the middens, researchers found a variety of marine shells, including abalone, indicating that gathering shellfish for eating and for symbolic and decorative use was a big part of their lives.

There is a link between eating shellfish and socio-biological advances in *Homo sapiens* who lived about 100 000 to 20 000 years ago, a period also referred to as the Middle Stone Age. It has been theorised that the fatty acids from shellfish provided significant nutritional benefits to early modern human populations on the coast.

Jump back to the present day, and I'm on a call with Anton Kruger, a commercial abalone diver and founder of the Commercial Abalone Divers Facebook group. Abalone has been part of South Africa's coastal diet for millennia and I'm keen to know what abalone trade is like for a commercial abalone diver.

From our conversation, I gather that the harvesting of abalone in South African waters and the rapacious desire for this mollusc in the Far East has created a flood of criminal activity that is seemingly out of control because certain stakeholders are being assisted in rule-breaking activities by people in the Department of Forestry, Fisheries and the Environment (DFFE). This corruption is exacerbated when officials confiscate tons of abalone and then sell it on and keep the earnings for themselves. In the early 2000s, a marine biologist employed by the department – Angus McKenzie – went to key sites to evaluate abalone colonies. He would literally count stock. The results were specific and there were regulations governing how much abalone could be taken from each zone.

This strategy helped abalone, in the zones where numbers were low, to reproduce. On his passing, Angus was never replaced. No one is checking, and harvesting practices today are not durable. 'These days, everyone is harvesting at Robben Island and this is simply not sustainable,' Anton emphasises.

Anton is in Hermanus and through his phone I can hear the sounds of cars and the chatter of people. His concern is about many aspects of abalone commerce, but is rooted in the sustainability of colonies that have diminished rapidly over the years. Divers are plunging to 16 metres just to find a few, sometimes only one.

Abalone was unregulated until the 1960s, when what was the Department of Fisheries introduced the first quota for the commercial sector. With a total quota of 2 000 tons per year, harvesters were taking out huge amounts, with recreational harvesting increasing the take to 3 000 tons per year. This was not feasible. In 1986 the quota was lowered to 640 tons per year, with an individual quota set at about 20 tons per year and recreational allowance at 1 000 tons per year. In the 1990s it was further reduced in response to declining abalone stocks and increased illegal poaching.

The approved total allowable catch (TAC) for 2025 is 41,6 tons. As Anton tells me these numbers, it is glaringly obvious how quickly this resource, which has been a part of people's daily diet and life, has been depleted. Anton doesn't agree with the new quota as he believes it is inflated and unsustainable. He is worried about the Robben Island abalone colonies because both commercial divers and poachers are taking massive amounts from them. 'Already at this stage both poachers and commercial abalone divers scour an area until they find a patch that's been overlooked and then clear it out.'

These patches are often functioning breeding colonies and there can be a hundred big abalone – which can weigh up to 100 kg – packed into an area of two square metres. It's easy for people to harvest every last one of them. Abalone need to be next to each other to reproduce as fertilisation occurs externally, and if they're not close enough this can't happen. 'I see a few geriatric abalone in hotspots, but no young abalone. It tells me they're not breeding,' Anton confirms.

When Anton goes diving for the mollusc, he combs the entire area around his boat. 'I search as far as my air line goes, then my crew pull me back in and I do the same in another direction. When I was on the Cape Peninsula, I only harvested a handful of abalone doing this. It just shows you how little they are reproducing.'

Anton is pushing for a rehabilitation method to be put in place. He'd like to do this through a densification process in Onrus River where the abalone are moved closer together so they can multiply. Private security would watch over the abalone and keep them safe from poachers. He would then implement abalone ranching by taking spat (young abalone just after the larval stage) from farms and placing each one by hand in the ocean – in crevices, between rocks and under sea urchins, where they can be safe and left for three to five years to grow. It would entail getting funding for the first three years. The way he sees it, the eventual harvesting would then cover the costs of this ambitious project.

I ask him if commercial abalone diving is worth the time, effort, overheads and laborious administration. He tells me that a few years ago a diver could get R1 000 per kilogram, but today a kilogram will earn the same diver R650. Anton's dad was a commercial abalone diver in the 1960s and, in those days, he was paid 10c per gutted and out-of-the-shell kilogram. It was about 1986 when abalone started being marketed to the Far East, increasing the demand and bringing a surge in poaching. By 2006, poaching, along with corruption within the DFFE was rampant and the newly upgraded Hawston Harbour had become a poaching hotspot.

Large gangs from the Eastern Cape began entering the illegal fray and by the time Covid hit in 2019 poaching was completely out of hand. Zones were so depleted that Anton remembers finding a mere 19 abalone in six hours of diving off Pearly Beach in the Overberg. By 2023, other areas had become depleted and Anton remembers how he picked seven abalone during a six-hour dive between Hangklip and Rooi Els, in the Kogelberg Biosphere Reserve in the Western Cape. The numbers in that area were so dangerously low that the department closed it to harvesting.

connection

As I listen to Anton explain the red tape required, I realise that there are numerous steps in the abalone harvesting process: getting a quota, placing phone calls to officials, filling out catch records in triplicate, supplying satellite signals to show your location, counting and weighing the catch. It sounds watertight, as if it should prevent illegal activities, but it doesn't.

When I ask him whether he eats abalone, he tells me no, because numbers and weights are all agreed upon beforehand with the buyer, so there is nothing left for him. 'You make a deal and you don't touch any of that abalone, it gets exported to the East.'

For him, the mollusc and the harvesting of it are threaded through two generations. While his father never acquired a taste for it, Anton did. As he reminisces about its texture and flavour there's nostalgia and a longing in his voice. While for many it is a delicacy, for Anton it was a regular part of his diet and he used to eat it grilled, steamed, or cooked in a potjie with cream, served over rice. While his life is intricately entangled with that of the shellfish, he can no longer enjoy it on his plate.

He misses it.

Dylan McGarry chats to me from his home in Kalk Bay. He has just returned from a trip to India and tomorrow he is off to hike in the Cederberg, so his day is packed with meetings. Still, he makes time. Dylan is South African Country Director with One Ocean Hub and Senior Researcher at the Environmental Learning Research Centre at the university currently known as Rhodes. With long academic studies in both fine art and science, he's at the intersection of creativity and marine knowledge. His demeanour is calm; he inhabits life, his life, with his entire being. While there are people who seem scattered, their attention fragmented, Dylan is all here.

We get onto the topic of sea mammals and the project that is decoding sperm whale communication – Project CETI (Cetacean Translation Initiative). This international initiative brings together people from various disciplines and their mission is ambitious and broad – a study of the patterns, tones and frequencies of whale sounds that will enable a translation of their language.

It's the first time that whales and humans will be able to converse, the first proper interspecies communication. It's a big deal, like discovering an enormous trove of treasure at the bottom of the sea. It is profound. It opens up a world, a universe, that we only really have a glimpse of now. Whales are at the top of their food chain, and we are at the top of ours. The large size of their brains means that they have emotional depth. Unlocking their intelligence could change how humans behave towards animals, for the better.

The ocean is whale home, it's what keeps them alive. Being able to understand them will give us new perspective on their interactions with each other and other species. Do they ever get lonely? How do they feel about pollution? How do they decide on migratory patterns? What are their favourite flavours? How do they love the sea? I wonder about how they feel the water, the subtle gradients of emotion, sexual desire, hunger. I would ask so many questions, but I'm aware that they'd be from a human point of view. My approach would already be flawed. But being able to talk to animals, really talk to them, is a dream come true for many. For me too.

I can see how understanding the effects of hunting, captivity, infringing on their territory and destroying their habitat will make their trials seem more human. Project CETI will give animals a voice in court, bringing them directly into our legal system. As we've done before, it's a way of humanising animals. But if I understand you and you understand me, if we speak the same language, we will have more respect for each other.

There is a lot going on behind the scenes in terms of animal rights, the rights of nature, communication between governments and civil society, and conferences discussing the protocols and procedures that would be most effective. I hope that the project will draw more curiosity and respect for the creatures of the sea, and more love for blue spaces.

Dylan agrees: 'It's where ocean heritage and multi-species communication coincide.'

Dylan has always been connected to the sea. 'I come from a long line of sailors and freedivers. My brother's a sailor. I learnt to freedive very young, and growing up in Durban we would surf. That's my cultural heritage. My uncle was a lifesaver and we did all that kind of stuff.'

It strikes me that Dylan is wearing a T-shirt the colour of a stormy Indian Ocean. He tells me that in 2019 he landed a global project, One Ocean Hub, which he co-directed with Elisa Morgera, who was then Professor of Global Environmental Law at the University of Strathclyde and is now the UN Special Rapporteur on Human Rights and Climate Change. She and Dylan had both worked with communities and conservation, and Dylan was familiar with the history in South Africa where people have been forcibly removed from their land in the name of conservation, so directing One Ocean Hub was a perfect fit. 'Colonialism and conservation are deeply entangled in this country,' he says. 'Conservation was often used as an excuse to treat people badly.'

So, Dylan and Elisa, together with other colleagues, formed a team of 180 researchers in five countries. 'We ran One Ocean Hub over five years. It was really trying to understand how to make better decisions around the ocean that are more inclusive and that really take into consideration not just the marine science, but culture and heritage and history and colonialism.'

They brought together artists, traditional healers, lawyers, marine scientists, economists, sociologists and people from other disciplines in Namibia, South Africa, Ghana, the Solomon Islands in the South Pacific and islands in the Caribbean to work on five different projects. Dylan led the ocean heritage one.

They were also involved with the court case in which fishers and activists stopped Shell's plans for seismic blasting off the Wild Coast. This victory was seen as a win for environmental protection and community rights. 'They won based on heritage and it was the first time in court in South Africa that the ancestors in the ocean were recognised,' says Dylan.

Dylan explains that for many people of Nguni descent – Xhosa, Sotho, Zulu, Tswana, even Venda communities and some Khoi and San communities – the ancestors are believed to be in rivers and in the ocean. 'The ocean is a sacred site, but it's also a site of necropolitics. We need to commemorate that.'

In a chapter that Dylan co-wrote with Buhle Francis for *Hydrofeminist Thinking with Oceans*, titled 'Grandmothers of the Sea: Stories and lessons from five Xhosa ocean elders', Gogo Nomalibongwe is quoted as saying that as someone who lives off the ocean, she has never been included in any form of governance, especially on issues such as MPAs – which have a huge bearing on her community. Nor has she been involved in the decision making about which species can be harvested. She says: 'I am hoping that the ocean can be what it used to be. We were able to go there uninterrupted and at the ocean, we will find a variety of choices of species that are [not] visible currently [...] So, I hope one day we will be able to go to the ocean as we used to so that we perform those rituals that our forefathers did to make species visible.'

There are many different eyes on the sea – watching its waves, mesmerised by it, longing for it, on its shores, on its surface and beneath it. Each has a different history. Shared memories rich with heritage. Personal experiences rich in context.

The sea belongs to all of us. It belongs to itself. It belongs to the animals that live in it. Chatting to Charlotte, Loyiso, Zolani, Stefaan, Anton and Dylan has opened my eyes to how everything affects everything. If we are to inherit the ocean, we cannot sideline indigenous knowledge. Nature is instinctive and inherently wise. It loves balance and diversity. If humans are to thrive, we need to mimic nature. We need to adapt our civil systems to the fluctuating rhythms of the tides, of the seasons. But human nature is corrupt and our systems complex.

connection

As I look out at the Indian Ocean the water's surface is disturbed by low-tide waves. There is a momentary lull as the roar hushes, the ocean inhales and then holds its breath. Time unfolds. The overwhelming feeling that the ocean is bigger than all of us consumes me.

And then the waves begin again.

kosi bay

In the ocean, I slip from my skin into the soul of the sea.

– Unknown

'Ow!' Instinctively, I pull my hand towards me. 'The fish are biting my fingers!'

I'm lolling in Kosi Bay estuary with a bunch of friends. The water is bath-warm and sublime. It's December, exquisitely hot and humid, and it's the period when loggerhead and leatherback turtles come to the beach to lay eggs.

We chat, a slow conversation that matches the rhythm of the flow and ebb of the seawater channelling into the estuary. The area is part of iSimangaliso Wetland Park in the northernmost part of KwaZulu-Natal on the border of Mozambique. The estuary is a system of four interconnected lakes, through which flows the Kosi River, coursing its way to the Indian Ocean.

The estuary is a breeding area for fish, a safe place for their young where food is plentiful. It has been named the aquarium because of the reef and the abundance of fish, flora, bright colours and protected biodiversity. We are close to the river mouth where marine water enters the estuarine system, a liminal place so dynamic and transient. It's perfect for snorkelling and the couple at the accommodation suggested that we start at the mouth and let the tide pull us inwards; in that way, there is little effort required for swimming.

I can feel the water pulling me, rippling against my skin, and I move my hand to get a better grip on the submerged sandbank. To stay in place, I sink my hands into the sand. The biting fish, small with teeth as sharp as nails, are still around and they've headed for my toes. 'Let's move away,' I suggest, 'before one of us loses a body part.'

Like a shoal of large fish moving in slow entrainment, we push away from the submerged sandbank and are carried with the tide to the other side of the river mouth, where someone has seen eels. I swim down to a rocky outcrop and hold on to a gnarly part for anchorage. There they are: beige and mottled brown, two eels peer out from between the rocks. Their eyes are black and rimmed with silver. They watch me and I watch them as they sway from side to side feeling the water and searching for food. We learn later that they are African longfin eels and that the females can grow up to 120 cm in length and are usually heavier than males. After feeding in fresh water for a decade, they turn silver, their eyes become enlarged and they return to the sea to breed.

I let go of the rock and swim away against the current to give others a chance to observe these estuarine inhabitants. The water from the sea makes the visibility great and I spot lionfish, their colours red and dark orange and white and black, their lateral fins undulating, their expression taunting. I lift my head and pull the snorkel bit out of my mouth: 'Guys, come check the lionfish!'

'Come look at these flutemouth fish, they're so charming,' a friend waves me over. We are like children discovering things. A shimmer of movement, the fish flick tails and disappear into the depths. The water is changing as the tide moves in quicker and thicker, turning up the sand and diminishing clarity. I roll onto my back and float, feeling the force of the current channelling into the estuary. The sky rips by. To be in the sea, in the estuary, is to feel the natural rhythm of things. It's to go with the flow of the day.

Barefoot, we're walking on Bhanga Nek Beach in the glow of an almost-full moon. The sky is a dark velvet pierced with stars. Bioluminescent phytoplankton trail the water. Our torches are off as the moon sheds an even light across the beach and lengthens our shadows. We're searching for signs of newly hatched turtles and then we see them: tiny tyre-like tracks on the sand that begin at a nest and end at the water's edge where the turtles have crawled to the sea. A few steps ahead, our guide crouches down and points his torch, on the infrared setting, at something.

It's a loggerhead turtle that has broken through its shell and climbed out of its nest. Hundreds of crabs scurry around it, nipping at its flesh. It is survival of the fittest, the strongest and the biggest in numbers. The turtle is moving slowly because the crabs have won. We move away and let it be, in the knowledge that of five hundred eggs perhaps only two survive to become fully grown.

Further along the beach we find two loggerhead turtles, the size of a child's hand, making a beeline for the ocean. They are guided by the moonlight reflecting off the waves. Their clumsy scrambling on the sand turns to graceful paddling in the water. After three or four decades, turtles mate and the females return to where they hatched to lay their eggs. The phenomenon is called natal homing.

On the beach the turtles' cycle begins again, continuing their epic, ocean-spanning existence. The ocean shapes their instincts.

swimming with the divas

I must be a mermaid ... I have no fear of depths and a great fear of shallow living.

– Anaïs Nin

The sea is silver, there is thick, low cloud, some of it rolling down the sides of the mountains. It is a silver-grey day in January, of even light and even temperature. The sun hasn't yet warmed the earth. I park at Long Beach car park in Simon's Town, thirty minutes early. I get out and watch the neon tow floats and swimming caps in the water. There is a group of swimmers training, a woman on a paddle board shepherding them. Someone exits the water and I guess she's part of the 6.30 a.m. swimming divas group. With a towel wrapped around her waist she walks barefoot to her car, opens the boot and takes out a water bottle. She pours water over her head and her torso, relishing it; it must be warm. I see someone else doing the same, except that her water is from a five-litre container.

The sea is the colour of stainless steel, flat as a mirror and perfect.

The 7.45 a.m. ladies arrive, they say it's a big group, we are about fifteen. They quickly pull me into their net with introductions and smiles. One of them, Pam, lends me her fins as we are the same shoe size. She is 74, bright-eyed and fit-looking. She spent thirty years in Joburg and loved it. 'It has an energy, the whole of South Africa does, actually,' she says.

Lisa is on the beach but isn't swimming. It's the second time we've seen each other in a week and a trust has built between us. 'A lot of people come here because they need a net, they need other people. They're going through hell and they're self-medicating; this is part of that. It's mostly women but we do see a man sometimes. There's no bullshit, you're in the water, you're swimming, it's personal. It's not about the material, here you're just who you are,' she says.

There is talk of someone who drowned on the Atlantic side. 'We don't know what happened, she could've had a heart attack or a stroke, her body just froze, but because of that Scott said: *please put your name and cell number on your tow float and fins, so it's easy to be identified.*'

I look at the fins in my hand and see Pam's name and cell number. It's a good idea. I'm introduced to Liesl, who tells me this is her second swim with the group and that she too was worried that she'd be left behind, because she's slow. I'm reassured that nobody is left behind, and that they take breaks to allow the slow ones to catch up.

Athambile arrives and it is wonderful to meet her in person. She is so gentle. Someone takes a group pic and then, like a big lumbering animal, we head into the water. After a few minutes of getting accustomed to the small surface waves and to the other swimmers around me, I put my head in and get into a rhythm of crawl stroke. I slow down my tempo; it feels better to go slower with fins. So, I relax into my body and into the water. I do four strokes then inhale, four strokes inhale, get into it. I am comfortably ensconced in the wisdom of water particles. I am aware of its depth and its age, although I fail to comprehend it because billions of years is an unfathomable time scale to a mere human.

I realise that I can tell the speed and tempo of the other ladies by their breathing. There is a spot on my forearm that I'd like to scratch. It's the sea lice. I let it be and after a while the sensation disappears. The water is soft, my fingers run through it as though it's silk. I'm unaware of time passing. The fins are amazing.

Once I'm in a rhythm with my stroke and my breath, it feels like sleeping. I am in an otherworldly zone, my mind calm, my eyes framed by the goggles, fixed on the green water alive with tiny particles, watching my hands and the blue and white colours of my rash vest as they alight in my field of vision.

We stop at a rock atop which are perched black cormorants, totally unperturbed by our presence. They are elegant as some peer out to the mountains and others to the horizon. I have seen fish, touched kelp, looked down at the ocean floor. I'm hoping to see a giant short-tailed stingray because this is their hangout. As we wait for a few swimmers to reach us the conversation is about swimming at Windmill Beach. 'Doesn't the kelp bother you?'

'No, I swam at high tide so I didn't really touch it.'

Athambile says, 'It doesn't bother me, it's like swimming in a forest.'

Another woman talks of someone who swims there in a bikini, for her skin to be better exposed to it. 'It's so good for you.'

We swim past the same blue boat we swam around during the ATB swim and carry on towards the white townhouses on Main Road. At our next stop, the ladies with smartwatches check the distance – just over 1 kilometre. 'Who wants to go further, to the end of the white houses?'

I raise my hand. Pam, who lent me her fins, and another woman, Theresa, also want to continue. They're fast, faster than me and I'm wearing fins. But I up my tempo and keep pace. I can feel the current is stronger and the water choppier here. I focus on my stroke, on my breathing. We reach the end of the white houses. Theresa carries on until she's about 25 metres ahead of us, but Pam calls her to stop and come back to us. We tread water for a few moments and then test the whistles on our tow floats just for fun – they work well and they're loud enough to be heard. I comment on their speed and stamina and they take the compliment, smiling. 'It's going to be more difficult swimming back because of the tide,' says Pam.

I'm not worried. It's like I've merged with the water. The fins help, of course. We swim against the tide and my body moves up and down with the waves. The current is getting stronger and the water more animated. It amazes me how quickly the sea changes, how unpredictable it is.

Finally, we emerge. In a semi-lying position, in the shallow water, I pull off the fins and when I step onto the sand, I immediately feel the pull of gravity on my legs.

Pam pours coffee from a flask into a cup and offers it to me. 'In winter we have whisky in it,' she says, provoking laughter. 'It warms you up.'

Another diva has Kahlúa in hers. I am floored by the generosity and kindness of these women, their willingness to make me feel included, and how they're going out of their way to make me feel at home.

As I stand on the concrete pavement where the tar of the parking lot begins, I watch water dripping off me, darkening the grey. I watch as slowly, and then quite quickly, it returns to its normal dry colour. The water melding with the air, rising upwards, invisible, to become cloud. To continue its journey. This liquid that supports life.

I start to shiver and they all say, 'Ooh, you'd better take off those wet things, you don't want hypothermia.'

I take heed and get changed from the boot of my car. Pam does the same while standing at the boot of hers. We chat across cars. 'There are two things I find unpredictable – the sea and wildlife,' says Pam counting on her fingers.

The sea has turned rough, when a few minutes ago it was undulating in smaller choppy waves. I've forgotten to pack underwear. I'm not the only one. 'Don't worry, we all go commando here,' says Kahlúa Lady as she puts her arm around my shoulders.

Lisa is still there in normal clothes talking about a guy who did Robben Island and had a mental breakdown while out at sea. 'It's difficult for an empath, who usually needs people around, to do this. People don't take that into account. You're out at sea, which can change at any time – currents, swells, there's the cold, then there's the sea life, and you have to deal with it. The boat lost him, he couldn't see it any more and he was surrounded by cold ocean.'

connection

Some leave and a few of us linger a while longer, enjoying the conversation. We talk about swimming, comparing it to other things, other sports and other practices. 'The more you run the better you get at it but it's not like that with swimming. Swimming is about technique. You can't drag your arms through the water because it uses up way too much energy, and if you're on a long swim you're going to get tired. Your legs need to be straight and not hanging down, you need to keep your energy to keep your legs up.'

'Swimming Robben Island is a big thing and so is Roman Rock.'

'If you're new you should train with a triathlete, they just keep going no matter what, they have great mental stamina.'

'You'll see more swimmers at Silvermine Dam, many of them need to clock over thirty kilometres of swimming a week to do the longer swims.'

The topic moves to the rabid seals and how there's been news of attacks on dogs and humans. Pam says that her Pilates teacher, who is also a nurse, will be administering rabies shots to her and other swimming friends later in the week. Heads nod and there are mumbles of approval. These ladies are willing to inoculate themselves against this virus so they can swim.

I can see how swimming becomes addictive. It is way easier swimming in the sea than it is in the pool, and way more fun. The feel-good factor is huge. My skin feels alive. I thought of none of the things that are troubling me. The sea takes them all away.

As I sit in the car and turn the ignition, I look out again at the scene beyond the windscreen – people dipping in the shallows, a dog on a surfboard being pushed by its smiling owner, a man in a kayak paddling out to the horizon, two dogs running together on the sand, people hanging around the food truck.

Later, I chat via WhatsApp with Athambile. It was wonderful to meet her and share the water with her. She tells me that swimming with fins has given her confidence in the group but also a false sense of ability. I agree with her. It was much easier swimming today with fins and I was able to do 2,1 km. I could've gone on for much longer too.

My skin is still salty. It's hours after my swim and I still feel good. My cells are humming with aliveness. It's so tangible, I notice it in my movements and my senses are heightened – colours saturated and I'm hearing all the different songs of the multitude of birds beyond my window, the tinkle of cutlery from downstairs.

I'm not sure if it was the sense of belonging – the women welcoming me into their tribe with wide-open arms, a perfect stranger letting me use her fins, the rhythm of swimming with a large group of humans, feeling like a sea mammal, marine life in touching distance, the feeling of renouncing gravity – or if it's all of this.

The social connection is real. I think of the spontaneous interactions I have on the beach and in the water – the parking lot, even. Swimming communities bring people together, and the sea is a great equaliser. I recall someone telling me, 'This is our socialising.' I can see from the swimming groups, like the swimming divas, that the shared experience of enjoying blue spaces enhances the lives of the participants. Waking up in the morning to go for an early swim with happy, enthusiastic people can only make your day, and your life, better.

I've left the sea on me. When I got back to the Airbnb I decided not to take a shower to let the goodness of the ocean settle into my skin and my hair. Seawater carries magnesium, potassium, calcium and iodine – trace elements that nourish the skin, ease inflammation and balance moisture levels. The brine itself acts as a natural exfoliant, sloughing away dead cells and drawing out impurities. Seawater is constantly replenished with organic compounds and charged with negative ions that calm the nervous system. The rhythmic push and pull of the tide stimulate circulation, which encourages oxygen flow and cellular repair. It's why wounds heal faster, why a salty swim leaves the skin glowing, and why floating, bobbing, dipping and swimming in the ocean feels like a deep breath for the body. I am so aware of how interconnected my wellbeing is with the sea. Even the thought of it makes me smile.

connection

The sea holds me as I float, weightless. Around me is the constant lap, lap of waves. A bigger wave lifts me gently, like a breath, reminding me that I belong here, we all do. The sea is in us, shaping our bodies, our blood, our stories. We are made of it.

And yet, it is changing. The water is warmer than it should be, the currents less predictable. Kelp forests thinning, coral cities fading, ecosystems changing. The vast ocean that once felt unknowable, like the one thing beyond our reach, is now calling to us – not in whispers, but in rising tides, in storms that hold more fury, in shorelines that slip away unnoticed until they are gone.

Still, I float. I watch the sun fracture into ribbons on the surface, as the sea holds the sky. It has always been this way – ancient and enduring. But now, it asks something of us. To listen. To care. To change.

The water cradles me. I try to feel my heartbeat as separate from the pulse of the waves, but I cannot. My body belongs to the water. I want this connection and belonging to last. I want to be part of the sea. I want the sea to go on telling its story.

epilogue

I'm in Sicily on the piece of land inherited by my dad and his siblings. On the horizon at that hazy connection between land and sky is the thin blue line of the Mediterranean. Its constant presence is like a compass for me – on this island I can never lose my way. I'm picking my way along a path overgrown with nettles and myrtle bushes. The August sun thrums on my skin and on the world. The shrill of cicadas is high-pitched and pervasive. Sand gets into my sandals and it prickles my feet. I am attacked by nature – mosquitoes, flies and other insects wanting a bite of me. The volcanic soil births intense colours – the fire and jade of insects, the elaborate silver gnarl of olive trees, the red of flowers, the sapphire and blue-black of lakes.

I continue down the path to the perfectly round twin lakes – i gorghi tondi.

When I was a child they were unfathomably deep. Since then they've been prodded by geologists and declared a World Heritage Site. I stand at the rim of the first one and look into its glossy depth. It is so dark I can't see further than a metre into it. These lakes still hold mystery for me.

I make my way to the coast, to the edge of this island, to the waters that were once merged with the waters in the lakes. I drive past the salt mines – their geometric lines and the pyramid shape of the salt heaps add to the calm of the afternoon. In my peripheral vision, salt crystals shimmer like small suns. I'm driving along a coastline that is steeped in history, meandering to Capo Boeo, near Marsala. The privilege of

epilogue

being in places that mean so much to my parents and ancestors is not lost on me.

I open the car door and the air hits me thick with salt, and the scent of brine and warm earth and hot tar. It's the scent of my childhood. In the distance low islands rise from the water – the Egadi Islands. I slip off my sandals and wander over the rocks until I reach the water. Everything in me feels suspended, caught between land and water, past and present. My feet are on the land of my parents and I feel different here. I am another person. Here I connect to my dad's childhood and my mother's memories of her childhood.

I watch as the water slaps the rocks where I'm standing; it's hypnotic. My gaze follows the rugged curve of the small bay near me. I walk there, over the rocks, careful not to slip on the green algae that marks the terrain.

I kneel at the rocky edge and trace my fingers along its rough contours and slick patches. The tide has drawn back, and there, in a shallow hollow, is a sea urchin, spines fanned out like a slow-moving star. It is still. The water bounces around it, magnifying its symmetry and the deep violet of its body.

I dip my hand in, careful, feeling the sea against my skin. It reminds me that the sea is not just something we admire from a distance; it is something we touch, something that touches us in return. Here, in this moment, on this rocky shore, I am aware not only of my own presence but of the presence of the sea and its creatures, of the way we belong to them as much as they belong to us.

notes and references

Prologue

The information about the global temperature rising I found here: https://www.theguardian.com/environment/2024/jan/08/global-temperature-over-1-5-c-climate-change (accessed 14 February 2024).

To read more about the people of the Sahara, see this article: https://paulsereno.uchicago.edu/discoveries/people_of_the_green_sahara/the_gobero_story/ (accessed 3 February 2024).

A brief history of water

The information about water was sourced from here: https://serc.carleton.edu/eslabs/drought/1a.html#:~:text=%22Water%20is%20life.,production%20and%20all%20living%20ecosystems.%22 (accessed September 2023).

Regarding the emergence of humans, about 2 million years ago, the genus *Homo* began to evolve from earlier australopithecine ancestors. This period marks developments in brain size and the ability to walk upright. Genetic data from a fossil belonging to *Paranthropus robustus* – an extinct hominin species that lived approximately 1,2 to 2 million years ago in South Africa – adds information to the branches of the human evolutionary tree. Using the data from 400 sequenced amino acids, the researchers confirmed that *Homo sapiens*, Neanderthals and Denisovans are more closely related to each other than they are to the two-million-year-old *Paranthropus robustus*. https://archaeologymag.com/2023/07/oldest-genetic-data-from-paranthropus-robustus-teeth/ (accessed 13 December 2024).

notes and references

Longest underwater kiss

Further information about the dive reflex in infants I found here: https://www.researchgate.net/publication/51608708_The_Diving_Reflex_in_Healthy_Infants_in_the_First_Year_of_Life#:~:text=Diving%20reflex%20was%20observed%20in,infants%20up%20to%2012%20months

This article explains the research in article above: https://www.popsci.com/blog-network/kinderlab/born-swim/ (both accessed March 2023).

A video of the longest kiss underwater by Beth Neale and Miles Cloutier can be watched here: https://globalnews.ca/video/9522837/couple-breaks-guinness-world-record-for-longest-underwater-kiss (accessed March 2023).

Ambitious human nature

Y-40 The Deep Joy, the thermal pool in Montegrotto Terme, near Padua, reaches a depth of 42,15 metres, making it one of the deepest pools in the world. The one in Dubai is called Deep Dive Dubai, and it holds the title of the world's deepest pool, descending to a depth of 60,02 metres.

To gain more clarity about what happened to freediver and well-respected safety diver Stephen Keenan, I read these articles: https://www.outsideonline.com/outdoor-adventure/water-activities/safety-diver-stephen-keenan-dies-during-rescue-dahabs-blue-hole/?scope=anon (accessed 22 December 2023). https://www.esquire.com/uk/culture/a44559088/the-deepest-breath-what-happened-to-diver-stephen-keenan/ (accessed 8 February 2024).

Enjoyment

https://www.theherald.co.za/news/2024-05-08-gqeberha-swimmer-amica-de-jager-devastated-after-being-left-out-of-olympic-squad-despite-qualifying/ (accessed 11 February 2025).

Rip currents

The quote is from an article that was published before Amica knew whether or not she had qualified to compete at the Paris 2024 Olympic Games. In the article she eerily says, 'In the end, it is Sascoc's decision'.

253

https://www.up.ac.za/swimming/news/post_3208008-tuksswimming-amica-de-jager-may-have-done-enough-to-qualify-for-the-paris-olympic-games? (accessed 11 February 2025).

Water, precious water, plastic everywhere

The study titled 'The deep sea is a major sink for microplastic debris' conducted by Woodall et al. was published in 2014 in the journal *Royal Society Open Science*. It is regarded as a pioneering study in an effort to quantify plastic fibres in deep sea sediments.

Regarding wastewater treatment facilities, a 2021 investigation revealed that 56 per cent of South Africa's 1 150 treatment plants were in 'poor or critical condition', with 265 in a state of decay. https://www.dailymaverick.co.za/article/2021-04-26-south-africas-rivers-of-sewage-more-than-half-of-sas-treatment-works-are-failing (accessed 4 February 2025).

For more information about average domestic water consumption visit: visionwater.eu

I quote from this article that appeared in *The Guardian*: https://www.theguardian.com/environment/2024/oct/16/global-water-crisis-food-production-at-risk? (accessed 4 February 2025).

The information about mussels used in biomonitoring comes from: https://www.iflscience.com/teams-of-mollusks-with-little-sensors-are-used-to-test-the-water-quality-in-warsaw (accessed 12 February 2025).

Jellyfish and goby fish

I garnered useful information from an article titled 'How a Little Fish Keeps Overfished Ecosystem Productive' by Elizabeth Pennisi. Published on Sciencemag.org on 15 July 2010 (accessed September 2023).

Agreeing to protect the oceans: The High Seas Treaty

The information about the measures South Africa has implemented to regulate commercial fishing I found on DFFE.gov.za (accessed 5 February 2025). While I've endeavoured to include the most updated information pertaining to the High Seas Treaty, changes and updates continue to be made. A useful website is highseasalliance.org. There is a lot of information about the High Seas Treaty and its progress, but during the writing of this book, I found the following particularly helpful: https://www.washingtonpost.com/climate-environment/2023/03/05/un-ocean-treaty-high-seas/ (accessed 2 November 2023). https://oceans-and-fisheries.ec.europa.eu/news/win-ocean-high-seas-treaty-signed-united-nations-2023-09-20_en#:~:text=Once%20ratified%2C%20the%20High%20Seas,30%25%20of%20the%20planet%20by (accessed 2 November 2023). https://mpa.highseasalliance.org/walvis-ridge#featured (accessed 22 February 2024). https://cmr.mandela.ac.za/Research-Projects/EBSA-Portal/Namibia/Namibian-EBSA-Status-Assessment-Management/Walvis-Ridge-Namibia#:~:text=Walvis%20Ridge%20Namibia%20encompasses%20the,demersal%20fish%20associated%20with%20seamounts (accessed 22 February 2024).

The human polar bear

I contacted Lewis Pugh's professional representatives, but I was unable to interview him. It was by luck that I met him in 2009 and interviewed him then. The information about his involvement in making the Ross Sea a Marine Protected Area and his Hudson River swim was garnered from various newspaper articles.

Inheriting the ocean

The song created by Zolani Mahola for the Sea Change Project will probably be called 'Amphibious Soul' when it is released, instead of 'Song of the Silent Forest'.

The information about the abalone shell finds at Blombos Caves comes from a paper published by Christopher S. Henshilwood et al. titled 'A 100,000-year-old ochre-processing workshop at Blombos Cave, South Africa. https://www.science.org/doi/10.1126/science.1211535 (accessed 13 February 2025).

More about early human exploitation of marine resources and how it is linked to socio-biological development can be read in a paper by Elizabeth M. Niespolo et al. titled 'Early, intensive marine resource exploitation by Middle Stone Age humans at Ysterfontein 1 rockshelter, South Africa'. https://www.pnas.org/doi/10.1073/pnas.2020042118 (accessed 13 February 2025).

acknowledgements

This book came into being with the help and support of many amazing people. My profound appreciation to the magical Sarah Bullen for her belief in this book and for energising my ideas – this book wouldn't have happened without you. To publisher extraordinaire Gill Moodie, an enormous thank you for your insight, clarity, vision and support, for welcoming me into your home and for letting me borrow your tow float and wetsuit. Thank you also for the long and stimulating conversations about swimming.

Huge gratitude to the fabulous team at Jonathan Ball Publishers, especially Kholisa Xhuma and Jané Rossouw, and Melanie Kriel for page design. A special thanks to Gretchen van der Byl for the gorgeous cover design. Deepest thanks to Angela Voges for your meticulous and perceptive editing – your sharp eyes and your gentle pen are angelic.

To Jane Woodhouse, Kathy Sutton – merci. To Elsemi Olwage for conversations about ocean heritage; your insights and guidance were tremendously helpful. A big thank you to Khaliq Dollie who provided a fascinating glimpse into the training of triathletes, to Scott Tait and the 'divas who swim with tow floats' for taking me into the fold of swimming in False Bay, to the marine law student who unpacked the High Seas Treaty for me, you know who you are. A special thanks to Bevan Dell for fact-checking some scientific information; all errors, if any, are mine.

I wish to express my warmest appreciation to each and every person I interviewed, for their time, their generosity with information and for answering my numerous questions. I find you all deeply inspiring and brilliant and visionary. Sincere and special thanks to the scientists and academics who answered my questions with grace and patience. I continue to be in awe of all of you!

To my dad for sharing his love for the sea and instilling it in me, and for the recounting of his youth and his days in Sicily, I am forever grateful. To my mom, thank you for the polpette and cotolette, your tireless support and for being who you are. To my family, thank you for all your love, support and inspiration. Enormous gratitude to all the individuals I am privileged to call friends, it's a gift to share this life journey with you.

Thank you with all my heart to my husband and my daughters, for the cheerleading, and for putting up with me speaking my thoughts out loud.

This book is my love letter to the sea and its wondrous creatures — may they continue to ripple, flow and thunder.

about the author

Veruska De Vita has worked in PR and communications for 26 years and runs her own firm. She is a seasoned journalist with numerous pieces published in the *Sunday Times*, *Fairlady*, *Inflight* and *The Sunday Independent*. In 2012 she graduated with an MA in creative writing, with distinction, from Wits University. Her obsession with the sea began at an early age and she has always felt at home in the deep blue.

www.ingramcontent.com/pod-product-compliance
Lightning Source LLC
Chambersburg PA
CBHW062047080426
42734CB00012B/2579